Michael Ongel Ongel (handwritten)

W9-CGP-783

Christian Origins and Cultural Anthropology:

Practical Models for Biblical Interpretation

BRUCE J. MALINA

John Knox Press
ATLANTA

Unless otherwise indicated Scripture quotations are from the Revised Standard Version of the Holy Bible, copyright, 1946, 1952 and © 1971, 1973 by the Division of Christian Education, National Council of the Churches of Christ in the U.S.A. and used by permission.

The classifications used in Figure 1. Grid and Group Matrix of Mary Douglas and explained in the course of the first chapter are from Sheldon R. Isenberg and Dennis E. Owen, "Bodies, Natural and Contrived: The Work of Mary Douglas," *Religious Studies Review* 3 (1977) pp. 7–8 and are used here with permission of the authors.

Some of the material in chapters 5 and 6 has appeared in different form in Bruce J. Malina, "The Apostle Paul and Law: Prolegomena for an Hermeneutic," *Creighton Law Review* 14 (1981) 1305–1339.

Table 3. Modes of Adaptation to Anomie is reprinted with permission of The Free Press, a Division of Macmillan, Inc. from *Social Theory and Social Structure* by Robert K. Merton. Copyright © 1968, 1967 by R. K. Merton.

Table 4. Styles of Norms is reprinted with permission of Academic Press and Donald Black from *The Behavior of Law* (p. 5) by Donald Black. Copyright © 1976 Donald Black.

Library of Congress Cataloging-in-Publication Data

Malina, Bruce J.
    Christian origins and cultural anthropology.

    Bibliography: p.
    Includes index.
    1. Ethnology in the Bible. 2. Bible. N.T.—Herme-
neutics. 3. Sociology, Biblical. 4. Christianity—
Origin. I. Title.
BS661.M34   1986   225.6′7   85-42824
ISBN 0-8042-0241-9

© copyright John Knox Press 1986
10 9 8 7 6 5 4 3 2
Printed in the United States of America
John Knox Press
Atlanta, Georgia 30365

Preface

This book is the result of intellectual model building by someone interested in interpreting biblical texts. It can be of use to anyone interested in the interpretation of social interaction in terms of broad, comparative models. It is an exercise in "kitbashing," a word that deserves a place in problem solving and theory building (in German, *Kitbaschierung*) since models and "kitbashing" go together. The word is a common term used in model railroading where it refers to taking a number of individual models and constructing a new piece from useful parts of those other models. In sum, "kitbashing" is selective model building, and that is precisely what this book offers. It contains a highly selective collection of social science models put together with a view to surfacing some of the broader dimensions of the implicit meanings found in the behavior portrayed in and represented by the New Testament writings. The models have been chosen with a view to their usefulness for generating a "big picture" or overview within which to situate the contemporary New Testament interpreter (student and scholar alike), the first-century A.D. Hellenistic authors and audiences of the various early Christian texts, and the personages peopling those texts. Since the book is about meanings, it must deal with social science perspectives because meanings are always rooted in social systems.

The book has been written with the usual problems of contemporary college-educated persons in mind, especially those who grapple with an adequate understanding of the Bible while pursuing careers in various technologies: medicine, law, dentistry, business, and the like. These persons form the fictional, implied readers of this book and are ably represented by upper-level undergraduate students of Bible and religion. The impatience of these students with scholarly biblical studies is in many respects not unlike that of ministers and concerned laypersons who wade through a mass of biblical commentary yet fail to see the point of it all or how it all hangs together. The "big picture," overview approach is highly suited to obviate this problem. It provides tentative articulation in place of implicit and impressionistic individualistic intuition, suggestive generalization in place of the incoherent amassing of data and detail. Perhaps the best feature of the approach is that it is consistently comparative, heading off ethnocentrism from the very outset. The approach as presented in this book presupposes and requires the information generally provided by scholarly New Testament introductions along with some knowledge both of the methods of form criticism, redaction criticism, and tradition criticism and of the history and historical geography of the period. It is not meant to be a substitute for such information and methods, yet it can serve to assess their value and meaning.

The book, then, presents a broad framework for a comparative study of the social context of the New Testament documents since it presupposes that the meaning communicated in the texts is to be found in the social system common to the social context and the texts. The framework is adopted from Mary Douglas (1973; 1978; 1982 with Wildavsky). This work is not an interpretation of her "thought," nor is it concerned with reproducing her ideas properly and adequately. Those acquainted with her ongoing work will quickly see that the discussion of weak group perspectives differs notably from Douglas' changing standpoints, while the four additional lesser cultural scripts, after Thom, are not in her works at all. Similarly, this work does not intend to be an adequate presentation or reproduction of the works of the others whose models I have shamelessly "kitbashed": Donald Black, Paul Bohannan, Robert Merton, Marshall Sahlins, Talcott Parsons, Rene Thom, Hayden White, and undoubtedly others as well. I trust that they will not take it amiss to find themselves within the grid and group matrix of Douglas. The originality of this book consists in its "kitbashed" quality, the simplification of much of the technical language used in the original models, and the recurrent suggestions concerning how the models can aid in fixing implicit New Testament meanings in some comparative way. However, the formulation of new relationships and the posing of new questions do contribute to the progress of a body of knowledge. To the demurrers of those biblical scholars and historians innocent of contemporary social sciences (e.g., Meier in Brown and Meier 1983: 14 n. 17), it might be pointed out that this work falls within the category of "qualitative" social analysis (cf. Bogdan and Taylor 1975; Schwartz and Jacobs 1979) or what the British rather grandiosely term "new paradigm research" (cf. Reason and Rowan 1981). While available quantitative data for "number-crunching" analyses of the first-century Mediterranean world are not as scanty as some might think (cf. Thornton and Thornton 1983; and, of older studies, Semple 1921; 1922), this book belongs within the "new paradigm," "qualitative" camp and takes an overview approach.

Further, as is typical and normal in overview approaches, no attempt has been made to draw out every conclusion, to point out every correlation, or to articulate every possible objection. That is the métier and joy of persons whose cognitive styles focus on detail. While such details are very important, here readers are urged to stretch the models to their limit, to draw further conclusions, to multiply correlations, and to come to grips with the dimensions of the models undeveloped in this book. In this way the purpose of such models can be better realized since they are meant to generate more explicit, articulate, testable understanding.

At this point I have the pleasant task of recalling with affection all who contributed to this work. In the first place, my thanks go to my wife, Diane, for reading through all manuscript drafts, for offering numerous, valuable suggestions, and for supporting the work and its author to the end. The book was first drafted at the Ecumenical Institute for Advanced Theological Studies in Tantur, Israel, during the spring of 1981, thanks to a Creighton University sabbatical grant. The support of everyone at the Institute at that time is greatly appreciated, but special thanks go to Professors Foster R. McCurley of the National Office of the Lutheran Church in America, New York City, T. Raymond Hobbs of McMaster Divinity College, and Obinnah Aguh, C.SS.P., of the Sorbonne and of Lagos, Nigeria, for their interest and daily dialogues; and notably to Heather Hobbs, R.N., for reading through the first draft and sharing many useful observations. Then Professor John H. Elliott of the University of San Francisco proved himself a prompt and helpful friend through encouragement and criticism which greatly contributed to the decision for a shorter and more readable version of this work. Finally, my undergraduate students at Creighton deserve a vote of gratitude for having mastered much of the material in this book, repeatedly showing me how practical good theory can be.

Bruce J. Malina
Creighton University

Contents

List of Figures and Tables

1.

Textual Meaning and Cultural Scripts

INTRODUCTION

For believers, the Bible is the Word of God. For unbelievers, the Bible is a collection of ancient Middle Eastern documents. Whether as the Word of God or as ancient documents, the books of the Bible are meaningful configurations of language intended to communicate. While believers and unbelievers might differ as to who is the source of the communication, both would agree that the Bible does contain communication in written language. And both would agree that the Bible cannot function as word or document unless it is read. The markings on a writing surface can come alive only through the minds of their readers. How does a reader get to understand the meanings encoded in the wordings encoded in the spellings perceived in the markings on a page?

What Language Entails

The answer to that question holds the key to understanding the Bible or any other piece of writing. The question presupposes that what a reader sees in a printed or written text is spellings or, if the reader hears it read aloud, soundings (after Halliday 1978). In their own way these spellings or soundings express wordings. And the wordings in turn express meanings. But where do the meanings expressed in wordings expressed in soundings/spellings come from? Another way to describe this point is to note that spellings (orthography) and/or soundings (phonology) encode wordings (lexical items or words and syntactical constructions or grammar) which in turn encode meanings (semantics). Again, where do the meanings come from? The answer is the social system. "If we ask of any form of communication the simple question, What is being communicated? the answer is: information from the social system. The exchanges which are being communicated constitute the social system" (Douglas 1971 in 1975: 87).

All forms of communication encode and transmit information from the social system. Such forms of communication include consumption, cohabitation, and collaboration as well as command and conversation. Language is but one form of communication, even if the most significant, and common speech forms communicate much more than simply wordings and their encoded meanings. Rather they transmit a hidden load of shared assumptions, a collective and shared set of interpretations of reality that make up the culture of a particular group. To interpret any piece of language adequately is to interpret the social system that it expresses. If these observations are accurate, then the attentive Bible reader would have to find a way to proceed from the text to the social system that imparts meaning. The alternative is for the reader to supply his or her own meaning to the text.

This alternative is not new, of course. It seems to have been the general practice of Bible readers from the time that the biblical texts were removed from the cultural context in which they were composed. The result of this cultural transfer was that the literal, textual meaning of the biblical writings no longer made sense; the words in the documents no longer referred to the reader's/hearer's world and its furnishings, such as ideas, values, feelings, persons, clothing, houses, roads, and plants. Yet the documents were authoritative, sacred writings and hence had to make sense. Since they were the word of God for much of the past two thousand years, they had to offer authoritative directives for and solutions to situations which their literal, textual authors could not envision. In order to have the Bible work this way theories of spiritual interpretation were produced. According to such theories a distinction had to be made between literal meaning and spiritual meaning in the Bible. Literal meaning was produced by the study of the things to which the words of the Bible referred: for example, "the Promised Land" was Palestine; "Peter," the apostle and companion of Jesus. Spiritual meaning, on the other hand, was to be found in the study of the objects to which items mentioned in the text might possibly refer: for example, "the Promised Land" might be the U.S.; the "Exodus" might refer to the emigration of Puritans from Europe to the U.S.; and "Peter" might refer to the Pope. For those who have practiced such spiritual interpretation in the past as well as for those who do so in the present, these meanings derive from the true Author of the Bible, God! This search for the spiritual meaning with a loss of concern for the literal and the belief that the literal meaning was and is obvious and easily understood resulted in the fact that the biblical documents ceased to be treated as texts. Instead of being considered meaningful configurations of language intended to communicate, they began to be considered as revealed and inspired language puzzles intended to be solved in order to bolster some idea or piece of behavior required at a given time and place. "Text" usually refers to a sentence rather than a complete written work, and sentences are interpreted as though they were the bearers of meaning that texts essentially are. A walk through the history of biblical interpretation would more than amply bear this out as would a random viewing of the Christian Cable Network (cf. Steinmetz 1980/81, a historian who would resuscitate respectability for spiritual meaning, itself rooted in a loss of the sense of history; P. Burke 1970). For the fundamentalist preacher or learned biblical scholar, a sentence approach to the Bible results in a series of complete thoughts, but thoughts that are often unrelated and ultimately uninterpretable (e.g., "she did so"). Sentences yield complete thoughts but not complete meanings. To treat a biblical text-segment as though it were a text is to tear the fabric of meaning that a document was created to deliver. It also makes intelligent reading of the biblical texts impossible (cf. Malina 1983).

What Reading Entails

Reading theory is, of course, very important to biblical scholarship since all biblical interpretation is rooted in reading texts. What does reading a text entail? There are currently two major models of reading comprehension in vogue in experimental psychology (Sanford and Garrod 1981). The first might be called a propositional model. This model considers the text to be a supersentence. Now this is a logical perspective for persons whose training in language focused on wording, i.e., the sentence and word level. In this view the text being read evokes mental representations in the mind of the reader, which consist of a chain or series of propositions which derive directly from the sentences that constitute the text. The text is made up of sentences which in turn are made up of words. The reader basically performs two tasks: dividing the text into propositional units and then connecting the resulting propositions in some way. This connection takes place by means of some superstructure—a deep structure, story grammar, narrative grammar, or something of the sort. This is the kind of model that undergirds contemporary structuralist exegesis (Patte 1976). The difficulty with the model is that it cannot be verified experimentally, and the research of some experimental psychologists indicates that this is not what goes on in the mind of a reader (Sanford and Garrod 1981: 63–85). This propositional model of reading comprehension might be called the conceptual approach. It seems to be rooted in presuppositions about the nature and function of language that derive from the reification of highly abstract entities such as words and sentences. Words and sentences are not the end products of human speech interactions, but texts or units of communication are, and the human ability to communicate is the ability to mean (Fishman 1971; Halliday 1978; Hudson 1980). Hence "to language" is to mean, although not all meaning is communicated through "languaging." While the unit of thought is the word/sentence, the unit of linguistic meaning is a text. Now if a text does not present a chain or series of propositions, what does it evoke in the mind of a reader?

The second model of reading comprehension might be called the scenario model. This model considers the text as a succession of explicit and implicit scenes or schemes in which the mental representations evoked in the reader's mind consist of a series of episodes, settings, or models deriving directly from the mind of the reader and are then coupled with appropriate alterations to these episodes, settings, or models as indicated by the unfolding text. Here, too, the reader must perform two tasks: using the text to identify an appropriate "domain of reference," that is, calling to mind an appropriate scene, scheme, or model referred to by the text and then using the identified domain of reference as the larger frame within which to situate the meanings proposed in the text as far as this is possible. This model of reading comprehension does have some validation from contemporary experimental psychology (Sanford and Garrod 1981: 109–154). The scenario model might be called the social context approach, based both on presuppositions about language as spelled out above and in a belief in the text as the basic unit of language. "To utilize sentences, language users rely on grammatical knowledge as a general, virtual system. To utilize texts, people need experiential knowledge of specific, actual occurrences" (de Beaugrande 1980: 14). Once again, in order to interpret texts as meaningful communication some appreciation of the social systems which texts portray and in which they are rooted is indispensable.

For texts are the end products of languaging, and languaging is a form of social interaction. People "language" each other to have some effect. Conversation partners expect each other to refer to some common situation and to talk about the same thing. The same holds for writing and the production of written texts. However, the main difference between written and spoken communication is not one of modality (graphic/visual vs. oral/aural) but one of opportunities for interaction. In conversation, interruptions for the sake of clarification are possible, while in writing they are not. Hence writing burdens the writer with the need to elicit the appropriate model of the domain of reference in the mind of the reader along with the need to select appropriate wording to encode the meanings proper to a given domain. Good and poor style are indications of the writer's ability in this task and of one's considerateness of discourse.

From this perspective, should biblical writings be judged to be perennially contemporary, then their authors might rightly be considered thoroughly inconsiderate. They refer to situations and models of the world strange to twentieth-century U.S. experience. Without some attempt to reconstruct and enter the social world of the biblical authors, it would seem that one can only be an inconsiderate reader, ethnocentrically anachronistic in highly sophisticated ways. The best a contemporary biblical scholar might offer Bible readers is a way to get back to the domains of reference which derive from and are appropriate to the social world from which the biblical texts derive. All interpretation, it would seem, requires and ultimately rests on such models (cf. Malina 1982).

The purpose of this book is to indicate some useful ways in which the task of being a considerate reader of the Bible might be adequately accomplished. The problem, then, is how to move from a text to the social system that endows the text with meaning.

SOCIAL MEANING: SOME PRESUPPOSITIONS

The foregoing considerations of language and reading point to the fact that language is a representational medium of communication. Language produces a mediated picture of reality as human beings experience it. As one listens to or reads a piece of language, one must not only assign meanings and interpretations to what is being said or read but also supply a great deal of those meanings and interpretations even though one is not the speaker or writer. This means that the words and phrases (lexical items) and sentence patterns (syntactical constructions) behind the soundings and spellings of an utterance present the reader/hearer with something like a picture that is complete but out of focus with outlines blurred and details imperceptible. The reader/hearer then uses some common domain of reference, the social meaning system, to bring the picture into focus. Only, to begin with, the picture was not a photographic likeness but a highly symbolic, non-concrete representation. Interpreting and understanding what someone says or writes is a decoding process at such a non-concrete and symbolic level (cf. Halliday 1978).

Nature, Culture, Person

From where does one acquire the ability to supply the meanings and interpretations needed in linguistic communication? If the whole human race lived simultaneously and shared a common tongue, "Human," that encoded and expressed a common meaning system, this ability would be genetic, natural, but this clearly is not the case. If each person were to speak a unique, idiosyncratic language and had only unique, personal experiences, then communication would not be possible at all. Thus the ability to language and be languaged is not exactly personal, and if not personal or natural (no one speaks "Human") then the source of the ability must be cultural but with genetic predispositions and individual actualization. This observation simply underscores a common twentieth-century Western intuition that all people are entirely the same and entirely different, somewhat the same and somewhat different, at the same time.

Nature generally refers to the sameness of a set or class of objects under consideration whether persons, things, or events. To say that one studies nature is a shorthand way of saying that one studies sameness, similarity, and hence regularity and predictability. In the U.S., mainstream culture assigns this area of study to *science*, and such knowledge is called *objective* mostly because it deals with objects, with models of the human environment, including models of human being as part of that environment. This perspective constrains one to see only the one hundred percent sameness characteristic of all human beings at all times and presumably in all places as well. The area of sameness—of the objective, the scientific, the natural—usually never generates much passion. People simply do not argue about who has nicer blood cells, whose TV set has better electrons, or whose salt has uglier crystal formations. So long as the area of discussion remains some area of sameness it evokes little emotion, and those devoted to this area seem quite dispassionate. After all there are no differences to fight about.

At the other extreme lies the area of complete difference. In the culture of the U.S. mainstream the area of complete difference between an individual person and his or her fellow human beings is called *person* or personhood. This is the area covered by the word "I" and the area of which the word is felt to be used meaningfully. Most Americans tend to believe that I's are unique, truly individual and indivisible, and totally self-contained and sealed off from others presumed to be I's as well. Now if I's are truly and completely different, unique individuals, then they are incommunicable and, on the I-level, quite alien to other I's. The I's knowledge of the I is labeled as the area of the *subjective*. There is a whole current of authors and philosophers who revel in this aspect of human being. Often called existentialist thinkers, they focus on this single aspect of human experience, the person as incommunicable and encapsulated. They often magnify this aspect so that it is made to comprise the totality of human experience. Existentialists have had little impact in the U.S., it seems, because Americans have been quite aware of this aspect of human being almost from the beginning of the republic. In the U.S. view of human being this aspect is called individualism. Individualism does not frighten or bother most Americans at all as it seems to bother people from non-individualistic cultures.

Be that as it may, if the I is so hermetically sealed off from other I's, if I am unique and incommunicable, then how is it possible for persons to communicate? One answer lies in the insight that human beings are not simply unique individually and the same generically but that, in terms of collectivities, human beings are in fact somewhat the same and somewhat different as well. This area of limited sameness and limited difference is called *culture*. It marks the area of the "we" over against the "they," the area of collective communication and sharing, the area of the limited and finite range of persons, things, and events that a given group of people holds in common. Culture, then, refers to the area of shared and distinctive interpretations of nature that belong to limited and often clearly defined groups of "us" situated, of course, over against "them." This is the area of the *social*. To perceive this area, consider the following.

All people in the whole world break down into male and female (a scientific or natural fact), but what does it mean to be a male or female? Which statuses and roles are assigned to each sex? Human societies the world over have offspring (another scientific, natural fact), but what does it mean to be a child or to have a child? Is a child an economic benefit or a loss? Which child is of greater value, a male or a female? What does it mean to have twins or triplets? People all over the world have shelters (a scientific, natural fact), but what does a shelter mean to Bedouins, to Eskimos, to New Yorkers, to Midwesterners past the Mississippi? Is a shelter simply a place to sleep and get in out of the rain, or is it a place to flee for protection from other humans, to store one's wealth, or to use as a setting for consumption rituals like dinner parties? It would seem that all people experience physical environments, seasonal changes, and weather conditions (a scientific fact, once more), but what do mountains, rivers, deserts, storms, and seasons mean? Is the earth like a mother, not to be scratched, fenced off, or made naked, or is the earth simply one more item to be dominated by people and to be controlled and manipulated for human ends? The point is that human beings are somewhat the same and somewhat different when it comes to their collectively or socially shared interpretations of their common environment, including themselves as part of that common environment.

To sum up, a ready intuition shared in the U.S. is that human beings can be understood in terms of three dimensions: the natural, the cultural, and the personal. Further, these dimensions correspond to three forms of knowing: the objective, the social, and the subjective. Finally, and perhaps most importantly, the three areas are actually one reality because they are concomitant and simultaneous. Just as one's house or sweater can be considered a personal choice from among cultural objects fashioned from materials of nature, so too a person's ideas can be considered personal perceptions of cultural conceptions of natural experiences. If persons do in fact perceive the same experience in different ways, perhaps the first place to look for an explanation of the difference in perceptions is in the cultural conceptions that control both the interpretation of experience and personal perception.

All the persons and things human beings live and die for fall within the area of the social, the product of cultural conceptions. This is the area of the interpretations and meanings that people put on the persons, things, and events which generate satisfaction and dissatisfaction, war and peace, love and hate. The socially shared cultural is also the area that sets us off from other groups of "we's" that share our country, state, city, and neighborhood with us. Finally, the socially shared cultural is the area that sets us off from those groups of people in the first-century Hellenistic world that constituted the Christian movement of those days. Since it is the writings of that movement deriving from those times that New Testament students wish to understand and interpret, some appreciation of the cultural conceptions behind the perceptions articulated in the writings is necessary.

Language: Natural and Cultural

A cultural artifact such as language can be profitably considered in the light of the nature/culture/person model just presented. It would appear to be a scientific fact that all normal adult humans make a wide variety of meaningful sets of sound; in other words, they have the ability called speech. To focus on the samenesses of this ability is to study it objectively or scientifically. From this point of view speech consists of sounds, and the scientific study of language-sounds is called phonology. One may study all the physically differentiable sounds used by humankind (phonetics) with emphasis on either the biology of speech sounds (articulatory phonetics) or the physics of speech sounds (acoustic phonetics), and that would complete the scientific, objective study of language since, as soon as one moves into the area of sounds that enter into a meaningful contrast or combination in a given language (phonemics), one is in the area of the social—the somewhat the same and somewhat different. Of course the study of the social has ranges of emotional resonance running from simple, emotionally unattached meaning to the heavily emotionally drenched "meaningful." For example, one may take up the study of meaning-related sounds (phonemes) and make the phonemic observation that English uses "b" and "p" as different sounds while Arabic does not or that English has "r" and "l" as meaning carriers while Japanese does not; these would be interesting observations. One may study the ordered relationships between small, meaning-bearing segments such as occur within words (morphology) and make the observation that "d" at the end of an action word in English indicates pastness; this too would be an interesting observation. One may study the recurring, ordered relationship between and among words in larger units like phrases and clauses (syntax) to learn the interesting syntactical structures of a language. However, the study of phonetics, phonemics, morphology, and syntax—known as linguistics—is devoid of emotional involvement, a trait typical of the natural, objective, and scientific. Linguistics tends to consider language as a system of structured sounds and looks for the regularities or samenesses in the system. Transcultural regularities would point to such samenesses, to the natural qualities of language. Linguistics dips into the social but only to withdraw again into the natural, thus maintaining its scientific boundaries.

However, there is a more focused social study of language, which treats language as a resource for meaning within a given group. Language here takes on the nuance of a verb, "to language" (this is the sociolinguistic perspective, cf. Fishman 1971; Halliday 1978; Hudson 1980). To language is to mean; to language is what a speaker/writer and/or hearer/reader can do. To language is a social activity, a form of social interaction much like buying and selling, marrying and bearing children, or ruling and being ruled. To language is to interact socially according to cultural rules and meanings. In this perspective New Testament authors languaged within the first-century Hellenistic world of the eastern Mediterranean basin. Once more, the understanding and interpretation of language leads to a social system whose meanings language realizes. The purpose of this book, again, is to develop a set of broad models for a comparative understanding of the social systems within which languaging takes place. A first step in this direction is to consider some basic dimensions of culture.

Culture

Culture refers to a system of collectively shared interpretations of persons, things, and events. It involves symboling persons, things, and events, endowing them with distinctive functions and statuses, and situating them within specific time and space frames. The ways in which persons, things, and events are symboled, endowed with functions and statuses, and situated in time and place result in socially appreciable meaning *plus* emotional anchorage focused on that meaning. Meaning freighted with feeling results in the meaningful.

This description may seem rather abstract. To see what it entails, imagine a group of human beings in some ostensibly monotonous physical environment, say, a sandy and drab wilderness. It seems best to begin with a group of human beings because the human group rather than the isolated individual seems to be the primary datum in any analysis of the human. Human experience begins in a group and needs the group, physically present or not, for meaningful survival and development. Consequently, it seems appropriate to begin with a human group in a sandy, otherwise featureless wilderness. Where is this group specifically? Some group member might draw a line around the group, and the members would immediately get to know where they were, namely, inside. Any other group of humans that might chance their way would clearly be outside. Due to the line in the sand the two groups would know both where and perhaps how they stand relative to each other. This bit of knowledge derives from an imaginary line made visible in the sand. In the ordinary world of human beings there most often are no lines in the sand. Rather, human beings make invisible lines and thus situate themselves socially and individually relative to others. Just as human beings make spatial lines in physical environments that empirically have no lines except those that human beings put and recognize there, they also make lines in memory and time. Ostensibly there is an ordinary, biological process called life running an undivided progression from conception to death. Human beings make imaginary lines through the process, called birthdays, infancy, adolescence, maturity, and old age. In the larger physical environment there is an ongoing planetary process marked by a recurring tilt in the earth's axis. The changes in the atmosphere resulting from this process are marked off by human beings into variously interpreted seasons, with the recurrence of one such cycle of seasons being called a year. The sun and the earth may not notice or mark such passings through a cycle but human beings do.

Culture is all about how given human groups in their environments draw lines though space and time. Human beings reveal the tendency to consider themselves as mini-models or scaled-down replications of the space and time processes which are perceived to exist around them, so human beings proceed to draw lines around and through themselves and their life processes. These are abstract, metaphorical lines marking off the inside and outside of a person. For instance, does the line marking off the inside and outside of a person end at the skin or at the clothing? If it ends at either of those points, then why do humans feel pain when a parent suffers? Why do persons ache when a brother or siste. dies yet feel nothing when reading an obituary in the paper? As for time lines, why does it seem quite suitable to pick up and cuddle a baby but somewhat embarrassing to do the same to that baby twenty or so years later? Why is a person's twenty-first birthday so significant in the U.S.? People simply do not feel neutral about such lines. The legal driving, drinking, or retirement age is generally a matter of great concern, a matter of meaning and feeling about oneself and others.

The omnipresence of such lines or demarcations in all human groups indicates that human beings have an overwhelming need to know where they and others stand. The variations in such lines further indicate that the fixing of social and personal positions happens by means of human-made lines, that is, arbitrary, conventional line sets through space and processes. Because of such lines there is a place for everyone and everything, and everyone and everything have their place. As long as everyone and everything are in their place, the world makes sense, people and things have meaning. Erase the lines and the result is nonsense, chaos, a loss of meaning. However, it is not an easy matter to erase socially maintained and personally assimilated lines. Any alteration in the lines will immediately draw comment from group members who will remind the would-be "eraser" where the lines belong. Clearly, people have to know where they are and where they stand, and they have to know where others fit in as well. In cultural anthropology the study of such socially contrived lines is the study of purity rules. Purity rules will be considered subsequently. At present a working description of culture must be developed.

Perhaps the foundation of culture lies in such line-making activity (B. Schwartz 1981). Yet, given the quality of U.S. society, perhaps a more suitable way to grasp what culture is about is to use the nature/culture/person model again. Culture means putting a definition, a delimitation, or a set of lines around the sameness of nature. Consider some features of human existence in terms of tutored U.S. perceptions. Humans are the end result of an ovum fertilized by sperm and brought to intrauterine term. Upon being expelled from the uterus, humans intuitively recognize mirror images of themselves in the male and female of the species to which they cling. They are taught to mark off, define, or delimit the ovum bearer of their existence as "mother" and to interpret the sperm contributor as "father." However, even the most scientifically minded in U.S. society do not celebrate "Ovum Bearer's Day" or "Sperm Contributor's Day." The reason for this is that in the area of culture males and females of the human group are not recognized simply as males and females. Scientists in the area of nature might use such designations, but once they get home after work their broods and mates give them second and third thoughts about the total applicability of the scientific, natural approach. To be sure, there is nothing wrong with the scientific approach or with scientists since they too are the result of cultural interpretation. For culture takes the one hundred percent similarity of the males and females around the globe and invests it with meaning and feeling by endowing those males and females with meaning and interpreting them as father, mother, son, daughter, aunt, uncle, and so on.

Culture, then, is a system of symbols, the result of a process of endowing persons, things, and events with meanings—with definition, delimitation, and situation in space and processes. A cultural group is a group of persons who share such a set of meanings and generally feel strongly about the meanings shared within the group. The system of symbols thus becomes a system of meaning and feeling, a system of meaningfulness. Tampering with the lines that define and delimit leads to confusion and ultimately to meaninglessness.

The language used by a given group of humans is a subset of the general symbol system of that group. As mentioned previously, speaking scientifically, language is articulated warm air (98.6 degrees F.) produced by a rather complex biological process with physical effect on the surrounding environment in terms of oscillating air waves. These oscillations or undulations of the air impact on the tympanum of a range of biological species but seem to have notable effect on members of the same species, which in turn register the tympanum vibrations in a set of brain cells. So much for language in nature. What culture does is to make appropriate lines through the undulating air, which allow for the perception of articulate sound that might encode meaning and feeling. To learn a language as a native speaker does is to learn the meanings and feelings as well as the uses of articulations of patterned air. To know a language is to have the ability to mean in terms of some language variety, and in terms of shared, regular patterns of biologically produced air. The ability derived from sharing regular patterns of sound and the meanings they encode is called understanding language. For example, a host of persons on the planet use methods of patterning air for meaning and feeling effect which are not shared by people in the U.S. Upon hearing them speak Americans simply do not understand the patterns produced by those people. On the other hand, Americans at times hear patterns of speech and think those patterns are their own; this happens most often when foreign diplomats use English to explain some issue or when people hear the Bible read in English in church. In these cases they will interpret what they hear as though it encoded the U.S. set of culturally shared meanings, as though Israelis and Soviets meant by "peace" what Americans normally mean by "peace," or as though Jesus meant by "Father" what Americans normally mean by that word. When patterns of language are really not those of a hearer's cultural group, they are simply misunderstood. What holds for meaning mediated through language holds for meanings in general: meanings can be understood, misunderstood, and not understood at all.

If language basically realizes or makes present meanings and feelings from a given cultural system and if the texts of the Bible are pieces of language, then to understand the documents of the Bible is to understand the meanings and feelings of an alien culture. To perform this task in some fair and adequate way, what is needed is a cross-cultural approach to grasping the meanings imparted by a foreign language. How might a reader of the New Testament situate himself or herself relative to the authors of the documents read so as to eavesdrop on their conversations with their first-century audiences? It should be clear at this point that any dealings with communications from alien cultures require the reader/hearer to play the role of eavesdropper. While this might sound rather tiresome, the point is that, until the human family invents and discovers a language that might be called "Human" (something like the emotionless univocal speech of mathematics), people will simply have to make the added effort to understand foreigners in an adequate cross-cultural way if they wish to interpret the meanings shared by alien groups. A useful and not too difficult step in this direction is the rather comprehensive model developed by Mary Douglas for comparative, cross-cultural understanding and interpretation (Douglas 1973; 1978; Douglas and Isherwood 1979; cf. Isenberg and Owen 1977).

DOUGLAS' GRID AND GROUP MODEL

In her book, *Natural Symbols* (1973; first edition 1970), and subsequently Douglas considers a number of contemporary societies through the prism of two variables. She calls the first variable "grid." By "grid" she means the degree of socially constrained adherence that persons in a given group usually give to the symbol system—the system of classifications, definitions, and evaluations—through which the society enables its members to bring order and intelligibility to their experiences. If human beings have to process their experiences through socially shared conceptions in order to produce perceptions of reality, then to what extent do people give full and undivided faith and loyalty to their socially shared conceptions and to what extent is that faith and loyalty withheld for various reasons? For example, persons in U.S. culture are led to believe that every effect has an adequate cause (conception); should one have the experience of having two dental fillings fall out within one week (experience), to what extent will that person perceive it as simply a case of loosened adhesive (perception)? Might one entertain the perception that one has been hexed by some malevolent person, thus putting the culturally shared conception in doubt? Grid is the measurement of fit between socially shared conceptions and human experiences. Douglas imagines a society's grid in terms of a vertical scale with those societies in which individuals almost always adhere to their culture's range of conceptions as "high grid" and those groups in which individuals doubt or waver in their adherence to socially shared conceptions as "low grid." On such a scale running from zero to one hundred, fifty would mark the midpoint, a midrange of conformity between experience and values or conceptions.

Along with this vertical scale Douglas lays out a horizontal scale called "group." "Group" refers to the degree of social pressure exerted upon an individual or some subgroup to conform to the demands of the larger society, to stay within the "we" lines marking off group boundaries. Human beings feel and perceive themselves as embedded within other members of a group along a spectrum ranging from full embedding (e.g., a toddler living in the psychological womb of its mother, always turning around to be sure mother is present and bursting into tears as soon as she is out of sight) to full disembedding (e.g., the hermit or the total individualist who never gives a thought to what others might think or say or do about what he or she does, acting as though he or she were the sole human inhabitant of the planet). The horizontal "group" axis likewise forms a scale, ranging from weak group on the one side to strong group on the other, with a midpoint (to which the value of fifty on a reversible zero-to-one hundred scale might be assigned) signifying group members who are half-embedded in and half-disembedded from a given group. If the vertical "grid" axis and the horizontal "group" axis are allowed to crisscross, the result is four quadrants (cf. fig. 1 on pp. 14–15).

FIGURE 1. Grid and Group Matrix of Mary Douglas
(Adapted from Mary Douglas 1973 and from Isenberg and Owen 1977: 7–8)

Weak Group, High Grid	HIGH

Purity: pragmatic attitude toward purity; pollution is not automatic; bodily exuviae are not threatening and may be recycled

Rite: used for private as well as public ends when present; the individual remains superior to the rite process; condensed symbols do not delimit reality

Personal Identity: individualism; pragmatic and adaptable

Body: viewed instrumentally, as means to some end; self-controlled; treated pragmatically

Sin: basically caused by ignorance or failure; hence viewed as stupidity or embarrassment with loss of face; the individual is responsible

Cosmology: the universe is geared to individual success and initiative; the cosmos is benignly amoral; God is a junior partner; adequate causality

Suffering and Misfortune: an intelligent person ought to be able to avoid them; totally eradicable

---

Purity: anti the purity postures of the quadrant from which it emerged

Rite: anti the rites of the quadrant from which it emerged; effervescent; spontaneity valued

Personal Identity: no antagonism between society and the self; but the old society of the quadrant from which it derived is seen as oppressive; roles of previous quadrant are rejected; self-control and/or social control are low; highly individualistic

Body: irrelevant; life is spiritual; purity concerns are absent, but they may be rejected; body may be used freely or renunciation may prevail

Sin: a matter of personal ethics and interiority

Cosmology: the cosmos is likely to be impersonal; there is individual and direct access to the divinity, usually without mediation; cosmos is benign

Suffering and Misfortune: love conquers all; love can eliminate

Weak Group, Low Grid	LOW

(left margin label: WEAK GROUP)

Group: refers to the degree of societal pressure at work on a given social unit (individual or group) to conform to societal norms.
—*Strong group:* indicates high pressure to conform along with strong corporate identity, clear distinction between ingroup and outgroup, clear sets of boundaries separating the two, and a clear set of normative symbols defining, expressing, and replicating group identity.
—*Weak group:* indicates low pressure to conform along with rather nebulous group identity (individualism), fuzzy distinctions between ingroup and outgroup, highly porous sets of boundaries between interfacing groups, and few or too many non-normative symbols defining, expressing, and replicating group identity.

Purity: strong concern for purity; well-defined purification rites; purity rules define and maintain social structures

Rite: a society of fixed rites; rites express the internal classification system of the group; rite symbols perdure in all contexts of life; permanent sacred places

Personal Identity: a matter of internalizing clearly articulated social roles; individual is subservient to, but not in conflict with, society; dyadic personality

Body: tightly controlled but a symbol of life

Sin: the violation of formal rules; focus is upon behavior rather than on internal states of being; rites are efficacious in counteracting sin; individual is responsible for deviance

Cosmology: anthropomorphic; non-dualistic; the universe is just and reasonable; personal causality; limited good

Suffering and Misfortune: the result of automatic punishment for the violation of formal rules; part of a "divine" economy; can be alleviated but not eliminated

Purity: strong concern for purity but the inside of the social and physical body is under attack; pollution present but purification rites are ineffective

Rite: a society of fixed rites; rite is focused upon group boundaries, with great concern to expel pollutants (deviants) from the social body; fluid sacred places

Personal Identity: located in group membership, not in the internalization of roles, which are confused; distinction between appearance and internal states; dyadic personality

Body: social and physical bodies are tightly controlled but under attack; invaders break through bodily boundaries; not a symbol of life

Sin: a matter of pollution; evil is lodged within the individual and society; sin is much like a disease deriving from social structure; internal states of being are more important than adherence to formal rules; but the latter are still valued

Cosmology: anthropomorphic; dualistic; warring forces of good and evil; the universe is not just and may be whimsical; personal causality; limited good

Suffering and Misfortune: unjust; not automatic punishment; attributed to malevolent forces; may be alleviated but not eliminated

STRONG GROUP

Grid: refers to the degree of socially constrained adherence normally given to the symbol system—the classifications, patterns of perception and evaluation—through which the society enables its members to bring order and intelligibility to their experiences.

—*High grid:* indicates a high degree of fit or match between the individual's experiences and societal patterns of perception and evaluation. The individual will perceive the world as coherent, consistent, and entirely understandable in its broadest reaches. Values consist of distinct sets of priorities.

—*Low grid:* indicates a low degree of fit or match between an individual's experiences and societal patterns of perception and evaluation. The world is largely incomprehensible. Values are scattered in various configurations, hence consist of desiderata.

Having constructed these quadrants, Douglas situates the societies she has studied in terms of their grid/group variables and ends up with a scatter diagram. She then proceeds to chunk or abstract the similarities found in each of the quadrants and thus produces four cultural schemes or scripts typical of groups within the respective grid and group quadrants. As can be seen from the accompanying diagram, Douglas' scripts include such categories as purity, rite, personal identity, body, sin, cosmology, and suffering and misfortune. It is important to realize that, since the traits of each cultural script are chunks or abstractions, they will not be found in any society in the terms listed in the diagram or the following explanation. Chunking (a college "problem solving" word) is basically a process of abstraction in which only similarities are retained while differences are discarded. For example, given a bag of presumably edible, concrete, individual items, one might sort them by noting similarities among them while discarding differences, then group them by similarity into Jonathan apples, Winesap apples, Delicious apples, and so on. The set can be further chunked by noting similarities again and disregarding differences, resulting in a bag of apples. Apples, of course, do not exist in the concrete; rather, "apples" is a way of abstractly referring to a group of concrete items in terms of their perceived similarity. Provided points of similarity can be found, the chunking process may proceed further: apples, pears, bananas, oranges, and tangerines can be chunked at a still higher level of abstraction as fruit; and fruit can be chunked with similarities in vegetables, meat, and fish as food; and the chunking need not stop here. Some philosophers would take up all that exists in the universe and group it under some ultimate chunk like being. There are, then, various levels of the chunking procedure or abstraction. Why human beings chunk things in this way seems to be due to the fact that humans cannot keep more than seven (give or take two) disparate items in mind at once (G. Miller 1956). Hence people chunk to manage their multiple and manifold experiences, to be able to deal with them, and to understand and interpret them. What this bit of information from experimental psychology indicates is that any model dealing with more than seven separate items will be rather difficult to follow. Douglas' grid and group model has only four quadrants; hence it should prove easy to work with. It is only a model, however, a set of interrelated chunks derived from focusing on similarity and discarding differences. Since chunking is a process of abstraction, the resulting model is really an abstract simplification of some much more complex real world phenomenon or process. The purpose of models—of abstract human thought—is to generate and facilitate understanding and interpretation, to aid in prediction, or to allow for better control. By applying Douglas' model to understand and interpret the New Testament writings, understanding and interpretation should be facilitated because of the access to comparative social systems the model provides. Furthermore, since the first-century Mediterranean world from which those writings derive stands in the past, the model should provide for better retrodiction (what it must have been like in the past) than for prediction.

The purpose for presenting Douglas' grid and group model in this book is to suggest some way to locate and compare the social systems bearing the meanings realized in language—the language of the New Testament. The model, like all models, must be tested to see whether it fits the range of data applied to it in such a way as to make the data more understandable. In terms of the New Testament texts, where would the social interactions described in them fit on the model? If the typical American is the "middle class" American, the type of person portrayed on TV shows and commercials, where would the social interactions of this idealized mainstream American fit on the model? Where would there be probable areas of all too easy misinterpretation in terms of U.S. mainstream culture and the culture depicted in the New Testament Gospels? Models are made for their usefulness in handling complex data. A valid model is one that handles all the data in some satisfying and adequate way. A model that provides no room for relevant chunks of data simply cannot be validated and would require major or minor alterations.

Grid

As previously noted, every society shares at least one symbol system which classifies persons, things, and events and which patterns the perceptions and evaluations of its members. *Grid* refers to the degree of socially constrained adherence normally given by members of a society to the prevailing symbol system which enables societal members to bring order and intelligibility to their experiences. Grid points to the degree of match a person finds between the values, norms, and perceptions a society proclaims, such as the values persons learn from parents and relatives in the course of growing up, and the experiences one has in that society. High grid means a high match, low grid means a low match. For example, say parents teach their offspring by word and deed that they are equal to their peers and that, being members of the larger group, equal access to the various opportunities provided by the society is theirs by right. Other people have the duty of respecting their access to the same opportunities enjoyed by the rest of their peers. Suppose that an individual son or daughter of such parents tries for a job, is given a test, passes the test, and gets the job. That individual would perceive his or her society as high grid, since values and experience match. Suppose, however, one of the children tries for a job, and a whole host of indications leads him or her to suspect that acquiring the job will be thwarted either because of skin color, sex, religion, height, or weight. Here the individual will perceive a mismatch between a proclaimed value such as opportunity and experience. What results is low grid perception. A generation of Americans has believed that, if a male simply worked hard, was devoted to his family, and lived an upright and moral life, he would be blessed with success and get his house in the suburbs while his children would finish college. For the many immigrants and children of immigrants for whom this scenario worked, their experience would find them in the high grid range of our gauge. On the other hand, that group of Americans who share the scenario yet find that they can neither afford a house in the suburbs nor send their children to college would find a mismatch between socially proclaimed and held values and their experience; they would move down the scale and rank at the lower level of grid.

Thus *high grid* indicates a high degree of fit or match between the individual's experience and societal patterns of perception and evaluation. The individual located at this end of the scale will perceive the world as coherent, consistent, and entirely understandable in its broadest reaches. The values that a person learns and embraces in high grid societies consist of distinct sets of priorities; generally everyone knows what counts in life and where one's main efforts should be focused.

Low grid, on the other hand, indicates a low degree of fit or match between an individual's experiences and society's patterns of perception and evaluation. Low grid individuals embedded in low grid groups find the world largely incomprehensible or bewildering. Values are known and publicly proclaimed, but most often they are unrealizable. Because the core values held by and holding society are not realizable, people consider the values to be a list of things to be desired but, given the world as it is, the values simply point beyond the abilities of humankind as people experience them.

Group

Group, as noted above, refers to the degree of social pressure at work on a given individual or group to conform to the norms of a society. Group refers to the degree to which an individual perceives himself or herself embedded in the larger group or groups in which the individual is emotionally anchored, for example, the family, the neighborhood, the city, the nation. For average U.S. persons weak group is easier to understand than strong group, hence weak group will be the starting point.

Weak group indicates low pressure to conform socially along with rather nebulous group identity. Weak group is individualistic. It evidences fuzzy lines of distinction between ingroup and outgroup and highly porous boundaries between interfacing and interacting groups, while the changing of group affiliations is an easy matter. Weak group is characterized by individualism. Individualism refers to a model or conception of "the person as a bounded, unique, more or less integrated motivational and cognitive universe, a dynamic center of awareness, emotion, judgment, and action organized into a distinctive whole and set contrastively both against other such wholes and against its social and natural background" (Geertz 1976: 225). What this means is, first of all, that the person perceives himself or herself to be unique and responsible for his or her own actions, destiny, career, development, and life in general and perceives other persons to have similar responsibilities along with the further responsibility of leaving the other person alone to do what he or she must. The individual person is above the group and is free to do what he or she feels right and necessary, normally using other persons, objects in the environment, and groups of people in the society to facilitate individually oriented personal goals and objectives. While this might be a poor articulation of what individualism means, it does more or less bring out what most mainstream Americans think they are or should be. For purposes of cross-cultural comparison, it is extremely important to realize, as Geertz notes, that this is "a rather peculiar idea within the context of the world's cultures" (1976: 225). It is as peculiar as the American notion and experience of monolingualism, the fact that most members of the society speak only one language. Although monolingualism is rather rare among the world's societies, it is perhaps not as rare as the individualism described above. Be that as it may, the pole opposite weak group on the horizontal axis is strong group, the next item to be considered.

Strong group indicates a great pressure to conform to socially held values, a strong corporate identity, and a clear distinction between ingroup and outgroup with clear sets of boundaries separating the two. In strong group societies individuals always feel themselves as embedded in a group, as representatives of the group, as needing others to know who they are and what they are doing. What this means is that the individual does not primarily perceive himself or herself as unique but as a group member. Group belonging and group location is primary and essential to self-definition. Furthermore, the individual would feel responsible, for the most part, to the group (not to the self) for his or her own actions, destiny, career, development, and life in general. The good of the whole, of the group, has primacy in the individual's life. The individual person is embedded in the group and is free to do what he or she feels is right and necessary only if the group shares the same judgment that the individual holds. The group has priority over the individual member, and it may use objects in the environment, other groups of people in the society, and, of course, the members of the group itself to facilitate the realization of its goals. The technical name for this type of individual is "dyadic personality." If a statistical survey of the planet's inhabitants were to be taken, it is highly likely that most of the world would be found to share this notion of individuality. This is an important point for New Testament study since it seems that the language of the New Testament texts encodes meanings from social systems peopled with dyadic persons and not with U.S. style individualists (Malina 1979; 1981b: 51–70). To make the point another way, for first-century Christians Jesus was not a "personal (i.e., individualistic) Lord and Savior," but a "dyadic personal (i.e., the group's) Lord and Savior." As a category of perception this is a significant aspect of the social world of early Christianity.

Script Features

With the grid and group axes laid out, what remains to be considered at this point are some of the anthropological features of the scripts that emerge within the resulting quadrants. In figure 1 on pp. 14–15, these features consist of rather technical categories like purity, rite, body, and cosmology. To make the scripts serviceable it would seem necessary at least to define and describe these categories.

Purity refers to the system of space and time lines that human groups develop to have everything in its place and a place for everything. As explained above human beings find themselves in an environment that undergoes process. To make sense of the environment and its attending processes, human beings draw lines through them. The results of such line drawing are social time and social space. Social time refers to the marks through cosmic processes like years, months, and days, as well as the marks through personal processes such as childhood, adolescence, maturity, and old age. Social space refers to the areas marked off by the borders people draw up, such as that between the U.S. and Canada or between one's yard and one's neighbor's. All such lines are socially contrived. The process of enculturation leaves individuals with the ability and the constraint to perceive reality through the lenses of socially shared conceptions produced by such line drawing or definition. These conceptions include the boundaries marking off the inside and outside of both the individual physical body and a person's shared social self, the social body, and it seems that the abstract, philosophical categories developed in a society are likewise socially derived chunks of line drawing resulting from marking off similarities from differences as socially perceived.

It is an axiom in cultural anthropology that boundary markers setting off socially conceived space and processes are rather tenuous and tend to be ambiguous; hence they are often a source of anxiety and conflict (Douglas 1966; Leach 1976: 33–34). If the boundaries are socially contrived, they can readily be erased by altering the conceptions held by members of society. For example, the nationalization of private property (such as after the revolution in Russia or the nationalizations of various industries in England and other countries) can be conceived as a social process of rearranging lines marking off "mine" from "ours." Erase the line and it can all become "ours," depending on one's social location. Thus such line drawing creates social meaning, with greater anxiety about lines in low grid societies and almost no anxiety about lines in high grid societies.

The category "purity" (and its opposite, "pollution") refers specifically to the socially shared map of space and time with special emphasis on lines and boundaries. When persons, places, or things are within their lines or boundaries, they are pure, clean. When they are out of place, they are unclean, impure. While Americans do not use the words "clean" and "unclean" or "pure" and "impure" in this regard, we do have terms for the category of purity, such as "deviant" (meaning outside socially contrived lines) and "normal" (meaning inside the lines) or "legal" (meaning within the explicitly articulated boundaries sanctioned by the political institution) and "illegal" (situated outside the legal lines). An easy way to grasp what purity is about is to think of dirt. What makes some rooms, houses, or parts of a city dirty is the judgment that matter is out of place in some way. Farm fields are rarely dirty even when filled with dirt. "Dirt" is, in fact, a socially contrived category used to refer to something out of place. Thus a wad of mud out of place on the dining room floor is quite in place in an adjoining garden. Cleaning a room is a procedure of rearranging matter and putting what belongs into its place; hence it is a purification procedure. An unclean person is a person out of place or one for whom there is no place marked off—a deviant. For instance, what makes a dirty, unkempt, and shabbily dressed person in an exclusive restaurant a deviant is that the person is patently in the wrong place. Deviance, impurity judged of persons, better fits the special category of sin to be considered below.

In sum, purity is about the socially contrived lines through time and space that human groups maintain in order to create and discover meaning. Leach has observed that "all human beings have a deep psychological need for the sense of security which comes from knowing where you are. But 'knowing where you are' is a matter of recognising social as well as territorial position. So we make maps of social space by using territorial space as a model" (1976: 54). Purity is about such maps of social space and social time.

Rite goes hand in hand with purity. Once a group has a set of lines, there are all sorts of reasons and occasions for focusing on the lines, either to maintain them and strengthen them or to cross them. Social behavior concerned with maintaining or strengthening purity lines are ceremonies, while those concerned with crossing lines are rituals. Ceremonies like family Thanksgiving celebrations, Christmas, and Sunday worship have their focus on those within a given group and reinforce the lines that mark them off from other groups. On the other hand, rituals, such as crossing the lines between being unmarried and being married, being sick and being well, and being legally innocent and being declared guilty, have their focus on the transition to some new, socially recognized state with a resulting change in status or role for the individual concerned. Ceremonies, then, celebrate the status quo while rituals look to line crossings. Given the achievement orientation of the U.S. mainstream, Americans have a large number of rituals ranging in importance depending on the value ascribed to a given line. People collect large numbers of line-crossing certificates, all commemorating rituals, which include receipts from grocery stores to the sheaves of paper produced with the purchase of a car or house. Such line-crossing certificates basically certify to everyone in society that a person did indeed follow approved ritual in crossing socially sanctioned property lines. Marriage and death certificates point to similar underlying rituals as do diplomas, state certificates of various types, and all the paperwork that characterizes ritually conscious U.S. society. But every society seems to be ritually conscious, and not all of them underscore rituals with the issuance of a piece of paper or parchment. In sum, rite with its ceremonies and rituals deals with the maintenance or crossing of boundaries in social time and social space.

Personal identity looks to answer the question, "Who are you?" As might be expected, answers to this question will run along the group axis, then fan out at either end depending on the grid. In mainstream U.S. society, persons would like to be known in terms of their individual selves, their psychological personality traits, and their individual achievements. They are not content with being identified solely as the son or daughter of, say, Henry Smith. Nor are they content with group or occupational designations as adequate descriptions of personal identity. However, people on the strong group end of the spectrum might answer the question precisely in terms of "sociological" roles or of group affiliation alone. Note how in the Gospels Jesus is described in terms of social roles (prophet, healer, teacher) or group affiliation (of Nazareth, Galilean). The New Testament lacks any indication of the type of psychological biographical information that Americans come to expect in descriptions of who people are. In any event, cultures do indeed vary in how persons are expected to identify themselves along the axis from individualism to dyadic personality.

Body refers to the physical person, the person as a physical, living human being. Human groups make and maintain lines through social time and space, thus mapping out the social territory of the group. If one were to look for a portable road map of that social territory, the place to find it is in the way people map out and regard their individual, physical selves. Anthropologists suggest that the way individuals map out the time and space dimensions of their physical persons offers a rather perfect scale model of the cultural group to which they belong. In the U.S., for instance, to enter the physical body of a person and tamper with its workings, an intruder must have two qualities for socially approved access: one must be competent and bonded. These are the qualities a person seeks in a dentist or a physician. Similarly, to enter the physical space that surrounds one's physical body and serves as an extension of it, that is, one's house or apartment, in order to tamper with its innards—its plumbing or wiring—the one allowed entrance must be a competent and bonded plumber or electrician. Finally the U.S. Department of State and its passport officers require visitors to be competent (passports and visas indicate this) and bonded (they are not to become a financial burden to the country). This set of examples points to a very valuable model for the study of social groups, a model called *replication*. Replication refers to the application of a set of norms or rules in similar, metaphorically identical sets of lines: the physical body; the extended physical body (the house); the social body.

Another instance of such replication can be seen in the way persons in the U.S. become members of basic belonging groups, for example, the family, church, or nation. Membership in these groups derives from either birth or law. Persons become family members by birth or by becoming an in-law. They belong to a church either by birth or by "conversion" matching a church's law. They become members of the nation either by birth or by "naturalization," that is, by law. The purpose of these examples of replication at this point is to demonstrate that as a rule the individual physical self is a portable road map of the general social body. The rules followed by a group of married couples at a party together, telling the males to keep "hands off" the wives of the others, are replications of the rules followed by political officials telling the Soviets to keep their hands off. Hence to gain insight into the boundary maintaining procedures used in the U.S., one can study either a married couple's socially learned behavior or read presidential foreign policy warnings. The rules will be metaphorical alternatives of each other.

Some time ago in the cartoon strip called "The Wizard of Id," the knock-kneed knight addressed his rather lumpy lady with the words, "What's a nice person like you doing in a body like that?" The distinction between body and personhood, between body and soul, involved here bears importantly upon the individual and social body replication previously noted. Douglas (1969: 69–80) has suggested that discussions based upon the dichotomy of the individual into body and soul, body and personhood, body and mind, matter and spirit, and the like, generally replicate social concerns about the relationship between the social body and the individual. In other words, body/soul dichotomies influence assessments of the group axis. Doctrines such as those common in philosophy and religion which use the human person as their metaphor and which define the relation of soul and body or spirit and flesh are likely to be especially concerned with social relationships. Conceptually, as mini-model, the body or flesh symbols the social or society, while the soul or spirit symbols the individual or the personal. Thus flesh is to spirit, body is to soul, as society is to the individual member of that society. Given this dichotomous and socially contrived separation of the unitary human being, three configurations are possible.

(1) Soul is greater and more important than body; spirit is greater than matter. This conception replicates the view that individual liberty is greater and more important than societal demands. Therefore there is emphasis on freeing the individual from social constraints. Such emphases as denigration of matter and insistence upon spontaneity, freedom, and "spiritual" values imply the rejection of society in its established form. In the Christian tradition this conception is further replicated in the theological and creedal statement that Jesus Christ is simply God, that there is/ was nothing human about Jesus the Messiah at all. Another replication of this model is insistence on the paramount, chief, and exclusive value of simply saving one's soul. Christian living is perceived to be entirely the work of God, of the Lord, with no human cooperation required or demanded. Outside the Christian tradition this conception develops the following characteristics: feeling, emotional expression, and direct experience are what ultimately count; attention is directed inward; individual self-reliance is emphasized; orientation is toward the inner realms of human experience; there is diminished concern for the well-being of others; no concern for mutuality; emphasis on the courage to be alone, to being apart; the individual is at odds with the surrounding world, with defects being the world's fault; society and the social are illusory. Such doctrines and dogmas offer ready clues as to what is happening in the societies of the people who would insist on them so much.

(2) The second configuration conceives the body as all important or more important than the soul, should there be such an entity as soul. Matter is all important or more important than spirit, if spirit indeed exists. This conception replicates the view that societal demands are all that count and are all that have a right to exist. The emphasis in groups that hold such a view would be to bind the individual to social constraints, to insist upon the total and all embracing rights of society, with no rights ascribable to the individual at all. Public values will then tend to denigrate and put down the individual and the purely spiritual. In the Christian tradition this conception is further replicated in theological and creedal statements to the effect that Jesus is simply man, that there is nothing divine about Jesus the Messiah at all. Christian living is entirely the work of the

human person who really does not need God at all. Other ideologies of this sort insist that there is no God at all or that only an ultimate materialism really exists. Thus another replication of this model is the insistence on the paramount, chief, and exclusive value of better material conditions of life, of saving the social body at all costs even if all economic wealth has to be put into the military and nuclear bombs without end. Other replications entailed in this conception include: the intellect, reason, and planning alone are what count; attention is directed outward to the material world, to material opponents; reliance on outward authority is emphasized; orientation is toward the outer, material world of objects; responsibility for being an individual is relinquished; intimacy is rejected; emphasis is on the courage to be a part of something larger; the individual is at odds with the surrounding world but defects are the individual's fault; individuality is an illusion. Again, doctrines and dogmas such as these readily clue in the attentive observer to what is happening in the societies of the people who hold and are held by these conceptions.

(3) Finally, in the third configuration spirit is conceived as working through matter, the soul as working through the body, with the individual conceived as an embodied soul or an ensouled body. This conception replicates the viewpoint that the individual is by nature subordinate to society and finds freedom within societal forms and institutions. Both society and the individual have rights and obligations which have to be played out in terms of the harmony of the whole. In the Christian tradition this conception is further replicated in theological and creedal statements to the effect that Jesus Christ is God-man in inseparable unity. It is also replicated in the model of Christian living as entirely the work of the human person and entirely the work of God. As for replications of this perspective outside the Christian tradition, these would include: valuing both feeling and intellect; alternating attention so that both the inward and the outward are taken into account; emphasis on interdependence; orientation to the whole field of human experience, inner and outer; concern for intimacy and mutuality; emphasis on courage both to be apart and to be a part; the individual is in harmony with the surrounding world, with both society and individuality being constitutive parts of reality. Again, doctrines and dogmas such as these offer ready entry into the social world of those who espouse them.

These body/soul replications can be readily noted in the way people in the Christian tradition speak and think about the Bible. Those who hold that God speaks directly through the Bible, that the Bible is the word of God without qualification, rank with (1) above; the soul is all that counts; society has no rights over the individual, hence there must be laissez-faire in economics, education, and religion. Then, those who hold that the Bible is simply a record of the past or merely the religious views of humans comparable with any other ancient views fit into (2) above; the body, matter, is all that counts; the individual has no rights; the society owns and is all. Finally, those who hold that the Bible is indeed the word of God but in the words of humans, hence entirely the work of God and entirely the work of human beings, fall into (3) above; both matter and spirit count, both society and the individual count (for the ambiguous this-worldly and other-worldly, social and individual dimensions of this position, cf. Eisenstadt 1983).

Sin, the next item in the scripts, refers to deviance, and deviance derives from the perception of pollution. As previously mentioned, pollution is the perception of people, things, and events as somehow out of their proper place. Just as dirt is matter out of place, so the deviant, the sinner, is one who disturbs the social order by being out of place or by putting someone or something out of place. Of course a society that allows its boundaries to get blurred or its lines of definition to be flaunted and disrespected is a society courting chaos. Chaos is the state or situation of having no lines at all, hence no meaning at all, since there is no place for persons, things, and events, and nothing is in its place. Simply in order to have, make, and keep sense, every cultural script will have something to say about sin or deviance.

Cosmology is the more traditional word for physics and its branches. It refers to the way in which social groups perceive their universe or world to be outfitted and to function. How, in fact, does the world run? Does it operate like a gigantic machine with which, if necessary, people can tinker to get it to run the way they want? Or is it a system run by some being responsible for its course, hence suggesting that people would be the wiser if they rolled along with the flow of cosmic events? Is the force behind cosmic and physical processes a "what" or a "who"? If people are "whos" (persons) who are superior to "whats" and the cosmos is a "what," the resulting type of technology is readily known. And if humans who are "whos" (persons) dealing with a universe set in motion and maintained by a superior "who" (person), the type of approach to technology and manipulating the world can likewise be readily inferred.

Suffering and Misfortune refer to whatever puts a halt to the processes and situations that human beings consider essential to their well-being, from a stomachache or headache to an earthquake or premature death or famine. Human beings the world over seem to ask why such deviations occur in the course of their well-being. To make life livable, cultural scripts offer answers to such why questions, and what is rather curious is that these answers are highly similar in societies inhabiting the same quadrant.

The script categories presented thus far are those found in figure 1 on pp. 14–15. Of course more might be added. In her lecture, *Cultural Bias* (1978), Douglas treats of nature, cultural process, time, human nature, and society in terms of grid and group. Her observations in these areas will be incorporated into the next two chapters which deal with each of the quadrants in detail.

2.

Strong Group Script Elements as Meaning Fields

INTRODUCTION

Theoretically speaking, for social life to exist at all human beings need to accept and adhere to some common set of "rules of the game." The situation of a group of persons living in society is much like that of a group of persons wishing to engage in sports. "Sports" as such do not exist; the term refers to a highly chunked, abstract category of behavior in a quite generic way. When human beings agree to engage in "sports," they inevitably have a specific sport in mind. Specific sports essentially consist of a set of all embracing rules, a "sports script," which enables participants to know what each is doing, allows participants and observers alike to assess the quality of play, and focuses the energies of the players and their fans on some specific outcomes. Cultural scripts are very much like team sports rules. All participants are expected to know the rules, and their performance is judged in terms of the ideal styles and purposes of the game. Even if the game is shoddy and poorly played, like a beginner's sandlot baseball game, all still know it is actually a baseball game, interpret it as such when they watch it, assess performance in terms of rather idealized examples, and share socially agreed upon assessments of outcomes in terms of "more or less." People can talk for hours about how great the World Series or the Super Bowl was last year, yet they could not say anything at all about those events unless they knew the rules of the game. Yet where are the rules of the game during a game? They might be printed in some rule book, but first and foremost they are in the minds of players and spectators alike. They control behavior on the court or field and set expectations, and knowledge of them is presumed by participants and observers alike.

If the cultural scripts belonging to respective grid and group quadrants are like the rules of team sports, then what happens when persons from weak group/high grid judge persons from strong group/low grid is much like what occurs when football players judge baseball players by football rules. More often than not, this is what U.S. Bible readers (presumably from weak group/high grid society) do when they read the New Testament (presumably from strong group/low grid society). Of course the results are hilarious to one aware of the different sets of rules. But what of the person who thinks the scenario in a given New Testament book represents performances of the same set of rules the reader holds dear? The result is an ethnocentric interpretation—the judging of all persons in the whole world in terms of one's own culture on the presumption that, since "we" are by nature human, so if anyone else is human then they should and must be just as we are. Such "Archie Bunkerisms" may have been funny on TV, but they can be disastrous in the minds of a Moral Majority or some other political action group that would have one believe that Jesus of Nazareth was a blue-eyed, blond-haired, Bible-belt American. If he was not a blue-eyed, blond-haired, Bible-belt American, what was he? What set of rules did he presume was shared by the people he dealt with? What social script provided the "rules of the game," the set of meanings that he held in common with his audiences? To help answer such questions the typical features of the grid and group quadrants have to be considered. At the outset it should be noted that the scripts typical of each quadrant are polythetic typologies. "A polythetic typology is constructed by grouping together those individuals within a particular sample which have the greatest number of shared features. No single feature is either necessary or sufficient" (Bailey 1973: 21; cf. Douglas 1978: 15). Hence while a given group might not evidence all the features listed in a given quadrant, it can profitably be placed in the quadrant if it reveals at least some traits of the script without contradicting the remaining ones.

STRONG GROUP/HIGH GRID

To begin with, consider the strong group/high grid quadrant of figure 1 on pp. 14–15 (upper right-hand corner). To help imagine who and what might be involved, I suggest that some contemporary examples of strong group/high grid social groups include the elite and controlling segments of the Soviet Union, China, West Germany, Switzerland, and the Vatican. In the New Testament period inhabitants of this quadrant included Roman elites along with the elites of co-opted subgroups within the Roman Empire, such as the Sadducees and the Herodians in Palestine and the *decuriones* of the various municipalities in the empire. Some may find it surprising that societies as similar and dissimilar at first glance as the Soviet establishment and the Vatican or the Roman imperial elite and the Sadducees of the Jerusalem Temple played or play according to the rules of the game that follow. While the classifications of given societies or segments of them within respective grid and group quadrants might initially seem improbable, they deserve to be tested in terms of the model. As noted previously, models are simplified approximations of more complex real world realities; their value consists in the understanding that they can generate and the interpretations that they can corroborate. They are not intended to be statements of absolute truth, and they need to be validated. Moreover, they are abstractions based on similarities only and are constructed by shedding the concrete and rich differences that clothe the similarities.

The description of this quadrant in figure 1 on pp. 14–15 begins by noting that the script involves strong concern for purity. This, of course, means strong concern for boundaries, for marking off who is inside and who is outside, who is above and who is below. The Iron Curtain, the Bamboo Curtain, and other such curtains are physical and metaphorical manifestations of boundary-marking purity rules. Purity or boundary-marking lines define and maintain the social structure. The lines of strong group/high grid mark off a society into hierarchic shape with a structure like a pyramid consisting of many horizontal layers (on hierarchy cf. Herbst 1976; Wallace 1981). Here persons fall into social position by *ascription*. Ascription refers to the fact that persons do not have to strive to achieve a given social position; instead they are simply placed into the social position they hold by various irreversible procedures. They fall into their statuses in the pyramidally structured society by actual birth or by some type of fictive birth, that is by means of a ritual that has the irreversible effect of actual birth, such as inauguration into certain political offices, into a church, or into a corporate role. Just as the individual has no control over his or her birth, so the individual has no control over being born a priest in Israel, being assigned by the party as party secretary in the Soviet Union, or being appointed head of the church by God in the Vatican. Roman emperors were likewise divinely appointed through birth and connection with the right families.

According to this script, vertical social mobility is not a generally available option. A person belongs to the status in which he or she was born or ritually reborn. For example, someone higher on the status scale may lift up a lower level person by some ritual (adoption, marriage), and thus the elevated person henceforth remains in the new status, but such interstatus interactions would be rather rare. Such societies are societies of fixed, permanent, and unchanging procedures for line crossing. Should a person find himself or herself out of place, there are fixed rituals for getting back to the proper place, such as public confessions, fines, and formal apologies. Rites will express the internal classification system of the group. This means that there are prescribed forms for celebration and ritual, for dealing with socially contrived lines. For example there are proper ways for passing into the presence of superiors, "natural" (such as parents and grandparents) and "social" (such as local commissars, bishops, or mayors). The ranks ascribed to persons are usually publicized by rituals (inauguration or ordination procedures), and the rank thus symboled endures in all contexts of life. Emperor, pope, party secretary, and king remain in their roles continuously and normally for the rest of their lives. There is no role switching allowed or expected. While most military institutions such as the U.S. army are strong group/ high grid in most respects (cf. Janowitz and Little 1974), a U.S. general in a department store is normally a customer, not a general, and it is quite normal for him or her to symbol this change of status by not wearing an army uniform off base. Similarly, according to the U.S. Supreme Court's interpretation of the U.S. Constitution, there are two systems of justice under the Constitution—one military (strong group/high grid) and one civilian (weak group/high grid)—and in the strong group script, enlisted military personnel cannot sue their officers (Chappell v Wallace, 103 S.Ct. 2362). Multiple scripts can be and are the rule in complex, immigrant societies such as the U.S. Yet even here individuals tend to live the script that commands their loyalty. But in strong group/high grid societies or groups it is quite normal to wear one's symbolic status all the time. Titles for all ranks are permanent and enduring, and everybody who is anybody has an appropriate title.

Moreover, just as persons have their status by ascription and perdure in that status indefinitely, the same holds true for places. The topography of the main places where people in this script live out their lives is rather permanent. A palace location, a temple location, and a homestead stay in the same place and with the same lineage through generations. The very thought of altering such locations is tantamount to altering the structure and fabric of the society replicated in these locations.

As to personal identity, individuals embraced by this script are normally dyadic personalities, with individualism found only among persons at the pinnacle of hierarchies. For example, a Roman emperor, a pope, a provincial governor in the province, or a bishop in the diocese occupies a unique and singular status at the top of some hierarchy, and hence all are in fact individuals who can act "individualistically." But all persons below them on the hierarchical scale are dyadic persons. The dyadic persons in this script know exactly what is expected of them. People are expected to internalize their roles, to be what they are labeled to be, and to live accordingly. This is why one's title can and must be used at all times. Thus the individual is embedded in the society; his or her self-image is defined by and supported by society. And all perceive the situation to be proper, natural, normal, and necessary with no thought given to the possibility of things being any other way.

The physical body, as the portable road map of the social body, will be tightly controlled like the society at large. Patterns of sexual intercourse, disposal of bodily wastes, and emotional displays tend to follow fixed and limited lines. Yet constraint is not perceived to be stifling but liberating, necessary, and normal, a sign of life as it should and must be lived.

Sin or deviance is always the result of being out of place, but place is defined by formal rules. The very fact that a person is out of place suffices for the deviant label; whether one intended to deviate or not is simply beside the point. Good or bad intentions are simply not taken into account as significant or as affecting the situation in any way. Consider here the priestly rules that disbarred a person from temple worship in ancient Israel: being crippled, suffering a nocturnal emission, or having a skin rash (Lev. 15:1–33; 21:16–23; 22:1–7). These rendered a person unclean, out of bounds. Similarly, touching the ark of the covenant quite accidentally and unintentionally (2 Sam. 6:6–7) sufficed for the death penalty because of the central importance of the ark symboling God's presence. The deviant individual is responsible and must undergo proper purification rituals which might entail twenty years in Siberia for taking a loaf of the State's bread or for delivering a letter for a friend. But the ritual is efficacious; one can be rehabilitated by means of the ritual.

In the strong group/high grid perspective the universe is considered to be in the control of persons, of "whos." Hence when something significant happens the question is not what caused it but who caused it. This perspective is called *personal causality* (and there will be more about it later). Personal causality urges persons to seek the cause of their benefits and difficulties in persons outside of themselves. For instance, if one purchased a new car that proved to be defective, logical behavior in terms of personal causality would be to go to the factory where the car was manufactured, seek out all responsible for its production, from factory manager to crew chiefs to the assembly line workers, and then to take revenge on all of them and insist they make restitution with a new vehicle. Obviously this is not the American way.

Further, should some benefit or difficulty befall a person and no other human being can be found who might have caused it, for example, a sudden toothache due to infection, strong group/high grid individuals would blame some non-visible human being. Non-visible human beings might include groups of conspirators, persons capable of hexing at a distance, or invisible, human-like beings called spirits, angels, or demons. The point is that everything that happens is caused by a "who," by a "you," by a person, and meaningful survival in the system develops from knowing which persons are involved and how to deal with them. Strong group/high grid systems normally know exactly who is responsible and how to deal with them; a modern array of identity papers and cards is but a recent manifestation of such concern. This approach to the forces that shape and determine life is called anthropomorphism, a word that literally means "human-like-ism." The

significant and meaningful forces that shape human life are normally perceived in terms of human similes (e.g., "the sun rose like a man out of bed")
and metaphors (e.g., "the wind was a stabbing pain"). Anthropomorphic
views of the world prefer to envision the processes that affect human living
in terms of human-like analogies or comparisons. People in the U.S., on the
other hand, prefer machine-type analogies, for example, a marriage "breaks
down," people get "turned-on" and "turned-off."

A final point about strong group/high grid practical physics is that the
universe is perceived to function extremely well with everything developing
and evolving as it should, much like a perfectly growing organism. Whatever
occurs, then, is necessary, proper, fitting, due, and inevitable. If something
negative happens to some individual or other, that can only be because that
individual is at fault. Thus in strong group/high grid, persons are guilty until
proved innocent. In the Soviet system only the guilty are charged in courts;
if they were not guilty, they would not be on trial. In the Vatican perspective
the church is always good and right and proper; deviation is always the fault
of the heretic charged with deviance.

Consequently, suffering and misfortune are necessarily due to the conscious, subconscious, or unconscious violation of the cosmic order by the
person suffering. There is a fixed and determined order to human living, an
order transcending, overarching, and controlling the lives of individuals and
societies alike, a divine plan or natural order. What happens has to happen,
and because of this fixed order the organically unfolding thrust of the process must be realized; communism has to win out in the end, the Roman
Catholic Church will prevail, the Chinese people will maintain their Middle
Kingdomhood. Strong group/high grid perspectives see the outcome of their
evolutionary purpose to be as inevitable as the growth of an oak from an
acorn, given proper conditions. Just as the developing oak must twist and
contort, be bent and bound back, so too human suffering and misfortune are
part of the organic growth process; they can be alleviated, but not
eliminated.

The strong group/high grid features just described are listed in figure 1
on pp. 14–15. However, there are other traits of this quadrant that might be
profitably considered. To begin with, strong group/high grid might best be
imagined as a triangle with a number of horizonal lines marking off distinctive *castes*. Where a person might fit along such a stratified triangle is determined by *ascription*. Ascription means being assigned a place in society on
the basis of some inherent and unachieved quality such as age, sex, birth, or
fictive birth (e.g., adoption, marriage, and divine election). Stratified, ascrip-
tion-based society is perceived as good, just as nature is good; there is no
sharp line separating society and nature; society as it exists is natural.
Strong group/high grid develops great pressure for intellectual coherence,

with elaborate theorizing about nature—nature meaning "reality" as untouched by humans or even new humans untouched by other humans, for
example, a baby right from the womb. Intellectual effort is expended to
elaborate a transcendental (transcultural, universal) metaphysics or philosophy which seeks to make explicit the match between society (and its institutions) and the purposes of God (the ultimate All) and nature. Intellectual
coherence requires explanation of both the society's boundaries over against
outsiders and the society's internal, separate, graded compartments and
their relationship to the whole. Synecdoche (part for the whole and whole
for part, e.g., man is microcosm) is used in metaphors of society and nature
to underscore their isomorphic structure and reciprocal support. Obviously,
then, going against nature is to court disaster. Unnatural behavior, whether
in humans or non-humans, is reprobated. The ultimate All (God, Mind, Process) sustains both society and nature. Theories of natural law flourish as do
doctrines of atonement and complete, once-for-all, divine interventions on
behalf of society. Unenculturated beings that need to be enculturated (e.g.,
children, animals, plants) have to be disciplined. Arguments premised on the
value of example and deterrence would justify the inflicting of physical pain
on such beings in their own interest. Consistent training programs in this direction are likely to be developed (e.g., plants consistently trained to fulfill
their nature and fit society).

The cultural process is one by means of which people produce meaning by using mediating materials. The processes of languaging and of defining persons, events, and things to mediate meaning were discussed
previously. In strong group/high grid the use of space evidences highly developed attempts to elaborate complex metaphors of symmetry, inequality,
and hierarchical relationships. Gardening is used as a means of justifying
and expanding the view of society as hierarchized, disciplined, and compartmentalized. Formal gardens present ingenious arrangements dominated by
design, with topiary, clipped borders, trees trained to weep or looped to give
light. Cooking likewise replicates social perspectives. Thus the edibility of
food would depend upon the part-to-whole pattern which projects social
structure and moral values on nature. Hence there is great emphasis on
class-specific foods and their availability and preparation. Finally, since nature is held to be on the side of the ultimate All (God, Process, Mind) and of
the good society, medical practice and therapeutic procedures will show
great trust in nature. Nature will cure on its own given half a chance. Rest,
sleep, and proper nourishment for signaling the sick status will achieve cure
without leaching, bleeding, purgations, surgery, or other violent intervention
into the human organism. A lock-and-key theory of science points to a technology in which the right formula has power to work of itself, *ex opere operato*, regardless of human intentions. Time is on the side of the physician.

Further, time is a community resource; hence the group imposes on its members required participation in leisure and group celebrations and rituals. Since everyone in the group is there for life, there will be a full demographic range of social representation. Time and death are part of the closed life cycle which the group encompasses and transcends by its own persistence; the life of the group is primary, far outspanning the individual. People who grow old in strong group/high grid have no reason to conceal the physical marks of aging. There will be distinctive styles of communication for each generation in speech, dress, and food, and each age cohort will be ready to claim the rights appropriate to itself. Fewer disappointments lie in wait for the old; they know how to behave, they represent the successful continuity of the group, and they are needed at the numerous group-celebrating ceremonies. Strong group/high grid is the best cultural script in which to grow old.

Strong group/high grid attitude toward youth depends on a major factor that falls outside this static, typological, grid/group analysis. If the group is successful in attracting and holding resources and in closing the channels of information from outside so that its theory of values is credible and is seen to match experience, there may be no generation gap. The upcoming generation will be loyal and open to the task of reproducing the social fabric. But this, of course, depends on how well the group manages its heritage and tradition. The grid must be experienced as high in the perception of the young.

Important group events are the main content of memorials and celebrations of times past. Since strong group/high grid exists in a longer time span in regard to both the past and the future, the sudden arrival of the millennium is simply not credible. The record of society's past from its foundation to the present is broad and deep. Plans have been laid for an evolving future, so it is contradictory to expect the end of the world soon. As a result, strong group/high grid evidences a strong sense of the past (but often without a sense of history, cf. P. Burke 1970) which is intended to justify the present and to which individuals owe undivided loyalty. Traditions, the presentness of the past, are part of nature, and the more the society is ordered by points of segmentation on a chronological scale (periods of the past), the more discriminated and the longer its perception of time past. The same would apply to a well-stepped and discriminated future.

Dimensions of human being that carry heavy social resonance include health and sickness, individual abnormality, death, and personal relations. In strong group/high grid the sick role is an accepted, well-exploited means of organizing group solidarity and thus of mustering support for the infirm. Failure to show sympathy and to offer help serves well for blame pinning and for clarifying social alignments. Strong group tends to make a public show of admiration for the courage of the sick but, since the universe is just in high grid, causes and responsibility for ill health have to be sought out. This perspective will create a fertile ground for the credibility of contamination theories and for linking moral causes with physical causes for sickness. Accusations of responsibility for sickness are used to trace lines along which full membership in the group might be ambiguous (significant for resident aliens, visiting foreigners, or transients). The trend of accusation acts as a control upon persons in weakly defined or poorly embedded roles. Readiness to care for the infirm derives from the way in which the sickness of an individual can be used to strengthen the group's sense of solidarity; it tends to be status specific, of course. Finally, the person who does not worry about his or her looks or health is admired, which points to worthwhile dedication to others, again usually in a status specific way.

Death, like heroism in suffering, is one of the ways of earning public recognition. Dying is much discussed, and altruistic ways of dying are given high salience. Typical symbolic stories nourishing group awareness tell of lives laid down for group survival or betterment. Funerals are an exacting public affair where tears flow without shame. Ceremonies of warm support for the bereaved are consistent with their status being ruthlessly exploited for group purposes in funerary rhetoric. Everyone goes to funerals; they are judged as a major ceremonial form; everyone knows how to put on a good one.

In strong group/high grid the right to take life is a matter of public concern. Attempts by the individual to abrogate the community right will tend to be disapproved (e.g., suicide, voluntary euthanasia, and abortion). Unless it is in the group interest, strong group/high grid will disapprove of any private ways of taking life.

In strong group in general and in strong group/high grid in particular the only unforgivable deviation is disloyalty. Therefore physical eccentricities including physical differences can easily be tolerated among other group variations, unless the group is marked off by definition based on some physical feature (e.g., skin color, hair color/texture, or height). Dwarfism, tallness, fatness, and large noses are part of the group's inheritance. If physical oddities can be recognized as part of a defining genetic strain, being seen as a "chip off the old block" is a positive value. But unusual physical handicaps come in for the same kindly treatment as long-term sickness—commiserated and somewhat exploited.

Since ascribed relations cover nearly every aspect of life in strong group/high grid, friendship is likely to be formally organized on universal principles such as being born in the same year, sharing a name, and being at the same school, college, or regiment. There will be, by definition, minimal scope for choice. Great control of procreation and of inheritance by prescribing the channels for permitted sexual relations, with a web of proscriptions over all sexual activities, is typical of this quadrant. Marriage is a valuable stake; hence single women of marriageable and childbearing age are a source of group dishonor, ritual defilement, and shame. To sustain the justification of their exclusion from equal opportunity within a given status, there will be theories of innate sexual capabilities to explain the female's relative position. Strong group regularly splits human nature into defilable and defiling women on the one hand and men relatively free from impurities of sex, except by contamination with women, on the other. Since women have to be subjected to meet the imperious demands of strong group over procreation, sexual pollution is always part of the cosmos put to use in threats and justifications.

So long as the grid is high, so long as values and experience match, change of any sort apart from the rather imperceptible, slow, and organic type noticeable in biological organisms is simply inconceivable. If experiences and values matched, how could one envision or imagine change? It is the high grid quality of life in strong group/high grid societies that gives their members a sense of inevitable permanence, of lastingness, of endless duration. But grids can drop. In strong group/high grid situations grids drop mainly due to external interventions such as war, conquest, unremitting famine, and plague. When such phenomena occur people will find it difficult to see how their experiences might continue to match socially held values; the grid drops. The result is a strong group/low grid situation.

STRONG GROUP/LOW GRID

For New Testament study this is a most significant cultural script, since it seems that nearly all the New Testament writings apart from the Gospel of John derive from persons socially and emotionally anchored in the strong group/low grid script. Contemporary examples of societies in this quadrant might be any country with four or more effective political parties: France; Italy; Turkey; Israel; or Greece. Similarly, the majority non-elites of democracies such as England or Germany, as well as the peoples subject to Soviet elites in both the Soviet Union and the satellite countries, would fit. In the first-century Mediterranean world this script seems to have been common to the groups of people under Roman domination—the various cities of the empire such as Corinth, Thessalonika, Ephesus, Philippi, and Colossae, as well as the cities of the Middle East such as Jerusalem, Antioch, or Alexandria, and specifically those segments of the population that did not fit into the collaborating framework of the Roman Empire. Thus the various Palestinian factions like the Pharisees, the Zealots, and the Jesus movement group can best be understood in terms of this cultural script.

As mentioned previously, strong group/low grid deals with individuals who define themselves in terms of their groups and their embeddedness in groups yet who find that the values held by the group and/or holding the group together cannot be verified in experience. The existence of this quadrant will normally be recognizable by a proliferation of competing groups, each attempting to be self-contained, to win out over its competitors, to defend its gains, and to consolidate its holdings. Thus, to follow figure 1 on pp. 14–15, there is strong concern in the respective groups about maintaining social boundaries, but the boundaries seem porous. The inside of the social body is under attack; there are informers, spies, or deviants present. The same holds for the physical body that replicates the social body; there are possession by hostile forces and a controlling and irresistible wickedness within the individual as well. Thus all kinds of pollutions and impurities (people, things, and events out of place) are present and cannot be effectively removed.

As far as rite is concerned, strong group/low grid is much like strong group/high grid in that it generates societies of fixed rites. However, the rituals and celebrations of this quadrant tend to focus on group boundaries rather than on stable caste classification. This means that initiation rituals which bring people into the group are of major interest and concern, e.g., circumcision for Jews, baptism for Christians, initiation procedures at Qumran, and marriage for all groups. There is an abiding concern to ferret out persons who do not belong within the boundaries, with fitting rituals for expelling them beyond group lines, like expulsion, shunning, or excommunication. On the individual level, the replication of the social level, there are rituals for casting out unclean forces from the individual body (exorcism) which usually work much like the ritual for casting out unworthy individuals from the social body.

This situation of porous boundaries and competing groups stands in great contrast to the solid, hierarchical, pyramidal shape of strong group/ high grid. In the low grid quadrant, as groups form and reform anew, permanence is no longer to be found outside the group; and where the group is, there is stability. Sacred place is located in the group, not in some impersonal space like a temple. The group is the central location of importance, whether the Body of Christ, the church, for Christians, or the synagogue gathering for Jews, or the philosophical "schools" and trade guilds of many urbanites of the Roman Empire. Discourse within these groups, whether words of a portable Torah, the story of Jesus, or the exhortations of the philosopher-teacher, becomes the mobile, portable, exportable focus of sacred place, in fact more important than the fixed and eternal sacred place of strong group/high grid societies.

As for personal identity, group membership becomes the primary focus for self-definition. In strong group/low grid it is not one's status in a pyramidally shaped hierarchy that counts but one's group affiliation in terms of overlapping memberships, for example, in kin group, occupational group, city or village legal status, and ethnic and fictive kin group. However, it seems that the kin group (family) is always primary with other groups replicating kinship values and structures (for the first-century Mediterranean world, cf. Elliott 1981). That is, people who belonged to groups like church or synagogue or trade were like "brother" and/or "sister," forming fictive kinship groups, groups *like* the kinship groups of the culture in question. Social roles, the sets of rights and obligations in terms of which individuals relate to each other, are rather confused in the low grid situation. No one is sure about rights and obligations, and these features become prime topics of discussion and debate. Strong group/high grid offers clearly defined, well-delineated sets of permanent and enduring roles; not so in the low grid counterpart. Such confusion and uncertainty about roles is what low gridness entails by definition. Due to such uncertainty about rights and obligations, especially outside one's group, individuals find it difficult if not impossible to judge where others stand on the basis of their behavior. External appearances are dissociated from internal states. One might appear to be living out a social role but might not be the person that the role would indicate. Thus warnings not to judge people by externals abound in this quadrant, although the only data available for assessment are externals.

Like the social body, so too the individual body is plagued by boundary problems. Strong group/low grid is as formal and precise as strong group/high grid in the use of titles, in interpersonal interactions, and in the maintenance of all semblance of order, regularity, and self-control. However, in the low grid situation social control, like self-control, is under attack and can break down quite easily. Bodily boundaries, like social boundaries, are all too porous; invaders penetrate all too readily, whether evil spirits, wicked thoughts, perverse ideas, or uncontrollable urges. Sin, evil, strife, contentiousness, factions, and divisions of all sorts are in the heart of the individual (so the heart has to be continually monitored), as well as in the core of the social body (which also has to be continually monitored). But the heart, the inside, is ultimately inaccessible to human scrutiny. What is discernible is the works of the heart which reveal what is in the heart, although even these can be deceptive.

Consequently the body, social and individual, is not a symbol of life, not a representative of the best of all possible worlds in the best of all possible times (as it is in strong group/high grid). Rather the body, social and individual, needs to be transformed much like the times have to be transformed, and, since the body is not a symbol of life, what happens to the body is not of great consequence. The body, social and individual, is a means to some larger transformation, some broader final state, some other end.

Sin is deviance. The sinner, the deviant, is one who disturbs the social order by being out of place or by putting someone or something else out of place. In strong group/low grid scripts deviance is seen as penetrating and then lodging itself within persons and groups mainly because the boundaries are so porous. Consequently, internal states of being, individual and social, are more important than adherence to formal rules. However, formal rules are still valued; the law must be obeyed; the enforcers of formal rules must be respected. In sum, strong group must be accepted even if grid has its problems. Since strong group mainly points to emphasis on social structures (means) while grid points to social values (ends), strong group scripts are heavily concerned with social means, social structures, and social institutions. But the low grid situation makes the existing structures appear to be temporary, transient, and essentially unsuitable for the job of realizing the values that they should, that is, the values of the grid. Hence social structures like kinship and government and their replications in various groups are perceived as passing, rather temporary phases of life to be respected but not worthy of full commitment. In fact it is possible to live without them at all. In the world of the New Testament noteworthy alternative structures arose, such as celibacy (Cynics), hermit living (John the Baptist), and alternative kin groupings of a lasting kind (Qumran, Pythagoreans).

Cosmology, the way in which persons perceive their physical environment to be outfitted and to function, is like strong group/high grid in some respects. Like the high grid, the low grid script perceives the world in terms of personal causality and explains events anthropomorphically. However, it differs radically in its assessment of the ongoing processes of the universe. Strong group/low grid, unsure of the state of purity boundaries, tends to see the world in terms of a dualism in the sense that there are warring forces of good and evil with the evil outside and penetrating the good inside. "This world" serves as antithesis to some other world. "This world" of hostile groups and conspiracies that thwart the best and noblest human aspirations must be evil; those in our group are good, no longer part of "this world." In such circumstances the universe, like the social world with its competing and controlling groups, is obviously unjust and whimsical. Thus the fact that the Roman occupying forces in Palestine or, in the case of contemporary multiparty societies, the central government or the party in power are unjust and whimsical is quite normal. Thus this world, as untrue, unjust, and evil as it is, is obviously under the dominion of forces hostile to human beings.

Since the world of human experience is so whimsical, it follows that suffering and misfortune are not automatic punishments for anything in particular but generally are unjust and unwarranted intrusions by some personal causes into the life of the individual or group. They can thus be attributed to malevolent forces (conspiracies, enemies, evil spirits, or wicked persons). Since this world, like our group and my body, needs to be transformed, suffering and misfortune cannot be expected to be eliminated. At most they can be alleviated for a time. Thus in the world of Jesus those healed by Jesus would not thereby presume that they would never get sick again, much like the persons raised by Jesus still have to die.

Strong group/low grid society might best be imagined as a network of interrelated sets of circles in apparently haphazard order (Boissevain 1974). Each circle represents a group related in multiple fashion to other groups while vying with still other groups in the attempt to acquire what the society considers significant and to maintain those acquisitions in spite of porous boundaries. While the group might appear to be acquisition oriented to outsiders, it might be more accurate to describe the main criterion of strong group/low grid as *acquisition maintenance*. The problem is how to maintain what one inherits, has ascribed to him or her, or acquires. Life is a constant challenge and hassle. Thus strong group/low grid perceives all human beings as divided into insiders and outsiders. Outsiders are hostile, actually or potentially, while insiders are continually disappointing expectations. Both nature and society have their rotten core.

There is no elaborate theorizing, no pressure for intellectual coherence. There is a bias toward single-issue theorizing that best supports the small group's decision to opt out of wider social involvement and identification. These features, of course, are typical of most of the New Testament texts, as the script would predict. The insider/outsider division is replicated in the division of nature into good creatures who stand for us and evil creatures who stand for them. We are vulnerable, lovable, natural victims in a predatory world; they are menacing, predatory, untamable, uneducable, poison contaminants that need to be purged. Dispute resolution takes the form of unmasking "wolves in sheep's clothing" and expelling the evil from the ranks of group members. Political and moral problems can be resolved by using nature in moral justifications; a recognized class of denatured human beings provides a way of resolving such problems (denature = unnatural = unenculturated = deviant). Scapegoating and expulsion make sense because of the inevitable enemy within; witchcraft models are most at home in this quadrant. While theories of natural law are valued, internal states of being are more important with doctrines of rescue from the impossible low grid situation (salvation) being prominent. Finally, animals and children, if they are to be domesticated and fit within the group, have to be disciplined; there are no inhibitions about using exemplary and deterrent physical punishment on them in their own interest. But there is no consistency in the application of such discipline.

While ambiguity and porousnesss are the prevailing conditions of social intercourse, the individual finds societal identity difficult to ascertain. Since nothing at the societal level defines him or her, the model of the smaller group, the village, or the small city section, fenced around, copied, and recopied from larger to smaller contexts, is an easy one on which to establish a generalized dyadic personality. Thus the small, closed groups typical of this quadrant use a recursive pattern of external boundaries at all levels; village or city-quarter boundaries will be clearly demarcated, as will compound and house boundaries. Within the house, the main rooms, kitchens, and lavatories are likely to be segregated by rules which protect individual privacy. Gardening is characterized by marking off or "hedging around" the different plots such as vegetables, front and back, and flowers. Gardening is essentially functional, that is for the produce, and is not considered a hobby, means of exercise, or recreation. As for cooking, the classification of edible food will replicate insider/outsider boundaries, with a prohibition against eating carnivores. Lambs and wolves have their different claims to be classed inedible. For those parts of nature which are immediately edible strong group/low grid adopts a long and complex, boundary-passing process for transforming the raw into the cooked. There is often little possibility of recognizing the original object once it has passed through the culinary process. Since danger is in stronger focus than is enjoyment, there is often a restrictive attitude to drink, drugs, and smoking. While being conservative in its tastes strong group/low grid has no objections to or predilections for packaged and highly processed foods. Great value is placed on denaturing natural products to render them edible. As regards medicines, strong group/low grid has clear ideals of good and effective therapy, but they are inevitably frustrated in practice due to the wrong moral attitudes of doctor and patient alike. In its therapy this quadrant places special emphasis on the strength of bodily boundaries and on purging evil that may have intruded. Procedures can work *ex opere operato* provided patient and healer have the right intention (hence partly *ex opere operantium*). Violent interventions like leaching, bleeding, surgery, and purgations are effective.

Time is not a resource in short supply as is literally everything else. The boundaries of the group set the limits to the use of time. Low grid indicates that time will not be compartmentalized; hence it will be used quite flexibly with no rules against using work time or drinking time for promoting group concerns or against separating work from play or conversation time from politics and shop. New Testament missionary stories, like the behavior of Paul, bear out this point.

Old age is a convenient principle for settling dilemmas about precedence and becomes a source of status in itself. Hence there is no incentive to disguise the changes of age in personal appearance or to stay looking young.

However, since this quadrant generates rather frustrating social life, old age is likely to be a disappointment. Old persons must be careful not to draw to themselves the scapegoating energies of the rest of the community. Since everyone in the group is there for life, groups normally will contain the full human age range. Further, since they are not insulated or set apart in any special way, the young are likely to be so assimilated to the group that any disagreements between young and old will not be seen as a generation gap but as a conflict between insiders and outsiders.

Strong group/low grid groups are likely to set up memorials to important group events, but not of the same quality as strong group/high grid would establish. Being liable to frequent fission, the record of any strong group/low grid history from a given group's foundation will be briefer than that of the larger and more complex strong group/high grid because there are fewer points of differentiation. It takes but a few, telescoped steps to move from the very beginning of the world to the founding ancestor to the recent breakaways that led to the immediate present. Correspondingly, the future is less discriminated. As a result the sudden arrival of the millennium is more credible here. Strong group/low grid has a marked emphasis on the past; present action is legitimated by commitment to past data. But, due to both its insulation or withdrawal from broader, more complex society and its telescoped perspective on the past, it is likely to be syncretistically open to occult practices and promises emanating from non-authorized, antiestablishment sources. Thus the more strong group/low grid focuses upon and emphasizes its boundaries, the more its prophetic threats will be loaded with hate and vengeance.

The sick role works much as it does in the high grid quadrant. However, strong group/low grid seeks out causes and responsibilities for ill health, thus creating fertile conditions for the credibility of contamination or conspiracy theories and for linking moral with physical causes of sickness. Accusations of responsibility for sickness are used to mark off covert factional lines. Thus witchcraft or possession accusations will be challenges to existing authority, or vice versa. Readiness to carry responsibility for the infirm derives from the way in which an individual's sickness can be used to strengthen the group's sense of solidarity. Even for the heavy burden of chronic and/or major illness, there will be well-defined roles for bedside attendants and respect for those aiding the sick. The heroism of the attendant is due for praise as is the heroism of the sufferer, but chronic illness may well become the occasion for attacking broader society since the group sees itself as its victim. In that case the double heroism of suffering and care is also a further reproach against the larger society, first for causing the menacing conditions, and second for not supplying remedies and compensations. Finally, people who do not worry about their looks or show concern about their physical well-being are admired, normally for behaving thus on behalf of the group.

Death is treated much as it is in strong group/high grid; only it is often perceived as unjust. Similarly personal abnormality and handicaps are considered just as they are in the high grid perspective, but if they are negatively assessed then they are judged to be unjust.

As regards personal relations, since there is no system of ascribed relations in strong group/low grid, elective friendship is the norm. Friends are acquired and maintained; the role of "best friend" needs to be developed for the individual's support at times of life crises. Generally the elective best friend is institutionalized, but the search for allies is restricted to ingroup members. Allies are sought to promote factional advantage. Sexual relations follow the same lines set out in the high grid script; however, the boundaries here are somewhat porous.

In conclusion, it might be noted that just as strong group/high grid societies can change only if the grid comes down, so also strong group/low grid scripts can change only if the grid goes up. It seems that most large scale strategies for the transformation of strong group/low grid societies include plans for an ideal strong group/high grid future. For instance, Marxist-Leninist blueprints, all forged in strong group/low grid settings, planned for the raising of the grid, much as has been effected in the Soviet Union. Structurally, the Christian movement was not much different. Jesus' future rule of God entailed a strong group/high grid transformation to be effected by God, as did Paul's hope for a grid-raising coming of the Messiah with power, patterned after an imperial visit (in Greek, *parousia*). It is no wonder that, when the Christian movement was eventually transformed and firmly embedded within the strong group/high grid matrix of the Roman Empire by the time of Justinian (sixth century A.D.), theologians could talk about the Christian church as "God's kingdom on earth," a phrase still attractive and obvious to strong group/high grid theologians today.

On the other hand, strong group/low grid societies need not get their grids raised by some transformation or other but may simply linger on in the strong group/low grid quadrant. Such is the case with most of the societies of the Mediterranean today as well as with most of those in antiquity. Further, figure 1 on pp. 14–15 also points to another possible option for movement from the strong group/low grid situation. Individuals from strong group/low grid societies might become disembedded from the strong group and slide along the group axis into the weak group side. In that location the initially lone individual can entertain new visions of life, the weak group/low grid perspective. The next chapter provides a description of the weak group quadrants.

3.

Weak Group Script Elements as Meaning Fields

INTRODUCTION

In the grid and group matrix the main feature requiring classification on the weak group side of the horizontal axis is individualism. People who have used Douglas' grid and group model as first presented by her (1970) have been confused by the subsequent articulation of that model in her paper entitled *Cultural Bias*. The reason for this is that in the later paper her new weak group/high grid quadrant (she calls it "Square B," cf. 1978: 20–21 *et passim*) is in fact a description of the lowest rank of strong group/high grid. The result is that readers perceive the confusion and abandon the model. In this chapter the weak group scripts are presented in a way that does justice to the definitions of grid and group presented above. Consequently there will be some departures from Douglas' description. Furthermore, an appendix at the close of the chapter will expand the matrix into eight categories for reasons specified below.

WEAK GROUP/HIGH GRID

Weak group/high grid is characterized by individualism along with a general match between values and experience. As Geertz's comment on individualism cited above (p. 19) would indicate, this is a rather rare cultural script on the planet both in the past and at present. However, for persons in the United States it is perhaps the most important of the four grid/group scripts since it seems to be typical of mainstream Americans. But given the complexity and population flow of the U.S., there are also significant strong group/low grid collectivities, for example, the Amish, Hutterite groups as well as the various, newly arrived, close ethnic groups. Furthermore, there are also strong group/high grid groupings in the U.S., but these are generally temporary, depending on the exercise of certain roles such as the military, corporation executives, physicians, and lawyers during their working hours (cf. Deal and Kennedy 1982). While a few such persons remain in strong group/high grid for the larger part of their lives, most shed these occupational roles, the switch being marked by the rite of changing "uniform." They then generally revert to weak group/high grid normalcy typical of mainstream America, its TV shows and movies, its newspapers and magazines, and its multiple main streets, downtowns, or shopping centers across the country.

The purity concerns of weak group/high grid scripts are largely pragmatic or technique oriented. The word "pragmatic" covers a set of values that essentially bear upon the mastery, control, manipulation, management, and direction of the environment. This environment is perceived to consist of everything that surrounds the individual, including other persons, groups, and concrete physical objects from cityscape to countryside. The weak group/high grid social body, like the replication of that social body in the individual, prides itself on being in control of concrete situations and concrete processes. It believes it must exert active mastery over everything or everyone with whom it comes into contact. It looks upon social interaction as a game in which the technically competent achiever can take all and the competent man or woman inevitably wins if only allowed to compete fairly and equally (cf. Hochschild 1981).

What this comes down to is the presumption that boundaries are of value only insofar as they work for some practical goal or end. If they do not work, they should be changed. Sixty-five is a good retirement age, but if it does not work for the well-being of a large group of individuals then the age must be adjusted one way or the other. Older buildings are fine as works of art and historical markers, but if they stand in the way of necessary technological adjustments (called "development" in this quadrant) then they must be torn down for something "better," meaning more efficient. Practical know-how counts more than impractical, non-functional thinking. If the car of a physician, judge, or university professor should break down, it is not beneath the dignity of those persons to open the hood and get their hands dirty to start the machine running again. The same holds for the pipes and wires in their houses. The practicality that crosses socially fixed lines and boundaries is of greater value than the lines and boundaries themselves. Practicality knows no law. Since in the pursuit of practicality a person just might have to cross lines—a broken down car blocking an intersection might have to be pushed by lawyers, physicians, judges, or other notables to get traffic moving—then it is simply premature to view a person or thing out of place without reference to practical outcomes. Pollution, then, is not automatic; a person must be presumed innocent until proved guilty; possession is nine-tenths of the law. Since what counts is what is practical and what works, the bodily wastes of the individual and the social wastes of society are really not threatening. To work with such wastes is not demeaning. Hence engineering of every sort—civil, chemical, electrical, biomedical, and social—is good. Both bodily and social wastes should be recycled because such recycling is practical and pragmatically useful.

The distinctive aspect of weak group/high grid rites is that the individual remains superior to the rite. People in this quadrant feel that they can walk out on anything and often do—church services, movies, lectures, and even football games. As individuals they are above the rites of the group, whether celebration or ritual. Individuals in this script do in fact use a large number of rites; witness the great number of ritual certificates issued in the U.S., as previously mentioned. Perhaps the most frequent set of line crossings pertains to buying and selling, but there are also graduations, weddings, funerals, and a host of private rites such as buying and wearing new clothes to celebrate line crossings like a new job, a much wanted divorce, or a new season of the year. Thus there are private rites taking place in the confines of one's apartment along with the broader public rites from buying and selling to naturalization and governmental swearing-in ceremonies.

However, what is really typical of weak group/high grid scripts is that there is no single rite that can capture universal attention and serve to define, mark off, and embrace the whole of reality as experienced in such a society. The closest single rite in recent memory that came near to delimiting the whole of U.S. social reality was the celebration of the bicentennial of the country, July 4, 1976. However, such rites are rare since individualism is loath to allow a person to feel embedded in a group, much less in an entity like a national society.

As for personal identity individualism, as defined above (p. 19), is the norm. Whatever sets the person off from other persons, one's points of differentiation, is normally emphasized. When two Americans meet and talk for the first time, they usually spend the whole opening section of the meeting rite by emphasizing differences, thus setting up their personal identities. Similarities are simply not interesting as a rule. While the proliferation of the practical technologies with which the individual surrounds himself or herself seems to be pragmatically inspired (to save time, steps, and energy), the gadgets equally serve to keep the individual apart from other individuals and thus heighten the sense of individuality. Individually owned washing machines, telephones, and cars, for instance, keep people from face to face contact. Furthermore, since purity lines get drawn pragmatically, the individual tends to assess himself or herself (as do his or her superiors) in terms of adaptability, flexibility, and practicality, each rated quantitatively (how much, how many). The same holds for replications of the individual in discrete social bodies. For example, quality schools and quality education are normally judged in terms of how much they cost, how much teachers get paid, how many students are processed, the number of degrees awarded, books in the library, and buildings on campus. Because questions of quality are not amenable to pragmatic and technological assessment, the kinds of teachers and students or books and buildings are usually of secondary concern.

The body, individual and social, is viewed instrumentally, practically, as a means to some end. Individualism has its goals or ends located in some "soul" or "spirit" which is normally considered a private and individual matter. Douglas' model of the implications of body/soul dichotomy illustrates the ramifications of weak group/high grid and its focus on soul and spirit (cf. pp. 23–26 above). As a result the body, individual and social, is viewed as a means to some end. People can be used like things because the emphasis is on services rendered, their "bodies." Farms and factories hire "hands." The proper functioning of the self, of the body, is often compared to a machine for flawlessness, accuracy, and dependability. "Automatic" outcomes are highly praised in people, for example, in assessing the skills of sports heroes and the reliability of colleagues. Thus machine analogies continue to be common for interpersonal and intrapersonal experiences: turn on, turn off, tune in, tune out, break down, run down, run out of energy. The individual, like the social body, assesses himself or herself (or perhaps better, a unisexual "oneself") in terms of pragmatic output normally translated into terms of the least common quantitative denominator of exchange, money. Gross National Product and annual income perhaps serve better to judge and appraise individual social location and national self-esteem than any other norm.

Sin or deviance, as repeatedly pointed out, refers to people out of place or persons causing things or other persons to be out of place. In weak group/high grid such deviance is thought to be caused basically by ignorance, individual inability, or individual failure. Thus solutions to deviance often consist of ever increasing doses of education, information, and indoctrination to remove the ignorance, much as doses of medicine take away illness. If ignorance is eradicated and a person continues to be deviant, then training of a practical sort is in order to make up for the abilities lacking in the person. Acts of deviance are, more often than not, considered to be the result of stupidity rather than moral bent. Responsibility for individual behavior is assessed commensurately with a person's knowledge or ignorance; the individual should feel guilty about deviant behavior even if not caught. Individual conscience (or ego-image) is thought to be a great deterrent to deviance, provided the individual's ego-image falls within the grades of normality attached to high grid. While members of a corporate board who overspend and waste government millions are not deviant, a shoplifting individual certainly is. In the grid corporate structure protects the individual because corporations run according to strong group/high grid scripts while single individuals playing the buyer role on their own follow weak group/ high grid scripts.

The weak group/high grid individual is not only above social rites but also above and outside organic cosmic processes. This means that the universe as a whole and the earth in particular exist for the individual to use and exploit as he or she sees fit, a perception characterized by the value called "technologism." The universe and its regularities are observed and modeled with a view to predicting variables and controlling resources to the individual's own purposes. Such models of prediction and control of the human environment (including people as part of that environment) are commonly called "science," a great value in weak group/high grid society. Thus individuals are free to exploit their environment in a competitive way. Practices that physically "pollute" the environment might not be morally wrong but could be simply dumb in the long run. The cosmos is benignly amoral like a car or a refrigerator; it would be downright stupid to abuse it so as to render it inoperative. Rather, one should adjust it and make it work for individual success.

Significantly for the study of religion, individuals in weak group/high grid society naturally (i.e., culturally) perceive themselves as in charge of their own piece of the cosmos, their own lives, and their overall destinies. Any gods or God that might enter the picture are always subservient to the individual, a junior partner in the process of life. Some ultimate All (gods, God) is important but only when the individual loses control of the situation. God normally has a role like that of a waiting room attendant or secretarial pool member, to be called upon at the behest of the individual, not the other way around. Thus God-focused religion in weak group/high grid society is often a secondary, implicit, and private concern but highly important since the individual can be quite fragile and lose charge of things easily. Thus God the junior partner is still partner, even if junior, dealing with the devotees as a proud parent trying to steer a budding adolescent on his or her individualistic way.

Finally, in this cultural script suffering and misfortune are generally ascribed to ignorance and stupidity. People who use their heads and follow current "scientific" information should be able to avoid them. Just as the individual should be able to eliminate suffering and misfortune, so too the social body in its medical and "scientific" institutions believes suffering to be totally eradicable. Wars on poverty, cancer, or muscular dystrophy are fought with a view to total conquest and not simply as holding actions resulting in compromise situations.

Weak group/high grid might best be imagined as a ladder with a large number of rungs marking off quantitatively determined *statuses*. An individual's location on the ladder is determined by *achievement* assessed in terms of mass dimensions—bigger/smaller, more/less, heavier/lighter—and expressed in quantified terms (on achievement, cf. Spence 1983). Both the individual human being and nature are good, but those at the higher achievement rankings have to exploit the resources of nature, including other human beings, for the quick and large results required for maintaining what they have achieved. In the weak group/high grid ranking system the lower level individual experiences higher level individuals as anonymous and merciless, as putting him or her under continual threat of withdrawal of support and under pressure to deliver and make promises or lose credit. Society too is an unremitting source of worry as well as of rich prizes: of worry because of the need to compete in order to achieve and of prizes because of the outcomes of successful competition. In the competitive environment individuals tend to see corruption, self-seeking, and aggression as characteristic features of human social life. Nature is idealized as good and simple, yet to be exploited; hence a wistful sense of alienation from nature never wins out against the excitement and rewards of achievement. There is continual selectivity in the social environment here since the ranking system is open-ended, and achievement-oriented persons can therefore fail and contract on the size scale or they may succeed and thus expand on that scale. Because of this feature the quadrant is marked by intellectual vigor, requiring and demanding the highest standards. If the competitor is not allowed to get by with sloppy performance, why should anyone else whether musicians, cooks, waiters, or builders? In any field of competence weak group/high grid demands high levels of performance.

Human aesthetic achievements in the plastic and performing arts as well as in literature, film, and sports are much used as weapons of justification and legitimation in moral arguments; they function like tradition in strong group/high grid and like nature in strong and weak group/low grid. Sports and film "stars" as well as characters from fiction, television, and the movies serve as touchstones and criteria for assessing what is expected. Aesthetic achievement in the areas of sports, film, television, and literature indicates an aspect of social life separated from the dirty compromises of achievement in commerce, politics, or economics.

Self-expression and self-teaching are held to do the most justice to the idea that human beings and nature are essentially good. Hence, theoretically, children and animals need not be disciplined to fit into society. Yet there are inhibitions that prevent the theory from being espoused wholeheartedly. For there is simply too much to teach which cannot be imparted to little ones without contriving hidden controls and hidden disciplines that might directly manipulate them to meet general societal needs.

Space is divided into competitive and non-competitive areas. In the competitive area weak group/high grid individuals adopt high standards of spit and polish, tidiness, style in decoration, and elegance; this is publicly assessed space, strongly classified according to social rank. Non-competitive space, invariably a private area, may be untidy or mixed. The mixed private space replicates some of weak group/high grid's inhibitions about free expression in the enculturation process, as mentioned previously. Moreover, if gardening is a medium of social relations in the treatment of space, it is at once a medium of competition. Subtle contrived effects, such as plants brought from afar, cherished skillfully to thrive in unusual climates and soils, and made to look natural, are highly valued. The seasons are defied and color glows the year round. Elaborate landscaping enlarges the sense of space and gives a "natural" effect.

Relative to cooking, weak group/high grid treats food as one more medium of competition and achievement, so it prefers imaginative, innovative processes and rare products (but not necessarily new ones, since ancient skills and processes can be rare too). Its eclectic openness to fashion and its readiness to loosen boundaries for pragmatic effect bring zest to the search for culinary novelty. Cooking time is shortened for there is not the special value on denaturing natural products to render them edible, as is the case found in strong group.

Medicine, notably in its pragmatic aspects, belongs to achievement quite emphatically. The latest developments of technological science are the only medicine good enough. It is chic to know the names of new diseases and treatments and to be able to identify them. This quadrant values medical information quite highly. Medicine works *ex opere operantis*, the *operans* being the competent and bonded achiever whose role it is to deal with the sick.

Time is an individual resource ever in short supply simply because the individual's lifespan is the normative period for achievement. Age in itself is not a criterion of deference or discrimination. The absence of strong group implies that there is no way of conceptualizing what being aged means. The passage of time is not necessarily a criterion of intimacy or for distinguishing between old and new friends. In weak group/high grid's achievement-oriented cosmology, the harsh principles of selection may eliminate the aged and less competent from the living space of the present achievers (who can thereby drive the aged down grid and perhaps toward strong group). The aged individual thus tends not to meet people outside his or her generation. Personal appearances should be young and active in this quadrant. Tensions and disappointments are to be concealed. Living style ought be one of apparent relaxation and readiness to take on anything. Older men here will be quicker to adopt cosmetic aids, hair dyes, and youthful looking cuts of clothing; their walk will seem springy.

Weak group/high grid has tolerance as its hallmark. It does not close

off options, being socially and intellectually open. It tolerates the rising generation very well and generally defends its attempts at individuation. At
times the competitive achievement orientation of this quadrant undergoes
the paradox of sympathizing with rebellions disastrous to its interests. However, it can tolerate a great amount of mixture and confusion.

As for times past, the dead who have achieved become part of society's
heritage as well as harmless, non-competitive parts of the environment.
There is much scope for valuing their memory, especially in terms of entre-
preneurial energy (souvenirs, albums, fund raising). Weak group/high grid
submits claims of historicity to the same competitive, skeptical criticism to
which it submits every other idea. Ever testing and challenging perspectives
on the past, it gives rise to the "science" (social) of historiography. The future is recognized as full of uncertainty, as indeed it is, but this realistic
acceptance of a high-risk, short-term future does not make it susceptible to
millennial prophecies. Prophets of doom must validate their claims just as
anyone else, competitively. Weak group/high grid can take a long view of
history because of its refined critical apparatus and thus joins up with strong
group/high grid in its potential to withstand millenarian movements.

In weak group in general, people are not able to use the sick role to
muster support since there is by definition no abiding group that might harness their weakness to its purposes (yet certain provisional groupings might).
Here it is best to brave it out and say nothing about personal ill health, unless the individualist is suddenly going to be able to interest others in his or
her condition, as when the condition is of a prestige variety and offers competitive advantage to the sufferer. Yet it would be better not to seem off
form so as to avoid adverse judgments when selective procedures are at
work. Nothing is to be gained either by flaunting heroic wounds or pinning
blame on others.

Since the wiser course is to reject the sick role, the individual will try
to keep fit. The natural bias in the script encourages conversation about
dieting, good health practices, and exercise. Not to look after oneself or to
be unconcerned about one's looks is viewed negatively as an indication of
unwillingness to compete.

The care of the sick is a difficult problem since it is essentially an individual concern. Since the individual is to live by the basic principle of self-
fulfillment, then close relatives are absolved from sacrificing their lives to an
invalid, whatever the strength of the invalid's claim to self-fulfillment. Conflict of rights and obligations in this area are solved with the requirement of
professional help to be provided by the anonymous political institution free
of charge to those unable to compete unless this might totally suppress their
achievement orientation. But the self-reliance principle may shift to the welfare state for non-achievers because of the priority accorded to competitive

efficiency as a condition for realizing the full scope of individual development and achievement. Individual development and achievement ever remain basic referents for social assessment.

In unfair and unequal competitive situations individuals are free to leave their independent isolation to team up with others. Those afflicted with enduring handicaps, for instance, are urged to team up with others with the same difficulty, such as victims of multiple sclerosis, diabetics, and epileptics. It is quite acceptable for health "benefactors" to harness the weakness of such teams (organizations) for their own competitive purposes.

Death has no social place and hence no subject to celebrate publicly. Talk about death is rare. The ideal way of encountering death is unexpectedly, painlessly, suddenly. Death should occur when an individual is in a positive competitive position—after some achievement or before some disaster—so that death signals a competitive position better than living would. Widows are often screened out of social intercourse.

The weaker the group variable, the more burial is treated as a private affair, almost of hygiene. But the memorial service has its competitive features. As for the right to take one's own life (suicide, euthanasia, abortion), it is a private, individual concern, with abortion being on the social borderline and hence ambiguous. In general, the individual has an overriding right to control his or her own destiny.

In almost all areas of life weak group/high grid is tolerant, unsqueamish, and unshockable but not where physical and patent mental abnormalities are concerned. Such defects imply the incapacity to perform in competitive situations; hence they are embarrassing and are not subjects to joke about.

A physically or mentally abnormal child takes up precious time; it creates heartrending dilemmas for its parents. With grandparents and retired or widowed aunts relegated to their own institutional spheres, the small, socially mobile family is rather stripped for action and lacks redundant personnel to care for its handicapped. Therefore these are sent to institutions, thus strengthening the assumption that segregating behavior is both appropriate and inevitable. Professions specialized in helping the handicapped attract to themselves the symbols of individual self-justification and acquire some of the honor that is reaped by family bedside attendants in strong group.

There is tolerance for physical abnormalities which do not require lavish expenditure of time and care. In fact, by capitalizing on personal oddities the individual can emphasize his or her individuality and exploit it as a personal asset for meeting the demands of specialized competition, thus making a virtue of singularity of appearance.

Since personal relations are not ascribed, elective friendship is the norm. Every individual knows that he or she cannot expect to survive socially without the sustained good offices of at least influential acquaintances, if not friends. The rites and language of friendship are highly developed cultural features. But achievement often encourages a readiness to take on new and better friends/acquaintances, while constraints on time result in the replacement of old friends.

Given the basic principles of tolerance and individual freedom, one might expect healthy minded, untrammeled enjoyment of all phases of life, including sex, with "easy come, easy go" as the governing ethical principle. But the sheer competitive exclusion of the "strongest" male may turn sexual disappointment into a symptom of general failure. Hence there will probably be as much anxiety about sex as about any other part of this achievement-oriented, competition-ridden quadrant. Competition generates anxiety for a person to seem adequately virile and alluring and to be seen to be open-minded about sexual deviance, successfully holding one's own, and the like.

If individuals are engaged in unrestrained competition to achieve, if they wish for alliances with those more influential or wealthier than themselves, if they sift and screen and drop weak allies and seek to bind themselves to strong ones, they will be tempted to break down any segregation or exclusivity in the political or commercial domains by involving kinship with their other affairs. Thus marriage, women, and children become pawns in the game of individual achievement. Hence there is no reason to expect females to be accorded rights equal to those of males unless females are allowed to compete individualistically beside and along with males. Those individuals open to competing and achieving females would insist on fairness and rules guaranteeing fairness that lead to equal rights. But to those closed to equal competition, women will be a source of dishonor, ritual defilement, and shame, especially if marriage is considered such a valuable competitive stake that women have to be kept under control. This will be coupled, of course, with theories about innate sexual capabilities to justify exclusion of females from equal opportunity to achieve, that is, to compete fairly.

The foregoing weak group/high grid script should seem familiar and reasonable to most U.S. adults in the mainstream of American life. However, to their college-age offspring the script may sound somewhat contrived. The reason for this is that, in the U.S. socialization process, adolescence (now up to about age thirty) is a distinctive period duly marked off by purity lines. During this time the individual is expected to "find himself or herself" and decide what to do with life. Young people are permitted to live with their societal grid down, to live in weak group/low grid. They are at times joined in this quadrant by those who "refuse to grow up," meaning "up the grid." Consider weak group/low grid.

WEAK GROUP/LOW GRID

Individuals held by the weak group/low grid social script do not form societies at all. This quadrant forms a social transitional area. Its individualistic occupants form impermanent groupings of varying types and numbers. This quality of weak group/low grid should be quite obvious from the variables. Weak group refers to individualism, going it alone. Low grid means experiences and values do not match in the individual's estimation. To live in such a cultural situation on a long-term basis seems rather impossible for an organized society or large group of persons, and even individuals in this location need to live off some stable society. Society might be defined as a set of interpersonal relations that define social roles, sets of rights and obligations that persons play out toward each other in some predictable and assured way. Groups differ from societies in that groups have participants in various roles, but lack sets of relations that mark off the social roles. For instance, persons in a small town or city neighborhood form a society with interrelated roles such as mother, father, mayor, banker, and clergy. College students, on the other hand, may have the role of son, daughter, or student, but when with a group of fellow students they form just that, a group. The reason for this is that the student role does not relate the person to other students but to the educational institution. Be that as it may, weak group/low grid is characterized by rather impermanent groups.

Weak group/low grid individuals define themselves for the most part by what they are against. They are against the scripts from which they emerged. An individual from weak group/high grid experiences a drop in grid and finds himself or herself in weak group/low grid, a common feature of U.S. adolescence. On the other hand, dyadic persons from strong group/low grid somehow get dissociated from their group and end up experiencing the individualism of the weak group/low grid sort. Both share the trait of being against the scripts of the quadrants from which they emerged. For instance, most religious founders in European history had their conversion experiences while in this quadrant, for example, Francis of Assisi or John Wesley (cf. Turner 1969; Turner's *communitas* is typical of this quadrant; further, Dumont's "individual as value . . . conceived as apart from the given social and political organization, outside and beyond it, an outworldly individual" [1982a: 16] is another case of weak group/low grid emerging from strong group/low grid; cf. Dumont 1982b; Bellah et al. 1982; and Eisenstadt 1983). Hence to know what will be emphasized by persons with this script, one must know their previous social location.

In the U.S. it is rather easy to see the drop in grid taking place as persons in early adolescence begin distancing themselves from their parents in the process of adult, individualistic ego-formation. At this stage, early adolescents simply do not wish to be known as Henry's or Harriet's boy or girl; they want to be known by their own first name and for their own sake. They are quick to criticize their parent's values, accusing them of being too materialistic, too selfish, too whatever. A collection of all such "too's" will provide a list of how weak group/low grid individuals are against the purity lines of the quadrant from which they came.

The Hippies of the fifties, the Yippies of the sixties, or the war protestors of the seventies are typical examples of grid drops, and so are any recently founded California churches or newer members of any cult group. At the outset of their existence communes are simply gatherings for "doing one's own thing." However, if the group persists at all the individuals comprising it will either move out and up the grid (witness the rehabilitation to weak group/high grid of the Yippies and war protestors of the recent past) or, if the individuals insist on staying together, move over to form strong group/low grid (and sometimes even strong group/high grid) self-contained units. Thus runs the path followed by some of the abiding U.S. communes in Oregon and New Mexico, and such ran the line of development of the Franciscan Order and the Methodist Church.

Weak group/low grid individuals focus their attention on the grid, on values and ends. What such individuals envision is not a change in the shape of society but a change in the values of society. They are into cultural change, a change of goals or ends, while the conflicting groups of strong group/low grid scripts are concerned with social change, a change in the social structures used to implement values (e.g., Marx, Lenin, Paul of Tarsus, and even Jesus of Nazareth as depicted in the Gospels).

The manner in which weak group/low grid individuals oppose the lines of the quadrants from which they come results in the perception of a lineless existence, hence unbounded, free, bubbly, spontaneous, ready to smell the flowers, to feel the wind, to do anything that symbols lack of social boundaries. Rites used to cross social lines, such as marriage, are dismissed as immaterial and unnecessary. Use of titles toward others is a recognition of roles, of lines, of people in place; hence use is dismissed in favor of nicknames or simply "hey, man." The "man" is basic humanity unencumbered by rights and obligations that roles entail. The technical name for this lineless experience is "liminality" (Turner 1969). Liminality is an emotional high, the feeling one gets when one is free of social contraints or when one is between or above the lines comprising stable society.

Obviously such experience is not confined to adolescents. Not a few Americans perceive themselves in weak group/low grid, at least temporarily, when they are on vacation outside the country in an environment in which no one knows them in terms of their usual social roles and where the values of the society they are visiting are very unlike the values at home. People on such foreign vacations let their grids drop, more or less. They become fast "friends" with their previously unknown traveling mates, and together these experience a relative freedom unavailable at home. However, once the trip is over back they go to their normal roles quickly forgetting their companions on the trip. There is, of course, much more to say about liminality and the group feeling it engenders, but this simple description should suffice here.

As far as personal identity is concerned, people in weak group/low grid feel that they ought to define themselves in terms of their basic humanness, apart from all the "put on," "unreal," and fake roles of the societies from which they came. They tend to see that society as terribly oppressive, but they do not hate people in it since all should be free "to do their own thing." While doing their own thing individuals in weak group/low grid frequently discover and create configurations of values hitherto unknown. The hermit artist, composer, author, and saint are well-known figures. Weak group/low grid is the home of the genius loner who, like other weak group/low grid individuals, must still live off of the society that spawned him or her.

The physical (and social) body is irrelevant in this script. Spirit, soul, and emphatic idiosyncrasy are all that count. True life is in the soul, in the heart, in the mind, in love. Celibacy or profligacy are to be found in this quadrant. The reason for this is that total renunciation of sexual relations and ready sexual relations with everyone in one's group are both societally irresponsible. With their sexual stance both express the position that the human relation symboled by sex is of singular unimportance and that being husband or wife with consequent parent roles (societal roles, not group functions) is irrelevant.

Sin or deviance in weak group/low grid is a matter of what "turns you off," of what makes a person untrue to his or her true and inmost feelings, or of actions and thoughts which betray all that the unaffiliated individual stands for. In a sense sin here is the entire person not living up to the vision and insight that weak group/low grid experience unveils. There is little if anything social at all about such deviance in the eyes of the individual and his or her group.

Futhermore, individuals in this quadrant find the universe and the world simply there, wonderful to behold and good if only it were not for surrounding society which blotches it all. God or gods are immediately available; experiences of the divine occur quite readily and without the need for churches, synagogues, priests, or ministers. Visions of the divine, auditions of heavenly voices, inspirations, and insights are typical of this social location. Things that could not be seen before or sounds that could not be heard before simply come tumbling forth. All this is normal in this quadrant. How-

ever, the value of such insights for society at large is rather uneven. For instance, the insight of early adolescents that what their parents say and do is
dumb is not very fruitful. But the works produced by poets and artists as
well as the lifestyle created by saints in this quadrant can and have moved
generations of people.

So far as the ills and woes of society are concerned, weak group/low
grid individuals come to the all too certain conviction that "all you need is
love." The message is always that love, care, and concern can conquer all,
that love can eliminate the strife and contention which mar living on the
planet. The real problem is that love involves both the free crossing of purity
boundaries and the elimination of many of the purity lines that define and
delimit the sets of related rights and obligations that constitute meaningful
society. Love has something chaotic about it in that to some extent it necessarily eliminates the lines that constitute order and meaning.

Weak group/low grid social formations might best be imagined as
groupings of individuals each of whom feels he or she stands alone even in
the presence of other individuals. The main criterion for meaningful living in
this quadrant is *contentment*, a contentment deriving from opposition to the
social thrust of the quadrant from which the individual derives. Thus contentment for a person from strong group/low grid would derive from being
against the maintenance of what the group has acquired, from non-acquisi-
tion, while contentment for one from weak group/high grid would be seen in
the espousal of non-achievement.

Weak group/low grid defines the quadrant from which it derived (often known as "society") as not-nature, hence as artificial and unnatural. Nature is identified with weak group/low grid experience; and nature is good.
Society, on the other hand, is an obstacle to contentment, often simply evil.
Nature represents all that is innocent and despoiled by civilization (the other
quadrants); nature is civilization's victim with whom the weak group/low
grid individual identifies. He or she is ready to lend support and sympathy
to endangered nature which pleads mutely for protection against the blind,
anonymous forces which threaten every individual.

Weak group/low grid prefers a model of enculturation of children and
animals that does the most justice to the value of the natural goodness of
children and animals and to the evils of civilization. There are no inhibitions
preventing this model from being espoused wholeheartedly. Children and
animals can be allowed full self-expression and experimentation since there
is nothing definite to teach except not to be like those in the quadrant from
which a given weak group/low grid individual came.

Boundaries around public and private space are perceived to be fused
and hence confused. The public is seen as naturally private, and the private
as naturally public. Space markers are judged to be societal artifices and

hence unreal and evil. Natural uses of space are highly valued, while human-made boundaries can never be exclusive or sacred. The quadrant tolerates mixtures of space (public and private) well.

Gardening is carried on with a view to purging societal influences. There is therefore great emphasis on natural foods, grown naturally without competition and chemicals. Since nature is abundant, gardening proves how cooperation with nature yields abundance. Gardens tend to have a wild, untouched look.

As for cookery, the closer to its natural state that a given food item can be prepared the better. Denaturing food is considered evil, too much like denatured society. The division between animals and plants is underscored, with plants alone allowed as food. Animals should be neither killed nor disciplined but permitted to follow their own course without constraints, much like weak group/low grid individuals follow theirs. Fish seem to be ambiguous, fitting on the borderline between animals and plants and hence left to the option of individuals.

When it comes to medication, natural remedies are the best. Products of human technology in the form of medicines or therapeutic treatments ought be avoided as unnatural. Natural remedies work *ex opere operato*. Obviously theories of medicine will be homeopathic with preventive medicine, especially living a life in accord with nature, being the best procedure.

Time in this quadrant is not in short supply but is rather a boundless individual resource. Low grid means time will not be compartmentalized; it can and will be used flexibly with no norms dictating when something must be done. Age in itself is not a criterion for anything unless the quadrant from which weak group/low grid emerged ascribed certain values to age (weak group/low grid will then ascribe antithetic values to it). As a rule, because of the attenuated group dimension, there is no way of conceptualizing what being aged means or of showing age any recognition. On the other hand, since being natural is the hallmark of this quadrant, there is tolerance for the vagaries and ignorance of youth, with social and intellectual openness to new forms and no options closed. There is much mixture and confusion, often cultivated to maintain position against the other quadrants.

Traditions are part of evil society and hence unnatural like that society. This quadrant consequently lacks any straightforward historical sense, since the script does not offer any selective principle by means of which to construct a history, except for biography and this is normally autobiography. Living takes place solely in the present; memorials to individuals from the past are unnecessary. As a result, the stronger the degree of insulation from the larger society (insulation by antithetic opposition here) and the greater the extent to which an individual's interests are insulated from those of others, the nearer may the millennium be plausibly foreseen. Forms of insulation or withdrawal from larger society indicate less historical sense; thus there is greater likelihood of the individual's being more syncretistically open to occult practices and promises emanating from non-professional and antiestablishment sources.

In weak group/low grid people cannot use the sick role to muster support since there is by definition no group or team which can harness weakness to its purposes. Here one must brave it out and say nothing about personal ill health. For the lone individualist will not be able to interest others suddenly in his or her condition, having already spurned the judgment of others about everything else. The sick role is best avoided by living in line with nature, letting nature take its course, and using only natural foods and remedies. Since weak group/low grid is contentment oriented and non-competitive, it flaunts not looking after oneself or worrying about one's looks. Living naturally will take care of health as well. Again, emphasis will be on natural ways to keep fit but with the avoidance of unnatural modes such as dieting or exercise merely for the sake of exercise. Since the care of the sick is the concern of the sick individual, it may best be met by using societal welfare systems but *not* as a conditioning or preparatory agency for future competitive efficiency and achievement orientation. Contentment, not competition, is the condition for realizing the full scope of personal development, and contentment alone is the referent for assessing life (enjoying having a good time, a trip, a lark, a high).

As a rule, weak group/low grid individuals are not inclined to philosophy. They are unconcerned about an afterlife, lacking a group adequately sprinkled with old persons whose deaths might lead to reflection on death and dying. Thus persons in this quadrant have little to say about death. Individuals have the right to control their own destinies and hence to take their own lives or to practice abortion on their own bodies. But the quadrant is not without its problems here. Abortion, after all, is unnatural; babies readily symbol vulnerable nature under attack by civilization. Death is natural and should take place in a way that is enjoyable to the dying one and in a contentment-oriented way.

Physical abnormalities of greater degree, that is, those calling for lavish expenditure of time, care, energy, and thought, are simply eschewed if only because they are unnatural. Such abnormalities are obviously caused by sick society. Hence society should take care of such persons in whatever way it sees fit. Abnormalities of lesser degree, especially if natural, can be capitalized to emphasize individuality and singularity of appearance. However, physical and mental defects can imply an inability to be content. If they do, they are an embarrassment and have to be rejected; if they do not, then whatever contentment the individual is capable of ought to be sought and provided, including requisite drugs, sex, and food. Institutionalization would be considered cruel and crude since it cuts off the individual's possibilities for natural contentment.

Since personal relations are not ascribed, elective friendship is the norm in this script. However, animals and humans are valued almost equally. Friends are chosen according to the extent to which they can provide for individual contentment needs, with unannounced and unplanned visits or sporadic appearances. No loyalty or commitment is given and none is expected. With contentment as paramount goal, there is little anxiety about sexual relations, about seeming virile or attractive; open-mindedness about sexual abnormality is normal, although natural modes are preferred. Further, since there is general rejection of societal responsibilities, weak group/low grid can opt for either sexual continence or sexual profligacy. Females are not excluded from equal opportunity for contentment, with male-female symbolic power balanced. Thus, with the basic principle of following nature and with tolerance and personal freedom from everything and everyone else, weak group/low grid's governing ethical principle is a self-focused "natural-mindedness," perhaps best articulated as "easy come, easy go."

For the reader of the New Testament, the weak group/low grid script is very important since at least one significant writing derives from it, the Gospel of John (Malina 1985). To verify this in a rather indirect way, consider which Gospel is most quoted by Americans and provides significant text-segments for billboard signs, crusades for Christ, "born again" groups, and people who believe in Jesus as their personal (i.e., individualistic) Lord and Savior. Furthermore nearly all Christian reform movements based upon special revelations to or revelational experiences of individual reformers have their biblical moorings in John's Gospel (cf. Küng 1967: 191–203).

SOCIAL CATCHMENT AREAS

Up to this point the items listed on the cultural scripts specific to each quadrant of Douglas' grid and group model (fig. 1 on pp. 14–15) have been considered. As mentioned at the outset of this chapter, Douglas herself has redefined the weak group scripts in a rather confusing way. One reason for this may be the fact that four categories are insufficient to deal with all cases, because some groups fall into the cracks and do not spill over into adjacent quadrants. Rather, they fall into social catchment areas typical of each quadrant. For instance, since high grid social scripts call for stratification in somewhat clear forms, some persons, even a majority of persons in a given society, can find themselves at the lowest rung of the high grid ranking or status system. Yet, instead of facing downward to low grid and forming predictable groups, such persons continue facing *upward to the high grid systems* in which they are embedded. These lowest high grid rungs thus form a social catchment area in which one finds both the dropouts of the weak group/high grid quadrant and the lowest stratum of the strong group/high grid script. Thus the untouchables in India, slaves in the Roman Empire, and the politically ostracized in the Soviet Empire all fall into strong group/high grid catchment areas. On the other hand, individuals who either cannot or will not compete for achievement goals yet who highly value achievement in the U.S., the U.S. poor, stand in a weak group/high grid catchment area.

The catchment areas thus represent extreme cases, the lowest ends of high grid spectrums. These areas would have their own distinctive scripts. Typically, the weak group individual and the strong group dyadic person in this area would have no scope for vertical personal interaction; rather interactions take place horizontally. Autonomy is minimal with most of life at the control and behest of vertical superiors. Individual behavior is directed and ordained by the classifications of the high grid societal system, clearly and fully defined and without ambiguity. Moreover, there are no rewards to which persons in this area can aspire or achieve other than those for fulfilling their allotted station. Since by definition there are no group boundaries below such persons that might enclose them on some ranking order, they are usually excluded from any of the formal groups that may exist because all such formal groups stand above on the stratification scale. The symbolic forces which maintain such persons insulated at the lowest rungs are remote and impersonal. In strong group these forces are either the group's power of exclusion (keeping lowest ranking persons in their lowest conceivable place) or the competitive energies of acquisition-maintenance oriented strong group/low grid groups or a mixture of both. In weak group these symbolic forces are the rules of fair play governing achievement; these rules, of course, relegate non-achievers to a place off and below the achievement assessment scale. Obviously such lowest rung occupants are peripheral to all decision making, even though they might constitute the largest portion of the population of a given high grid society.

For persons in these catchment areas, understandings about how the world works are likely to be a thing of shreds and patches picked up eclectically from other strata in the system. The most adaptive response in this situation will be great passivity since there are no rewards and no escapes conceivable (high grid does this). Furthermore, since persons in this social location have continual and intimate experience of punishment (in strong group) or rehabilitation (in weak group), they can see nothing problematic about using discipline to train the young. As a matter of fact such persons have no special theoretical problem about using discipline in any phase of social interaction (i.e., punishment or rigid rehabilitation).

With regard to the use of space, people in this script follow the compartmentalizations enforced by topside society rather passively. Generally admired spatial arrangements will be reproduced without any special meanings attached to them. As for cookery, restricted experiences make people here highly conservative in their tastes. There may be special value in denaturing products to make them edible, while there are usually no objections to or predilections for packaged or highly processed foods. As for medicine, moreover, pills and well-colored remedies are seized upon like any occult recipes without more reason or theory than one needs to consult a horoscope.

Time is not a personal resource in this social location since by definition it is all plotted out by others. Consequently the sense of time is poorly developed and/or not a matter of concern at all. The normal population of this quadrant may consist of an above average proportion of the aged. If so, this population will be insulated, with no opportunity to interact with other generations in day-to-day affairs. Furthermore, if youths in this sector do not adopt the passivity posture suitable to this social ranking, their elders will be afraid of them and avoid them.

People here respect the burial places of their private dead. Any straightforward historical sense is impossible to develop since there are no special selective principles or particular vantage points from which to construct a history. There are no systematic criteria for judging or verifying predictions. Since groups and individuals in this location are withdrawn and/or insulated from topside, larger society and since they possess little sense of history, they are more likely to be syncretistically open to occult practices and future-oriented promises emanating from non-professionals and anti-establishment sources, much as persons in weak group/low grid situations.

When socially recognized, sickness can at least give a little respite from pressures to conform. Self-inflicted death is often seen as a solution to unbearable conflict, with or without a theory to legitimate it. If any social problems arise due to personal abnormality and handicap, they will collect and settle here, but there is no distinctive theory to explain how to cope with them, nor is any such theory expected to emerge. Finally, since the individual or dyadic person is here bereft of larger and broader group support yet must still face sickness and death, the ideal of a friend is warmly acknowledged. Too often, though, the social ranking and insulation imposed from outside and afar prevent friends from rendering notable help to each other. As for sexual relations, those forcibly insulated will take their chances when they can, theory or no theory, pollution or no pollution. The balance of power between males and females is rather in equilibrium.

In the social catchment areas of high grid the criterion for a meaningful life is *conformity*. Topside society sets the norms to which people in these areas attempt to conform. In strong group, people in this area conform in terms of compliance, going along with the system because that is what one ought to do, while in weak group, persons' conformity takes the shape of congruence, finding it fitting or appropriate to conform as they do.

High grid social catchment areas might be said to have their corresponding low grid equivalents in extreme weak group/low grid and extreme strong group/low grid locations. The extreme weak group/low grid location would consist of hermits in the strict sense of the word, loners who totally avoid any interaction with their contemporaries and live out the features of the weak group/low grid script to the nth degree. On the other hand, in the strong group/low grid extreme stand groups that perceive the world in terms of strong group/low grid scripts pressed to their ultimate, such as apocalyptic, chiliastic, millenarian, end-of-the-world groups by whatever designation one wishes to label them.

With these last two types, the grid and group model now numbers eight scripts (cf. fig. 2 on pp. 66–67). Perhaps that number is necessary and sufficient. Thom (1969) has demonstrated that the number of biological shapes perceivable in four dimensions is eight and that these shapes necessarily emerge in fixed sequences. Thom is a typologist, a mathematician working in terms of shapes rather than numbers. In his work Thom suggests that perhaps the number of ultimate and distinct social structures is likewise eight. Thompson (1979) adopts Thom's insights to social theory by demonstrating that social change can be described in terms of the mathematical shape called a catastrophe.

In terms of the grid and group model, a catastrophe is exactly what happens when the grid comes down to such an extent as to warrant a change in script from high grid to low grid, regardless of the group aspect. While Thom and Thompson do not utilize Douglas' grid and group model and while Douglas does not understand it in the way it has been depicted above for the weak group side, yet it seems that the insights of Thom and Thompson would bolster the position adopted thus far in this book, namely, that there are eight ultimate social scripts and that groups adopt and adapt to these scripts in terms of changes initiated, for the most part, by a drop in grid, with subsequent modifications due to alterations in group location.

CONCLUSION

Up to this point the items listed on the cultural scripts specific to each quadrant of Douglas' grid and group model (fig. 1 on pp. 14–15) have been considered. Four other variations, the catchment areas, have been added to these (fig. 2 on pp. 66–67). Each script offers a rather different vision of the world, a different set of emphases which enables people to see life in a certain way while preventing them from viewing it in any other way. Such cultural scripts form the lenses through which individuals view their experiences in order to form the perceptions that make their living meaningful.

To use the foregoing model intelligently, it is important to note that societies may be higher or lower along a given grid axis and deeper or shallower along a given group axis. For instance, in strong group/high grid some collectivities may be higher on the strong group scale than others or higher on the high grid scale than others. The model would invite its users to form scattergrams of social locations rather than neat pigeon holes. Furthermore, as intimated above, complex societies such as the ancient Roman Empire and most modern nations simply do not fit neatly into any single box in their entirety. Rather, such complex social aggregates contain sets of collectivities that fit into various social locations in the model. Thus a recent analysis of an unnamed modern South American country's religious institutions points to four distinctive forms, all strong group yet ranging along the grid and group axes as follows (taken from Desroche 1973: 113):

(1) the established Catholicism of conservative and aristocratic landowners; very high grid and very strong group;

(2) a social Catholicism originating in the enlightened part of the ecclesiastic hierarchy, cautiously interventionist in other social institutions but constrained by traditional social doctrine and high church authority; midrange high grid and midrange strong group;

(3) a protesting Catholicism of those aiming at the reform of both the religious institution and society at large with the aid of all persons of good will; midrange low grid and midrange strong group;

(4) an explosive, radical Catholicism among illiterate and subversive peasants seeking a quick transformation of society marked by the redistribution of land among the landless poor; very low grid and very strong group (typically millenarian).

To return to the problem set out in the first chapter, if language is basically a means of communication and if language ultimately communicates meaning from a social system, the scripts of the grid and group quadrants should enable one to see which meanings are encoded in language, depending on the social location of the speaker and his or her audience. The relevance of this problem for interpreting the New Testament should be quite apparent. For if people in the U.S. live in a weak group/high grid society for the most part with a goodly number of "poor" in the weak group/high grid catchment area and if the New Testament writings apart from John derive from strong group/low grid groups, then which meanings can be exchanged when a U.S. person reads the Bible? Is he or she really reading the meanings set down in the biblical writings or only reading his or her own meanings into the writings of the Bible?

FIGURE 2. Douglas' Grid and Group Model with Eight Scripts
(Diagrams adapted from Boissevain 1974: Herbst 1976)

HIGH

Weak Group/High Grid:
ACHIEVEMENT

Assessment scale indicates each person has overlapping competence with other societal members (= equality), with assessment performed on the basis of size/mass dimension.

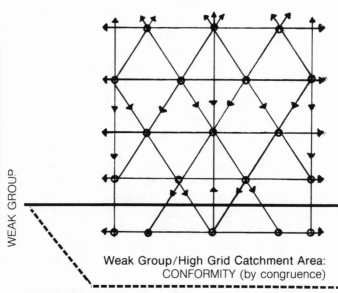

WEAK GROUP.

Weak Group/High Grid Catchment Area:
CONFORMITY (by congruence)

Weak Group/Low Grid:
CONTENTMENT

Assessment scale indicates each person is able to carry out all available tasks (= equality) in the quadrant; assessment rooted in depth of perception/experience.

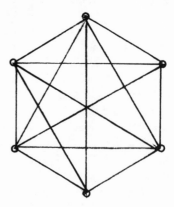

Weak Group
Low Grid   O
Extreme:
SOLITARY INDIVIDUALIST

LOW

GRID

Assessment scale indicates each person has a single social task, normally ascribed to the person by criteria other than personal ability, with assessment performed on the basis of vertical dimension.

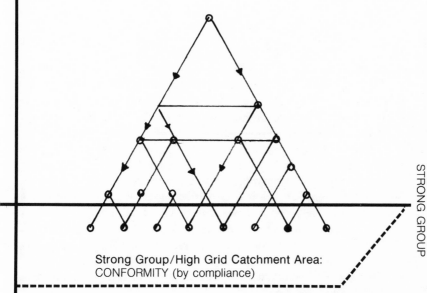

STRONG GROUP

Strong Group/High Grid Catchment Area:
CONFORMITY (by compliance)

Strong Group/Low Grid:
MAINTENANCE OF ACQUISITIONS

Assessment scale indicates each person linked to sets of others by means of networking, with assessment performed on the basis of horizontal dimension. Vertical positions are for patrons and brokers.

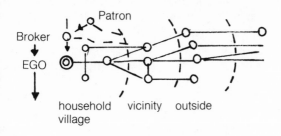

Patron

Broker

EGO

household   vicinity   outside
village

Strong Group/
Low Grid
Extreme:
SOLITARY GROUP

GRID

4.

Social Interaction in Grid and Group

INTRODUCTION

In the previous chapters four broad, comprehensive, comparative cultural scripts were considered. These scripts might be viewed as clearly marked off playing fields or courts. They show the in-bounds and out-of-bounds markings of the fields and describe abstractly a set of very general rules of the games to be played on the fields. The question considered in this chapter is: how should players proceed in the game? What style of game should they play when on defense and when on offense? The cultural scripts are rather static pictures of playing fields and general rules for playing on the fields. To envision the action that occurs on the fields requires some description of what constitutes a score, of the available styles of play, and of the expected strategies on both defense and offense. Human social interaction is not very different from strategies on a playing field. People behave as they do in order to have some effect on each other, to score points, as it were. This they do by playing according to the rules of the game, adopting various styles to meet their goals.

The Grid/Group Playing Field

The purpose of this chapter is to present a model of play appropriate to the cultural scripts marked off by grid and group. As a model of play, the model will include descriptions of how points are scored, the types of play available, the strategies used in these types of play, and methods for rating players. Like the grid and group model itself, these descriptions of the play that constitutes social interaction will be at a rather comprehensive level of consideration. The value of such abstraction is that the style and strategy of human interaction can then be applied to a number of societies. In this way it can contribute to the task of retrodiction, of getting back to the styles of social interaction and their meaning as portrayed in the New Testament writings.

At this point, then, the skills involved in scoring along with appropriate defensive and offensive strategies will have to be considered. Clearly it does not pay to be a good pass catcher when the rules of the game, like soccer, do not allow anyone to catch the ball except the goalie. It also does not pay to be a good center fielder when the rules require a good center. The strategies of being a good forward depend on whether the game is hockey, basketball, or soccer. Hence the question: given a field laid out by grid/group, what game can take place and which strategies are appropriate? As most people find out in the course of growing up, it is quite possible to play soccer, football, baseball, and even field hockey on the same playing surface. Yet, even on the same playing surface, the playing field is marked off differently; each game has different rules, requiring different strategies and different skills.

Grid/Group Interaction: A Complex Game

To imagine how play might proceed in any quadrant of the grid/group model, think of yourself playing baseball in one corner or a large play area in which a football game, a soccer game, and a field hockey game are also going on in the other three sections. Yet the fields are not clearly marked off. Rather, while you try to pay attention to your baseball game, the football game moves into your area of the field, and you are expected to switch to playing in the football game while keeping an eye on the baseball game. Should the soccer game come your way, you might then have to play some soccer with an eye on the basic baseball game and some thought to the football game still not entirely removed from your section of the play area. Along comes the field hockey game, requiring your participation so long as it is in your area, while some of your attention still has to be focused on the basic baseball game and the ongoing football game and soccer game as well. Each quadrant of the grid/group model is like a field with four floating games on it, and each game has its full number of concerned and interested players yet requires its participants to switch positions as another game moves into the playing area and still demands some attention to the original game. Furthermore, in pluralistic, complex societies a person might have to locate himself or herself in more than one of the grid/group quadrants in the course of a day. All told, this description is not a bad comparison for the normal types of social interaction that take up nearly all of a person's time and energy throughout a lifetime.

MEANINGFUL HUMAN LIVING: FOUR MAIN GAMES

Imagine a group of people of various ages and sexes in any concrete environment in ancient or modern times. What must this group do in order to survive in a meaningful, human way? Ostensibly, the group will have to *(1) adapt to its environment in some (2) purposeful, (3) meaningful, (4) social way.* Four elements have been marked off in this description because each one constitutes a separate "game" with its own forms of scoring, its own strategies, and its own ways of rating play on a scale from good to bad.

Belonging—Adapting in a Social Way

The first of the four games might be called "belonging" or "solidarity." Its type of play deals with the *social way* of being human. It implies a shared set of values, beliefs, language, feelings, and ideals that make up the group's definition of the truly human. This definition marks off those elements that constitute the integrity or wholeness of being human. Definitions of belonging take the form of a set of symbols marking off the truly human, thereby generating and requiring commitment, loyalty, or emotional anchorage in the group. All the individuals sharing the set of symbols clearly perceive each other as members of the group. The strategy specific to this game is called commitment, the ability of the players to activate the loyalty of fellow team members. A high rating in this game is signified by esteem within the group of players. This esteem is interchangeable with precedence, underscoring the horizontal quality of belonging: in and out; insiders and outsiders; first and last. To play well players need know-who information: know with whom one is playing, who is a member of the group and who is not, and who has significant esteem and who does not. This game is about proper ways of being human. Hence the set of symbols involved in the game forms the belonging system of the group. In U.S. society the belonging system would include the kinship and fictive kinship system—family and those to whom persons are related and/or who accept them because of who they are and not because of what they do or what they own—such as neighborhood groups, school groups, church memberships, and friends.

Meaning—Adapting in a Meaningful Way

Game two might be called "meaning" or "norms for truth and validity" or perhaps even "validation." Its type of play deals with *meaningful,* social ways of being human. It involves an overarching, general model of the order of existence in terms of systematized, organized rules that define normative reality. Meaning looks to worldviews (cf. Smart 1983). It deals with the norms of "truth" about persons, things, and events as they are and of a human being's relation to them, and it deals with rules of evidence that enable group members to prove things by reducing "facts" to the socially shared evident and thus producing evidence. Such a set of norms defining the "truth" of reality generates and requires the setting out of reasons and/ or proof by means of which one person exerts influence upon another. The strategy in the meaning game is called influence, the ability of players to persuade fellow players to act or think in a certain way by furnishing adequate reasons for doing so. Rating in this game is measured by degree of reputation within the group of players. This reputation is interchangeable with credibility, the depths to which an influential person is believed to have penetrated to produce the meaning and understanding that stand behind reputation. Meaning thus has a depth dimension; it involves getting behind and below the surface into the depths, the heart, and the unseen interior, and getting at the substance of the truth. To play well in the meaning game players need know-why information based on some know-that information. Once a person has the facts (know-that information) deriving from experience with the group in its environment, the game requires an explanation of the facts, hence know-why: know why things are the way they are and not otherwise and why people act or react the way they do. This game concerns establishing the norms of truth about people, things, and events. These norms consist of sets of symbols that form the meaning system of the group (e.g., the scientific method, the rule of law, and civil religion in the U.S.).

Collective Effectiveness—Adapting in a Purposeful Way

Game three might be called "collective effectiveness" or "the attainment of social goals." Its type of play deals with the *purposeful*, meaningful, social way of being human. It involves a set of goals to be attained by the group along with social structures for effectively acting to attain those goals as a group. Such a set of goals and the effectiveness in realizing them produce and require power, the ability to effect conformity. The strategy in the collective effectiveness game is called power, the ability of players to get fellow players to fulfill their obligations for the good of the whole group. Rating in this game is measured by a person's degree of authority within the group of players. This authority rating is interchangeable with one's position on some stratification scale, highlighting the vertical quality of collective effectiveness: superiors and inferiors, the high(er) and the low(er), superordinates and subordinates, supervisors and subjects, overlords and underlings. To play well players need know-how knowledge: specifically know-how about persons, how to get persons to do what they are supposed to do, how to make effective decisions on behalf of the group in such a way that group members will carry them out. The set of symbols involved in this game of social power forms the collective effectiveness system or political system of the group, such as government and all forms of group governance in American society.

Adaptation—Utilizing the Environment

Finally, the fourth game might be called "adaptation," in the sense of "natural resource utilization," or "resource utilization" and "exploitation of the environment." Its type of play deals with *adaptation to the environment* in some purposeful, meaningful, social way. It involves sets of ways in which people can be mobilized in order to extract and/or produce the whole range of life's "necessities" through work of all sorts. To utilize, control, and mobilize physical resources in a social way is essentially a process of mobilizing people who belong to or are somehow related to the group. The strategy in the game of adaptation is called inducement, the ability to have effect upon one's fellow players by providing goods and services for compliance. Rating in this game is measured in terms of wealth relative to other players in the group. This wealth is interchangeable with material advantage and the respect shown persons with greater or larger material advantage, thus underscoring the mass quality of inducement: more and less, greater and lesser, many and few, much and little, large and small. To play well players need know-how knowledge: specifically know-how as applicable to things and to persons considered as quantifiable things in this game; know how things work, grow, are useful, and can be produced and distributed for members of the group. This game is about developing resources and utilizing the physical environment. The set of symbols involved in this game forms the adaptive system of the group (e.g., economics and higher education in the U.S.).

Thus the hypothetical group of people under consideration would be involved with and utilize four games or playing procedures in order to adapt to the environment in some purposeful, meaningful, social way: a belonging system played with commitment (or loyalty), a meaning system played with influence, an effective collective action system played with power; and an adaptive system played with inducement (cf. fig. 3 on p. 73 and note the feedback loops from the meaning system to the other systems; the figure's circular shape indicates how impossible it would be to separate such interrelated and mutually impacting systems).

A group of people sharing these four components and hence required to play these four games simultaneously is no longer a simple group of people. It is a society; the games make up the group's societal system. Each of the simultaneous games has its type of play, its strategy, its rating of players, and, of course, its scoring method all based on the implementation of the main value that each game strives to realize: belonging, meaning, collective effectiveness, and adaptation to the environment (cf. table 1 on p. 73). If group members can successfully score in these games, their society will re-

FIGURE 3. Games Constituting the Societal System
(Adapted from Langness 1974:138)

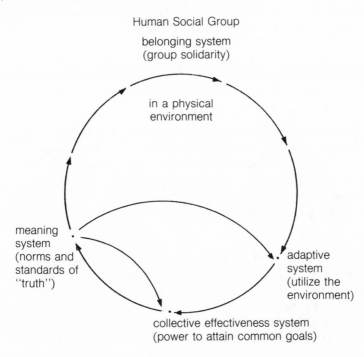

Human Social Group

belonging system
(group solidarity)

in a physical
environment

meaning
system
(norms and
standards of
"truth")

adaptive
system
(utilize the
environment)

collective effectiveness system
(power to attain common goals)

TABLE 1: Game Dimensions of the Societal System
(GSM = Generalized Symbolic Media)

	Game I	Game II	Game III	Game IV
Value (scoring)	belonging	meaning	collective effectiveness	adaptation
Subsystem (type of play)	know-who (belonging)	know-why (meaning)	know-how: persons (power)	know-how: things (wealth)
Medium (strategy of play)	Commitment (ability to activate loyalty)	Influence (ability to persuade)	Power (ability to effect conformity)	Inducement (ability to utilize goods, services)
Rating of player	Esteem	Reputation	Authority	Respect

The value of the GSM (commitment, influence, power, inducement) is evident only in terms of what each "says" symbolically in an exchange relation, a social interaction.

The GSM are symbolic modes/means of communication for effect in interaction.

main in the high grid quadrants (grid is a measure of value effectiveness). But, if they fail to score well, their society's grid rating will move down.

THE SYMBOLIC QUALITY OF THE GAMES OF LIVING

The Symboling Process

These four games seem to be basic to any complex society. However, it is important to see that the games themselves as well as any society that is made up of them are essentially symbolic. The games are symbol systems (cf. Geertz 1973: 90–125 for the generic features of symbol systems adopted here). Systems of symbols generally establish powerful, pervasive, and enduring feelings and motivations in people (the players) by formulating conceptions of value objects (the score) and outfitting these conceptions with such an aura of factuality that the feelings and motivations which the symbols generate are perceived to be reality. After all, the games constitute social reality. As noted in the first chapter, symboling refers to the process of endowing, imbuing, investing, or drenching people, things, and events with socially shared meaningfulness.

As an illustration of the process, take a pair of *homo sapiens*, male and female, who generate offspring. Their copulation is often socially interpreted as meaningful lovemaking. Upon conception of an offspring, the human pair receives a new social interpretation in terms of the prospectively meaningful roles of mother and father. Upon birth and incipient socialization, the offspring learns to interpret itself significantly as son or daughter and to relate to its genitors in terms of the symbolic roles of father and mother. The symbolic roles used to interpret the naturing and nurturing process among humans—father, mother, son, daughter—are rather powerful, pervasive, and enduring, since sons and daughters generally believe throughout their lifetimes that the male and female who generated them are "in fact" their mother and father. They probably will believe so "forever," and should anyone cause them to rethink their relation to their genitors—that in fact their roles as father and mother are simply culturally determined and merely symbolic—most offspring would continue to hold that there is nothing more real or more factual than the abiding reality of those persons who are one's father and mother.

This description of the symboling process exemplifies what goes on in all social systems and subsystems. The example chosen above derives from the belonging game. Concretely, it bodies forth in the kinship or family system. Kinship, as are economics, politics, religion, and education, is such a set of symbols. The whole societal system of any human group is a system of symbols made up of the subsystems that form the ongoing, simultaneous games considered above. The system of symbols that constitutes a society establishes strong, pervasive, and enduring feelings (emotionally anchored norms) and motivations (values) in people who are immersed in the system and who constitute the system. Individual human beings are socialized through the belonging system. Thanks to socialization, individuals are immersed in and held by the conceptions or models of meaningfulness shared by their belonging group. All that a person experiences will be processed through these conceptions. The resulting perceptions (often called "facts" and "truths") are then clothed with such an air of factuality that one's assessment of one's experience and the persons and things of that experience are thought to be realistic, true, and objective, just as one's mother and father are thought to be factually, realistically, truly, and objectively one's mother and father. Each of the four games considered previously is a symbol system that works as a subsystem to produce perceptions of what counts, of what is factual, real, true, and objective.

Symboling is about constructing, maintaining, and living out such systems of meaningfulness. Symboling is another way of describing both the social line drawing that allows for a place for everyone and everything and the emotional and social pressure to keep them in their place. Social interaction looks to the style of play required by a given game. It is all about effectively sharing, dividing, altering, and circulating the symbols that make up a group's world of meaningfulness, the symbols that enable human beings to adapt to an environment in some purposeful, meaningful, social way. Thus the four games or systems are symbol systems, and the style of play required in the games is one of symbolic, social interaction.

Symboling and Communication

Social interaction is, fundamentally, a form of communication. Communication might be defined as the process by which messages are transferred from a source to a receiver for a purpose. A source (Source) sends a message (Message) along certain channels (Channel) to some receiving individual or group (Receiver) in some situation (Situation) in order to have some effect (Effect) (cf. Rogers and Shoemaker 1971: 11). For instance, communication in terms of language is the process by means of which one or more persons (Source) present another person or group (Receiver) in a given situation (Situation) with an oral or written utterance (Channel) that encodes or stands for some social world object to which the utterance refers (Message), whose purpose is some reaction or outcome (Effect). Nonlinguistic social interaction is highly similar. For social interaction is also a process by which one or more persons (Source) present another person or group of persons (Receiver) in a given situation (Situation) with goods, services, actions, or a range of words sometimes written but usually oral (Channel) that comprise symbolic experiences encoding the real-world, human values to which the symbol refers (Message), with the purpose of getting some results from the interaction (Effect).

Just as people normally communicate with each other in language in order to mean, to share and impart meanings, so too people normally interact with each other even apart from language (e.g., with goods like cars, food, housing, clothing; cf. Douglas and Isherwood 1979) in order to mean, to share and impart meanings. Meanings are communicated in order to have some effect, to realize some purpose and, as in all communication, the message may be effectively received, garbled, muted, or turned into meaningless noise.

Symbols as Media of Communication

To return to the four games once again, recall that each of them has a specific strategy. These were called commitment, power, influence, and inducement. Each of these specific strategies is in fact a symbolic channel or means of communication encoding real-world values. For the strategies are like language in that they constitute the means for playing the game; they are means or media of social interaction. But they are strongly unlike language because they are not utilized to encode the whole of human experience as language is. Rather, the four are specific to the games or subsystems described previously. Consequently, they might be considered as specialized varieties of language. These system-specific, generalized symbolic media of social interaction encode complex, real-world persons, things, and events as defined by and contained in the subsystems (games) making up the societal system. Each subsystem produces its own strategy and specific generalized symbolic medium for social interaction. The media in turn serve to model the complex, symbolic interactions of the given subsystem (game).

Every generalization is a model, a simplified representation of more complex real-world phenomena. Human beings make models for the purpose of understanding, controlling, or predicting. The four strategies, the four generalized symbolic media, are in fact symbolic models. They are used for interactions within and between social institutions with a view to obtaining effects in the interaction. From the perspective of communication, a person (Source) embodying a given symbolic medium (Channel) applies the medium (Message) with a view to altering the attitudes and/or behavior (Effect) of another person or group (Receiver) in a given situation (Situation) in a direction which the source believes to be desirable. Here, however, the medium (Channel) and the message are identical. With these generalized symbolic media of social interaction, the medium is the message and vice versa.

Since the foregoing might appear somewhat abstract, for clarity's sake the reader might try the following test. Over the past year, you did or did not do many things because other people asked or told you to do or not to do them. Consider the following sentence and insert the roles of the persons who asked or told you to do or not to do something that in fact you did or did not do: "I did it because he or she was: my mother, father, sister, brother, friend, relative (= commitment); a doctor, lawyer, clergyperson, teacher (= influence); the police, mayor, president of the U.S. (= power); my boss at work, employer, foreman, customer, client (= inducement)." Now what is it about people who have these social roles that makes you do what they ask or tell you to do? This is what these symbolic media of social interaction are about. They are the symbolic means that people employ reciprocally to have each other do what they want and value.

GENERALIZED SYMBOLIC MEDIA OF SOCIAL INTERACTION

At a high level of abstraction symbolic media used in social interaction are reducible to four (Parsons 1969, on whom this discussion is based). These are:

(1) *commitment*: generally specific to the belonging system—the family or the extended family such as a group of friends, fellow church members, fraternity or sorority members, and neighborhood or town mates;

(2) *influence*: generally specific to the meaning system—the American way of life, the Western way of life, "democracy," institutionalized applied sciences and their representatives such as physicians, dentists, pharmacists, and nurses, and institutionalized learning and its rules of evidence as well as its representatives such as lawyers, teachers, and clergy as teachers;

(3) *power*: generally specific to the collective effectiveness system— government in all its forms such as representatives of the units of government from president down to local mayor and their extensions in the courts and the police systems;

(4) *inducement*: generally specific to the economic system which measures usefulness in terms of money in U.S. society—employers, customers, and workers of various sorts extracting and producing goods and providing services; quantity, such as amount of pay, gives indication of social usefulness and at the same time ranks a person on a scale of material advantage.

Commitment, influence, power, and inducement are like specialized languages within a particular social subsystem. Each symbols a type of relationship between persons with a view to obtaining results in social interaction. As symbolic models they represent the result of abstraction, of chunking a whole range of concrete interactions, just as money represents all kinds of goods and services since about the eighteenth century A.D. (cf. Carney 1973). Perhaps the easiest way to see how these symbolic media work is to think of them as functioning just as money does. Money, of course, is a symbolic and rather abstract means of exchange. It cannot be driven, listened to, lived in, eaten, or worn, yet people accept it in payment for labor, for goods, and for rentals. The main reason people accept this symbol in return for goods and services is that they believe others will accept it from them in return for the goods and services they might value. Thus, for a symbolic medium such as money to work in exchange interactions, the parties to the exchange must be willing to accept the symbol from each other as they surrender real-world goods and services for it. The "value" of money, then, is evident only in terms of what it "says" symbolically in an exchange relationship. Money likewise measures the value of concrete items in quite abstract units believed by all to be applicable toward the acquisition of concrete goods and services. If all of a sudden everyone in a given society refused to believe in the symbolic exchange and measure value of money, people would have to resort to bartering. What might one do, in a complex society, with five tons of grain, five hundred auto bumpers, ten thousand strokes on a typewriter, or seven hundred supermarket tallies, or what might one ask in return for a week's work? Could such items be stored in a city apartment? Could one readily find barter partners in one's limited circle of friends and neighbors for such goods and services? The significant point to note here is that the four generalized symbolic media function just as money does in complex societies. As will be seen, if the four were to become unacceptable to interacting partners, living in complex societies would come to a halt. Be that as it may, enough has been said about the four generalized symbolic media of social interaction (referred to henceforth as GSM). How might they be appropriately defined?

Commitment—The GSM of Belonging

Commitment is the capacity to command loyalty. As a GSM it refers to the ability to get results in social interaction by appealing to and affecting another person's personal, internalized sense of obligation, sense of duty, or sense of belonging but without reference to any threat of external sanction such as force or physical compulsion. Instead of such physical coercion commitment effectively urges loyalty by means of internalized sanctions such as guilt feelings, feelings of shame and disloyalty, or fear of disapproval. Commitment thus focuses upon those socially perceived areas of emotional anchorage which human beings develop from their experiences of belonging to or with certain persons and groups. One can readily call to mind all the persons and groups in which one feels emotionally anchored and has emotional investment, such as one's parents, spouse, children, siblings, relatives, neighbors, and friends. Should one of these persons activate commitment in order to get some results in interaction, one complies because of the implied threat of being shamed, humiliated, or denigrated in one's own self-esteem. The threat consists in effectively casting doubt on one's personhood, one's integrity, or even one's basic humanity. Thus, when people explain their activity "because my mother, father, sister, brother, friend, neighbor in great need" asked them to act, the trigger for their behavior is the GSM of commitment. On the other hand, exclamations such as "Is that any way for a son to treat his mother, for a Christian to behave toward one in need, for a mother to help her children?" evidence the sanctions that come from not responding to the activation of commitment.

As previously mentioned, the GSM are much like money. Money, as is all too well-known, can be an inflated or deflated medium of exchange. Inflation occurs when there is too much of the symbol in circulation and not enough goods and services to exchange for it. Deflation occurs when there are more goods and services available than there is money to exchange for them. During an inflationary period money is in too large supply—too much of the symbolic medium. During deflation money is in too short supply—too little of the symbolic medium. How would the inflation/deflation dimension apply to commitment? If one feels effective emotional anchorage in too many persons or groups, one's commitment will be inflated. On the other hand, if one feels effective emotional anchorage in very few people, then commitment will be deflated. Thus, in the former case, should a person belong to many clubs and service organizations, be married, have a number of neighbors who regularly call on him or her for help, and bring home work from the office or school, then which person or group can call on that person in time of need to activate commitment? Here commitment is inflated; in the end no appeals for help are answered effectively. On the other hand, should a person simply do his or her job, have very few friends, be unmarried, and belong to no clubs or service organizations, such a person would have few focuses of emotional anchorage in his or her social life. His or her commitment would be deflated with a very limited concentration and often a wide range of responses to appeals for results from those able to activate commitment. Commitments obviously are ranked in terms of priorities, but the broader the elements in the ranking, the more inflated the GSM of commitment is likely to be, while the narrower the scope, the more deflated the commitment.

To envision the workings of the GSM of commitment in the first-century Mediterranean world, one might imagine a Hellenistic city resident rather frequently appealing to the loyalties of fellow citizens in order to have something done for the city. Well-born citizens would often have multiple and perhaps conflicting loyalties (e.g., they might also be heads of households, members of fictive kinship groups that might be called "religious" associations, Roman citizens, retired army veterans, investors in intercity trade, and patrons of a small army of clients). The person with the great idea for the city might find commitment so thinly spread, so inflated, among those able fellow citizens that no results would be forthcoming in a given instance. In fact this was most often the case among the non-elites of the first-century Mediterranean world, that is, roughly ninety-eight percent of the population. In this regard, New Testament questions about "who is my neighbor" and "loving neighbor as oneself" are questions concerning the appropriate range of commitments. In the Gospels Jesus is frequently portrayed activating commitments, either to himself or to the God of Israel, among the persons with whom he interacts. The parable of the helpful Samaritan (Luke 10:30–37) focuses on an all too narrow range of commitment among the elite passersby, a typical problem in strong group/low grid society where elites have deflated commitment while non-elites have inflated commitment. On the other hand, in the strong group/high grid world of the Roman elites, the Roman emperor functioned as a universal patron for Roman citizens and non-citizen elites. Imperial clients sought to activate their patron's commitments on their behalf as might be expected among persons of honor, while the emperor rarely, if ever, took the initiative since the commitments he controlled were duly balanced (cf. Millar 1977).

Influence—The GSM of Meaning

Influence is the capacity to persuade. As a GSM, influence refers to the ability to be effective in social interaction by getting another person to decide to act in a certain way on the basis of reasons indicating that it simply makes sense to act in that way, apart from any other benefit that the other person might receive from such behavior. Influence works by persuasion; it presents another with reasons and information about why one ought to act in a given way, and it points out why it makes sense or can be to one's benefit to act or not to act. Influence thus looks to change opinions and attitudes so that intended actions might follow. The way in which a person wielding influence gets another to decide derives from the socially shared perception that the "influencer," as one who knows what he or she is talking about, is in command of the facts, is competent in the field, and hence ought be trusted and believed. This, of course, means that the person wielding influence can produce the facts or explain the "why" of things should the other person not take his or her word for it.

A person whose word is taken immediately and directly without explanation or proof has deflated influence. Conversely, one who has to explain in detail or needs to supply repeated verification for what he or she states has inflated influence. For instance, if someone yells "Fire!" in a crowded auditorium and no one reacts, that would point to influence so inflated as to be worthless, like worthless inflated money. In order to change one's influence rating into an acceptable symbolic medium, a person would have to persuade group members by actually showing people the smoke and the fire. The well-known story of the boy who cried "Wolf!" too often illustrates the same point; initially his influence was accepted as a suitable medium of social interaction. But as his evidence consistently proved unverifiable, his influence inflated off the scale to sheer worthlessness.

Influence is perhaps the main GSM employed in the course of the student-teacher interactions that mark the college years. Most of the time a student simply has to take a professor's word for it, especially in the sciences and health profession technologies. For various cultural reasons the professor of any area of "science" has automatic credibility in his or her field and hence has ready social influence. On the other hand, professors in the humanities and arts have to acquire influence, to demonstrate in some way that what they say is credible and verifiable. In other words, the only way to acquire influence is to "prove it," unless a society enculturates its members to believe that certain areas of knowledge are already "proved." These already "proved" areas in U.S. society would include those professions requiring public certification of competence, such as medicine, dentistry, law, pharmacy, and nursing. Like university teaching, these are positions of influence which function chiefly by means of the GSM of influence. Of course, reputation in these fields depends on the inflation/deflation level of the GSM of influence applied in social interaction by the influence wielder.

In the Gospels the whole debate about Jesus' credentials and credibility revolves about his influence rating. Paul, too, is much concerned about defending his "apostleship," that is, his credentials and credibility. Both Jesus and Paul are often required to "prove it" in various ways by various groups. On the other hand, some people simply accept their influence; these people believe what Jesus and Paul say without further proof and behave accordingly. As GSM, then, influence means getting people to believe and act according to what one says because of one's reputation for having better general or specific knowledge. Strong group/low grid singles out persons with deflated influence because in that quadrant influence is usually all too inflated. The notable adversary is one with deflated influence. Hence the direction of the interactions recorded in the Gospels and referred to by Paul indicates how Jesus and Paul have to deal with persons wielding deflated influence in their society.

Power—The GSM of Goal Attainment

Power is the capacity to produce conformity. As a GSM, power refers to the ability to get results in social interaction by simply requiring the performance of some binding obligation or duty. The power wielder is perceived to have the right to require others to perform some obligation because it is deemed necessary for the good of the group or the society in question. Power always implies the threat of external sanction such as force, compulsion, or fines. Inflated power is power with too little physical coercion to back it; deflated power has too much physical coercion behind it.

As mentioned previously, *inflated* influence can move off the scale to no influence at all. But with power, it is *deflated* power that moves off the scale to no power at all. For example, consider the sanction entailed in the use of nuclear weapons. The physical coercion entailed in the large scale use of nuclear weapons points to highly deflated power. Yet those societies having nuclear weapons cannot use them effectively since their use will not lead to the performance of binding obligations. Rather, the use of the weapons would obliterate the persons that power seeks to make conform. For power to work effectively it must find a proper balance between inflation and deflation, just as any other GSM must.

Perhaps an ideal instance of effective power was marked by the Roman Empire. The Roman emperor in the first-century Mediterranean world ruled some fifty-five million people with an army and navy of some one hundred and fifty thousand men (Hopkins 1978: 1–2). This of course was power, not brute force, since at any given time the emperor simply did not have enough physical force to keep every imperial subject in physical check. The emperor ruled subject peoples by power in that conquered peoples performed their binding obligations to the emperor and empire because of the perceived probability of physical coercion. There were few revolts in the Roman Empire because subject peoples recognized and acquiesced in the emperor's power and because the emperor himself believed he had such power. Again, as in the case of money, for power to work as a GSM it must be recognized and accepted by interacting persons and be exchangeable for a variety of "goods," that is, fulfillment of various obligations.

How the GSM of power functions in strong group societies might be somewhat difficult for Americans to understand because in the U.S. system power resides in the democratic populace which invests the power in officeholders on behalf of the common good. This is weak group/high grid power.

Now the power of the Roman emperor did not function like the power of the U.S. president does within the U.S. Rather, it worked like the president's power does when applied extramurally in dealings with other countries. Within the country, the president exercises influence rather than power, although most Americans confuse these GSM when talking about U.S. politics.

The New Testament world, on the other hand, was a world of mixed power. Deflated power was vested in the hands of elites: Roman officials for the empire, the Sadducee party controlling the Jewish Temple in Judaea. For the conquered and non-collaborating peoples of the empire, power was quite inflated. Since Jesus did not rank high on the power scale, he generally had no access to power at all, except when dealing with evil spirits and demons which were subservient to human beings (cf. Hollenbach 1981). Furthermore, in Hellenistic conceptions God or the high god was the ultimate wielder of power. Hence the closer one was to God in the hierarchy of power ranking, the more power one had. Consequently, after Jesus' resurrection Christians perceived Jesus as Messiah with the power of one "seated on God's right hand." This perception, of course, led to the problem of why this power was not effective at present. Paul, for instance, said it is in abeyance for the time being; for now Christians, like all others, are to accept the GSM of Roman imperial power and its replications throughout the empire (cf. Rom. 13 and chap. 6 below).

Inducement—The GSM of Adaptation

Inducement is the capacity to expropriate goods and services. As a GSM, inducement refers to the ability to lay claim on the goods and services of others because of one's social usefulness as replicated in one's social standing. Social usefulness in any society is generally symboled by a whole range of goods as well as rites employing goods, which are called consumption rites: dinners; parties; benefits. People perceived to possess greater material advantage are equally perceived to be more socially useful and hence to have greater claim to society's goods and services so as to maintain their social utility. In U.S. society, mainstream Americans pay collective homage to such social usefulness in terms of salaries, paychecks, fees, and tax loopholes and exemptions. Although many less materially advantaged persons might not agree, the cultural "fact" is that the wealthy are, by and large, more socially useful than the non-wealthy. The positions commanding greater pay are more socially useful than positions with lesser pay, and goods and services that cost more reflect the greater social standing and social utility of those occupying those standings, at least in the weak group/high grid U.S. system.

In this system, individuals and groups can, with relative and remarkable ease, occupy positions marked by expanding and contracting material advantage, positions of larger and lesser affluence. But in the strong group world of the New Testament social usefulness, a significant indicator of social standing, was based chiefly on the group of one's birth and, more rarely, on proved ability on behalf of some larger group. In other words, in the first-century Mediterranean world social standing was not a matter of inducement ability or wealth but of belonging. Thus significant social status did not derive from the accumulation of money, goods, or things but from birth into noble groups which commanded large resources of land and labor. Furthermore, in that world the index of group wealth was land rather than money or goods. Money did not become an all-purpose generalized medium of exchange until about the eighteenth century A.D. (cf. Carney 1973).

To return to inducement as GSM, inducement gets others to do what the wielder of inducement wants because the performance entails some benefit for the doer in the form of payment, gift, patronage, service, or help. Thus a person perceived to have inducement at his or her control can have recourse to a range of positive inducements to get the interaction to go his or her way. Again, inducement can be inflated, just as money can be, to the degree that the value of one's physical assets or socially acknowledged standing and service diminish; and it can be deflated to the extent that the value of such assets and standing augments. The fewer the assets and standings available in the society at large, the more likely that inducement will be deflated. On the other hand, if statuses such as citizen, senator, or knight in the Roman Empire become readily available to many people, the value of the status becomes inflated and less useful.

GSM Interaction

In the foregoing description of the GSM of social interaction the focus has been on the source, the person wielding the symbolic medium. The person on the other side of the interaction, of course, is the receiver. What benefits flow to the receiver in such symbolic transactions? By accepting and acquiescing in another's power, the compliant receiver is *not* physically coerced into obeying. Then, by performing the action sought by the one activating commitment, the person complying with the request does *not* get shamed or embarrassed into doing something. In this sense power and commitment are negative symbolic media since compliance does nothing to or for the receiver apart from avoiding the implied threat. Furthermore power and commitment are both concerned with having someone fulfill some pre-existing, relevant obligation. The obligation activated by power is rooted in the political or power system, that is, the forms of government aiming at collective effectiveness, and the obligation activated by commitment is rooted in the belonging system, that is, the kinship system and its replications such as fictive kinship and friendship. Finally, power is a form of social pressure coming from outside a person, while commitment is a form of personal pressure arising from within a person.

For students of the New Testament it would be important to observe that in the first-century Mediterranean world only the GSM of power and commitment had any real salience. Commitment and power were the main focus of social interest and social comment. This means that the aspects of human existence that won central attention were those of collective effectiveness symboled by power and those of human integrity or wholeness symboled by commitment. Consequently the main subsystems, the main games on the field, were the belonging system and the power system. These subsystems took on shape in the kinship and political patterns of the time and place. At the concrete level there were only two significant and discernible social institutions in the first-century world of the New Testament: kinship or family and politics or government. The other social institutions so clearly and distinctly discernible by us, namely, religion, economics, and education, simply did not exist as separate, differentiated, and distinct social institutions. Rather, these "modern" distinct institutions were embedded in either the kinship or the political institution of the societies of the New Testament period.

The fact that religion was not a separate and distinct social institution in the New Testament period might seem somewhat incongruous to people today since it is specifically contemporary "religious" institutions that use the Bible. However, it seems that first-century Mediterraneans would be hard pressed to talk about their "religion," if they knew what the word meant at all. Now it is true that first-century Mediterranean people did in fact provision their society; they had an adaptation system and an economic institution that realized it. Also they did share some overarching conceptions of the general order of existence and of appropriate behavior deriving from that order of existence; they had a meaning system and a religious institution that realized it. However, the point is that the only two social institutions of any salience at that time were kinship and government. Economics, for instance, was embedded in either the family or the government. There was a political economy and a householding economy but no formal economy with special rules and theories dealing with the provisioning of society and, of course, no special institutions from which the rules and theories might be derived. Economic systems which are embedded in other institutions are called substantive economies, and their study is the study of substantive economics (Dalton 1961; Carney 1973; Perinbam 1977; Lowry 1979.) Much of the contemporary world has a formal economics with a body of theory perfectly appropriate to the posteighteenth-century, separate, free-standing, distinct economic institutions typical of modern society.

Similarly, in the Hellenistic world religion was embedded either in the government (political religion) or in the family (householding religion), with a number of groups forming either fictive polities in which religion was embedded (e.g., the ethnics conquered by the Romans, such as the conquered Jews) or fictive families in which religion was embedded (e.g., early Christian groups and mystery religion groups (cf. W. Smith 1963). Drawing an analogy from economic anthropology, we might call first-century religion substantive religion, while modern U.S. religious denominations would be instances of formal religion. Moreover in the contemporary world a number of societies still have mainly substantive religion, for example, Japan and its ancestrism or Muslim countries with their Islam rooted in a polity, the *ummah*.

The main reason for underscoring this point is that scholars and nonscholars alike find it all too easy to apply theories of formal religion, for example, from the sociology of religion, to early Christianity as well as to first-century Judaism. Studies based on such procedures are simply inadequate, as inadequate as applying formal economic theory to the substantive economies of the past. At most such studies tell us what first-century people would look like if they were part of the twentieth-century world, but they are not. It would seem, then, that modern sociology of religion has little to offer the investigator of early Christianity and first-century Judaism since the formal religion models of the sociology of religion are quite anachronistic and inappropriate for the substantive religion of the New Testament period.

To return to the remaining GSM and their bearing upon interacting receivers, what bearing do influence and inducement have on those who comply? In contrast with power and commitment, compliance with influence and inducement always leads to a positive outcome for the receiver. By submitting to influence a person acquires information or proof or reasons which he or she did not have previously. By submitting to inducement a person obtains some positive goods or services. Thus influence and inducement are positive since compliance yields something positive, and neither is concerned with fulfilling previously binding obligations. Rather, influence looks to having the receiver think or act in a different way because it is good for the receiver, while inducement seeks to have effect on another's resources, both goods and services. As mentioned previously, in the first-century Mediterranean world inducement interactions were embedded either in the kinship system where they worked by reciprocity or in the political system where they worked by redistribution (on these aspects, cf. chap. 5 below). Influence, too, was embedded either in kinship or in political groups. The former would be an extended kinship-like group, called a fictive kinship group, in which members are "brothers and sisters" on the basis of some shared ideology, for example, "brothers in Christ" and the "son" or "children" of some teacher or deity. The latter would entail political-like groups, called fictive political groups, in which members hold office and look for limited collective effectiveness, for example, burial societies. Finally, influence is a form of personal pressure focused within the receiver, just as commitment is, while inducement, like power, is a form of social pressure focused on items outside the person.

GRID AND GROUP AND THE GSM

The question posed at the outset of this chapter referred to the manner in which play might take place on the fields marked off by grid and group. Ostensibly the style of play within each quadrant is determined by the prevailing GSM that the players throw at each other. For example, power and commitment derive their force from obligation, the ability to bind another person or to have another person feel obliged. Both of these GSM use negative sanctions or pressures ("Do what you are supposed to do, otherwise . . ."). Power affects a person's physical and social situation, while commitment affects a person's internalized self-image. Neither offers any positive reward for compliance, only punishment for non-compliance. Being based on obligations to others, with strong focus on those others to whom one is obliged, both these GSM bear qualities that clearly befit strong group. Consequently, it would appear that strong group works largely if not exclusively by means of power and commitment which oblige with negative sanctions.

On the other hand, influence and inducement are basically consensual. They derive their force from consent and prestation. Both employ positive sanction ("If you do this, then I will give you . . ."), with inducement externally affecting a person's physical and social situation and with influence internally affecting a person's opinions, attitudes, and judgment. Since both are based on individual and individualized consent, both obviously bear qualities that befit weak group. Hence it would seem that weak group works largely, if not exclusively, through influence and inducement which gain consent with positive sanctions. How then would the GSM fit into the grid and group model and into the flow of the action with the quadrants?

Strong Group and the GSM

Strong group works with primary emphasis on the GSM of power and commitment while inducement and influence are secondary. Strong group societies are thus social systems of obligation that gain consent from their members through obligation. They are therefore systems of *obligatory con-*

sent. Power is concretized in vertical classification (B. Schwartz 1981) while commitment is realized along horizontal dimensions (Needham 1973). Thus strong groups will be much concerned with superior/subordinate relations and the quality of interaction with persons on the social level. Since subordinate members of the group are subject in some way to the wielders of power and controllers of commitment, they would find the use of power and commitment closed to them. As a result, the only recourse open to subordinates is to employ the consensual devices of inducement and influence. In other words, social superiors ply their subjects with the obligating GSM of power and commitment while subjects, should they desire results in interaction with superiors, have only the consensual devices of inducement and influence open to them.

Furthermore, since power and commitment do not offer any positive sanctions or rewards for compliance, only punishment for non-compliance, there is no way a subject can get ahead and increase his or her physical and social resources by being obedient to a command of power or by fulfilling an obligation rooted in commitment. Consequently, with power and commitment being the paramount GSM employed by superiors in strong group social interaction, the members of the system are led to the perception that all goods are limited. The perception and consequent presumption that all goods are limited means that large areas of human behavior are patterned in such a way as to suggest that persons in strong group societies view their total environment (people, things, events) as one in which all of the desired objects in life, such as land, health, friendship, love, beauty, femininity, manliness, honor, power, loyalty, security, cars, cattle, and money, exist in finite quantity and are always in short supply. In addition, there are no ways to increase one's available quantities apart from wielding power and commitment, behavior that always takes place at the expense of other individuals and groups. Compliance with power and commitment never yields any increment or advantage for the person or group complying, only decrease and disadvantage for not complying. Thus the sum total of goods, including power and commitment themselves, is viewed as inherent in finite and limited nature. They are there to be divided and redivided, if necessary, but never to be augmented (cf. Foster 1965; Gregory 1975).

Consequently, subordinate individuals and groups in strong group societies must utilize the GSM of inducement and influence in order to have effect on their social superiors who utilize power and commitment. Thus subordinates will have recourse to forms of inducement, such as goods, services, or money, and forms of influence, such as requests, prayers, arguments, or persuasion of all sorts, in order to have power and commitment work on their behalf. More concrete examples of such inducements in strong group societies include payment, bribery, gifts, public works, sacrifices to God or the gods, and offerings in temples. More concrete examples of influence would include petitions and embassies to emperors, kings, or governors, prayers to God or gods, vows or other binding promises, and discipleship or clientship. Because strong group is not the American style, this all may seem rather strange. Clear examples of accommodation to strong group can be found in the "unfair" practices of a large number of U.S. corporations dealing with significant segments of various strong societies for a wide range of business purposes (the list is extremely long; cf. Jacoby et al. 1977). Such behavior was and is considered "unethical" by weak group Americans in the Congress and the press and among the citizenry. A most recent statement comes from Timothy E. Wirth, U.S. Representative from Colorado, who offers an official list of such nefarious cases in the ongoing discussion of amendments to "The Foreign Corrupt Practices Acts" (*Congressional Record*, 129 No. 54 [April 26, 1983] E 1859; cf. also Greanias and Windsor 1982). However, such bribery in a whole range of forms is perfectly "ethical" and normal in strong group societies. Whether known as *bustarella* in Italy, *bakshish* in Turkey and Arabic speaking countries, or *blat* in the Soviet Union, bribery is more or less an integral part of strong group life.

Finally, since in strong group an individual's or group's well-being depends largely upon having an inducement or influence effect upon the wielders of power and commitment, there is a common perception that every significant effect in a person's or group's life is caused by and depends upon a person; here impersonal causality, that is, technology, is of secondary interest, largely applied to the control of persons. Personal causality is tantamount to the conviction that every effect that counts in life is caused by a person.

Weak Group and the GSM

Weak group would work with primary and notable emphasis on the GSM of inducement and influence, with power and commitment secondary. In comparison with strong group, the GSM are in reversed position here. Weak group systems are systems of consent and acknowledgment that gain recognition of members' obligations through consensus developed among groups of individuals. They are therefore systems of *consensual obligation*. Lesser members of such societies see themselves as occupying social statuses different from those wielding influence and inducement. Status is gauged here chiefly in terms of material advantage, and those with less material advantage will find inducement and influence closed to them in their interactions with those who have greater material advantage. Consequently the less advantaged can only have recourse to the obligatory devices of power and commitment to obtain results in interactions with the more advantaged.

Thus the more advantaged ply their less advantaged fellows with the consensual GSM of influence and inducement, while the less advantaged ply their more advantaged fellows with the obligatory devices of power and commitment. This seems to be the case in the U.S. (e.g., on the role of inducement-advantage, cf. Hochschild 1981).

Furthermore, since inducement and influence offer positive advantage and positive sanctions or rewards for compliance, those who comply do in fact increase their physical and social resources. This increase consists of the rewards of inducement, goods and services of all sorts, as well as the reward of influence, information of all sorts. Consequently, with inducement and influence as the paramount GSM used by the more advantaged in social interaction, the members of the system are led to the perception that *all goods are unlimited.* Due to this perception broad areas of human behavior are patterned in such a way as to suggest that persons in weak group societies view their total environment, consisting of persons, things, and events, as one in which all the desired objects in life exist in "infinite" quantity and are rarely in short supply (for one instance of this view cf. Barbour et al. 1982). Further, there are many ways aside from inducement and influence to increase the available quantities of socially valuable goods. The basic reason for this perception is that compliance with inducement and influence always yields an increment for the person or group complying. Goods, like inducement and influence themselves, can be replicated, multiplied, and augmented indefinitely.

Less advantaged individuals a..d groups in weak group societies emphasize the GSM of power and commitment in order to have effect on the more advantaged with their inducement and influence. Examples of the power of the less advantaged include: voting procedures; accountability to the citizenry in the legal system; rioting (instrumental interpersonal coercion); and technology (instrumental impersonal coercion). Examples of commitment activated by the less advantaged include: the demand for recognition of publicly acknowledged human and civil rights, since these are to be legally recognized by all regardless of one's social standing; loyalty oaths required regardless of status or reputation; and political decisions made with a view to the consent of the governed.

Finally, since the well-being of a person or a group in weak group society depends to a large extent upon having coercive or commitment effect upon the wielders of influence and inducement, persons in these societies would tend to hold the view that every significant effect in the life of a person or group is caused by some individual adequate cause, be it personal or impersonal. The reason for this is that in weak group societies the individual perceives himself or herself to be in control. Control is exercised through coercive force and/or commitment effectiveness both over other people by means of voting, granting or withholding one's consent, and various legal ploys and over things by means of technology. Hence the social thrust in such groups is to enable the individual to understand and control both persons, for example, by means of psychology, sociology, or political science, and things, for example, by means of technology, with a view to self-externalizing mastery over people and things. This book is itself a product of weak group cultural cues. In sum, weak group societies tend to perceive reality in terms of adequate causality—every effect has an adequate cause, be it personal or impersonal.

Inflation, Deflation, and the GSM

The previous section of this chapter described the general style of play to be expected, in terms of the GSM, within the group dimension of the grid and group model. What of the grid dimension? What specific style of play and what direction of interaction might be presumed in each of the quadrants thanks to the grid dimension? As noted previously, the GSM are subject to inflation and deflation, much as twentieth-century money is. Consider each GSM in turn.

(1) Power deflation occurs when the effectiveness sought by the wielder of power results only through reliance on strict obligation and coercion with immediate and ready physical and social force. Power inflation, on the other hand, occurs when the effectiveness sought by the wielder of power requires the performance of some obligations that cannot be coerced, or it occurs when policy decisions cannot be adequately enforced.

(2) Commitment deflation occurs when the wielder of commitment experiences an overriding and rather total demand for a very narrow range of loyalties. Commitment inflation occurs when loyalties are spread so thinly and widely that demand for action based on some activated commitment cannot be fulfilled.

(3) Influence deflation occurs when those who can affect the decisions and attitudes of others are confined to narrow specialists, where untested positions matter little, or where intellectual virtuosos able to prove minute points are in the foreground. Influence inflation occurs when the decisions and attitudes of people are based on information that cannot be validated, where mere reputation or celebrity status alone sways people, where unverified bits of knowledge have effective impact on public opinion, or where there are many "influencers" whose relative merits cannot be readily evaluated.

(4) Inducement deflation occurs when all social usefulness is confined to a single social status, to one level or group in society, and remains there. This would, of course, be the highest, foremost, most advantaged, most cred-

ible status, depending upon which GSM has the highest salience. Inducement inflation occurs when statuses with no social usefulness are acknowledged and recognized as more or less equal to others.

Given these descriptions of GSM deflation and inflation, how would the GSM function in the respective quadrants of the grid and group matrix? The answer is based upon the truism that individuals as well as the groups they form act with a purpose, with goals. The perception and evaluation of goals is a function of grid. High grid location points to a *priorities ranking* in which values are well-articulated, coherent, and hence hierarchized and consistent in their effects; but low grid location indicates a *list of desirables*, of *desiderata*, and these make up a kaleidoscope of goals in which there is no coherent, articulated, or systematic order. Relative to GSM styles, this would mean that the higher one moves along the range marked by grid, the more deflated the GSM would appear, while the lower one moves, the more inflated they would seem. Thus each quadrant location might be described as follows.

(1) *Strong group/high grid* is a cultural location whose occupants perceive life in terms of distinct priorities. Superiors wield deflated power and commitment over their subordinates, and subordinates in turn ply their superiors with equally deflated influence and inducement. The GSM work effectively and hence predictably. Thus the embodiments of power, the topmost wielders of power, are in office "forever," or at least for life, and are succeeded in office in terms of a stable and predictable succession. Consider the length of tenure in po\.:er of the following: Roman emperors, Roman Catholic popes, Japanese emperors, the heads of the Chinese and Russian Communist parties, and the Sadducee high priests. These were more or less lifelong tenures, a feature explained by the way the GSM of power functions in this quadrant. Similarly, superior wielders of commitment share and demand a very narrow range of loyalties. They want more or less complete loyalty to the group or institution that they embody—the empire, church, party, or temple. On the other hand, subordinates in such systems find their influence and inducement equally deflated, effective only within the narrow focus in which these GSM are exercised. Such societies will predictably consist of a range of experts who know but a single field, for example, only chess, only Kant, only chemistry or physics, only priestly Torah, or only one type of law. If prayer is a form of influence and sacrifice is a form of inducement applied to superiors, then the effects of required prayer and sacrifice are known and effective. Prayer is influence applied to a superior, and superiors may cover a broad range from God and gods to local bureaucrats. In such praying, should a subordinate have his or her forms filled properly, terminology correct, style or bearing of request in order, then the prayer is heard, the passport is issued, and the

travel papers, building permits, or legal briefs are duly approved. Furthermore, the subject is always treated in terms of his or her social status, and most certainly rank has its privileges in terms of a share in the goods of society, with the higher rankings receiving first and appropriate choices of housing, food stocks, health care, and so on.

(2) *Strong group/low grid* location has its occupants see life in terms of a kaleidoscope of things desirable but in no specific order of priorities. A falling grid scrambles the priorities once fixed in high grid. The low grid entails the perception of uncertainty regarding the effectiveness of the inflated GSM that mark social interaction. The GSM work uncertainly and unpredictably; hence the "nothing ventured, nothing gained" perspective takes on the quality of virtue. The embodiments of power, the topmost wielders of power, appear to be capricious and their tenure in office is impermanent. Commitment functions very similarly. Thus loyalty, like office, is believed to be for a given time only, for a given need or crisis only, with highly unsure and unpredictable outcomes. For example, consider the "crises" of government that befall Italy, Greece, Israel, Turkey, or France? Or, to look at the first-century Mediterranean world, how many petty client states could have been certain of the duration of their king's rule which was always at the capricious whim of the Roman bureaucracy? Rulers in such systems have overextended loyalties, mainly to those who put them in power, might keep them in power, and might recognize their power, and to little else. On the other hand, subordinates in such systems find their influence and inducement abilities equally inflated, with no certainty of their effectiveness. Thus the main style of GSM interaction for subordinates in such cultural scripts is the "nothing ventured, nothing gained" perspective previously mentioned. Since the effects of required prayer are unknown, a host of unrequired prayers are added for insurance. Should a subordinate have his or her forms filled properly (although no one admits to really knowing what is a properly filled form), have the terminology correct (although no one admits to really knowing what is the proper terminology), or have the style of request in order (although no one admits to really knowing what is the proper style of request), then chances are that he or she still does not know if the prayer will be heard, if the passport will be stamped, or if the travel papers will be approved. The same holds for inducement or status. While all admit that rank has its privileges, no one knows what those privileges or their dimensions might be; hence it is better to overdo than to underdo, to use a bigger and better bribe than to offer less, and to shove for first place in line rather than to expect people to recognize one's rank and make way. With inflated inducement the usefulness of social statuses is put in doubt and, as a result, statuses with no social usefulness are acknowledged and recognized, for example, royal or noble families in contemporary "democratic" countries, in-

consequential government titles and awards, and the claim to status by recent and presumably temporary persons of wealth or by new lackeys of those in power. Strong group/low grid is a situation of instability, impermanence, uncertainty, and capriciousness in the workings of the GSM. Given such a situation, group members in this quadrant seek security as best they can while yearning for some secure stability to make living more meaningful. Consequently, it should be apparent that social concern for salvation or redemption (rescue and transformation of the social situation) is to be located typically in this quadrant, specifically at the lower end of low grid.

(3) *Weak group/high grid* can be conveniently exemplified by the contemporary U.S. mainstream. It is, of course, a cultural script which conceives of life in terms of distinct priorities, with the more advantaged wielding deflated influence and deflated wealth over the less advantaged. These latter, in turn, wield deflated power and deflated commitment in their interaction with the more advantaged. The GSM work effectively and predictably. Those who embody influence, the most credible wielders of influence (e.g., high level U.S. government officials, judges, professors), are presumed to have influence for life. For instance, note how former government officials of rank take up positions for continued effective dealing with the various central bureaucracies, both national and local, after their turns in office; ex-presidents, ex-senators, ex-cabinet members, or ex-department heads maintain their influence as a rule. Further, note how the most advantaged wielders of inducement, that is, the very wealthy, maintain and increase their inducement capacity, unaffected by monetary inflation, social changes, or changes of public officeholders. This all indicates that the GSM of influence and inducement are deflated in the system and function accordingly. Thus public officials in weak group/high grid systems function in terms of influence. Officeholders are to interact with their fellow citizens in terms of explanations, reasons, and facts and thus to solve internal problems; power applied to fellow citizens, for example, a soldier at every gas station during a fuel "shortage," is simply out of the question. Similarly, with deflated inducement national social usefulness, much like local social usefulness, is presumed to derive mainly from one level of society, that of the materially advantaged, and to remain there. On the other hand, the less materially advantaged in such systems find their power and commitment equally deflated and hence effective within the narrow focus within which the GSM are exercised. Power works quite effectively by means of voting; losers in an election step down without revolution or mobilizing the army or police "on the people's behalf." Wielders of influence and inducement can be removed from public office quite predictably. Power also works very effectively by means of technology which eventually filters down to most of the individuals active in the system who might want to apply the technology

or to have it applied to them. Further, commitments are generally focused on and within the individualistic boundaries typical of weak group. Self-interest is predictably paramount and effective, for instance, in terms of the types of contracts into which an individual might enter, such as marriage, purchase, or job. Outcomes and effects are rather well-known and understood.

(4) *Weak group/low grid*, again, is marked by a kaleidoscope of poorly defined sets of desirable outcomes in no order of priority. For individuals in this quadrant the GSM work quite uncertainly, often ineffectively and unpredictably. The GSM are inflated. As previously noted, this quadrant is a transitional location marked by ad hoc groups rather than by enduring societies. Within such groups those perceived as more advantaged due to inflated influence and inducement hold their central positions of influence, often called "leadership," on the basis of little if any information, factual knowledge, or proof of any kind. Such central figures are rated as highly advantaged even in the face of extremely little if any social utility. For examples of groups emerging from weak group/high grid, consider the central figures of Hippie, Yippie, and SDA groups or the materially advantaged central figures of Acid Rock, Punk Rock, or New Wave music. In this quadrant the GSM of influence and inducement, as inflated as they are, point to rather temporary and wavering leadership and status. For example, the weak group/low grid "stars" of American young persons of weak group/high grid origins last only for a given generation. Their successors follow capriciously and unpredictably since their fans eventually move out of the quadrant either up the grid to weak group/high grid, as most U.S. mainstream young people do, or across the group axis to strong group/low grid, as the experience of U.S. communes indicates. As for the less advantaged in this quadrant, the followers, they would perceive their power and commitment to be equally inflated. In the U.S. context the weak group/low grid individual's power over the more influential or more advantaged is seen to be inflated ("Voting never changes anything, so why vote?"). As far as the interest in technology is concerned, instrumental mastery over the environment only ruins the environment. In other words, in this quadrant the GSM of power is perceived to be ultimately ineffective and impractical; hence it is simply useless. Nothing can be changed with power since ultimately nothing can be enforced anyway. The inflated commitment of individuals deriving from weak group/high grid is manifested in unfocused loyalties either to other individuals or to specific anti-ideologies. Such inflated loyalties are articulated in oscillating allegiances perhaps to individuals with whom one is willing to have sexual relations or to religious or political ideologies one is willing to adopt and be held by.

These examples deal with weak group/low grid individuals coming to that quadrant from weak group/high grid societies, notably U.S. adolescents. What of individuals who come into this quadrant from strong group/ low grid by sliding across the group axis? Obviously the most significant thing that happens to such individuals is the reversal of the operative GSM. For a subordinate from strong group/low grid, the new location in weak group/low grid generates the experience and perception of having power and commitment, even if they are inflated. Because of this switch, new perceptions and orientations of values emerge. A superior from strong group/ low grid finds his or her previous control of inflated power and commitment transformed into the influence and inducement characteristic of strong group subordinates. For both the superior and the subordinate previously in strong group, the weak group/low grid experience offers a vision of new values. Should these individuals return to their former strong group/low grid world, they might readily attempt to implement the new values recently experienced by means of new social structures. Weak group/low grid generates alternate values while strong group/low grid develops alternate structures. Values mark general directions of behavior while structures are social means for realizing values. Thus the low grid person newly returned to strong group from weak group would readily imagine new social structures to realize the values and vision experienced in the weak group. In the context of the models presented in this chapter, it would seem that such diverse persons as John the Baptist, Jesus of Nazareth, Paul of Tarsus, Francis of Assisi, John Wesley, Lenin, and a host of strong group creative geniuses drew their vision and call for new values along with appropriate changes in social structure from their experience of a period of weak group/low grid reversal of GSM. The Gospel of John, on the other hand, does not bother with structure but simply inculcates new weak group/low grid values.

Figure 4 on p. 97 sums up this chapter by presenting the GSM of social interaction within the larger frame of the grid/group matrix. The figure also sets down some of the generalizations drawn from the strategies and styles of play. These generalizations should serve to suggest the types of conceptions and perceptions group membership in the various quadrants might develop concerning goods and causality. The purpose of these considerations is to set out some approaches for discerning social meanings encoded in the language of texts. On the basis of this chapter, what might a U.S. reader expect to find depicted in the strong group/low grid texts of the New Testament, of course apart from the Gospel of John, a weak group/low grid text? And what would John portray in terms of the social scripts sketched out here?

FIGURE 4. GSM in Grid and Group

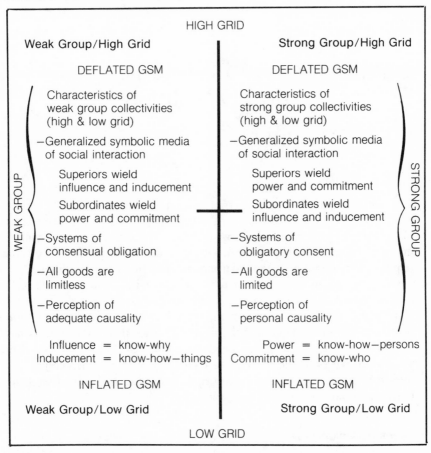

Group: refers to the social definition of the interacting personality.
—Strong group: dyadic personality, replicating the group body as inviolable; action oriented to the collectivity; agents assessed in terms of birth and inborn qualities of sex, age, race, family status; persons judged by ascriptive standards and qualities unrelated to performance; all judged by status-specific standards.
—Weak group: individualistic personality, replicating the individual body as inviolable; action oriented to self-interest; agents assessed in terms of performance, hence judged by achievements; all judged by the same standards regardless of ascribed qualities.
Grid: refers to the degree of inflation or deflation of the operative generalized symbolic media of social interaction.
—High grid: deflation = too few wielders of the GSM and too much of the goods the GSM stand for: force (power), focused loyalty (commitment), facts and proofs (influence), social utility (inducement).
—Low grid: inflation = too many wielders of the GSM and not enough of the goods the GSM stand for: ineffective force (power), diffuse and unfocused loyalty (commitment), conflicting and unverifiable facts and proof (influence), lack of any great social utility (inducement).

5.

Game Plans and Strategies: Processes and Directions

INTRODUCTION

To summarize up to this point, after a brief introduction to the grid and group model, the typical cultural scripts lodged within the quadrants of that model were considered. Subsequently, the four generalized symbolic media of social interaction were described. These GSM mark off the games required for adapting to the environment in a humanly meaningful, purposeful, and social way. This chapter will deal with the dimensions of the action that takes place when people in given social groups ply each other with power, influence, commitment, or inducement. The way the action flows will obviously determine the main strategies used by people to have effect on each other. The means people use to have effect on each other are the generalized symbolic media. The focus here is on *how* people use these means. What game plans and strategies do people devise? How does the action flow in human social interaction?

Types of Action Flow

If all the types of human social interaction were chunked in terms of their similarities, they would fall along a range marked, on the one hand, by the back-and-forth movement called reciprocity and, on the other, by a movement toward some central point and then out from it called centricity. Reciprocal, back-and-forth social movement can be found in Christmas gift giving. Centric, toward-the-center-and-out-again movement can be found in taxation and other forms of redistribution. Of course there are some people who refuse to take part in either social movement. These would be the stubborn individualists, unwilling to share and unwilling to allow themselves to be controlled. Such extreme non-participation in the normal flow of social interaction is usually called rudeness, selfishness, and a number of other names. Talking aloud during a movie or lecture and shouting and screaming outside the open windows of a church during services point to individualists who refuse to reciprocate. Such persons act off the scale of social interaction and are tolerated in few societies, weak group/high grid U.S. being one of the few.

At the other extreme and equally off the scale of social interaction stand those groups that seek to control both the reciprocal and the centric movements of all the people in their society, with controlling group members excepted. Such controlling groups monopolize all the GSM of the society for their own purposes, unwilling to let the majority under them participate in significant reciprocal and centric ways. Such minority elite control of all social interaction is called agglomeration or, more commonly, totalitarianism. Such total control of social interaction is equally off the scale of human interchange and, when found, can normally be situated at the extreme corner of the strong group/high grid quadrant.

However, it seems that human relations are normally mutual relations and hence avoid the extremes of utter individualism and agglomeration. Mutuality at the social level would imply reciprocity on the one hand and centricity on the other, with a combination of forms in between. Reciprocity is a vice versa movement between two parties, individuals or groups. It is a "between" relation of back-and-forth movement marked by the action and reaction of two sides or two distinct social interests. Consequently, reciprocity is based on the social fact of sides and is rooted in the purity lines that mark off the inside from the outside. The common English word for this relation bridging distinct social interests is sharing. In terms of the GSM of the previous chapter, power on the reciprocity wavelength entails power sharing, normally called consensus. Commitment on the reciprocity wavelength entails loyalty sharing, sharing oneself, one's children, and one's group, and this is precisely what commitment is about. Such commitment often entails living in the same place (coterritoriality) and offering one's children and relatives in marriage (cohabitation). In other words, cohabitation and coterritoriality usually replicate and mark off areas of commitment or shared loyalty. Influence, in turn, when put on the reciprocity range of the scale, involves sharing the cultural story one lives out, sharing the personalized sets of meanings used to interpret human living. Reciprocal story sharing is called conversation. Finally, inducement on the reciprocity wavelength involves sharing one's goods with others, social consumption. Thus consensus, commitment, conversation, and consumption are all ways of expressing the back-and-forth movement of reciprocity in terms of the GSM.

Centricity, on the other hand, is a form of pooling by members of a group; what is pooled moves in the direction of some central party (individual or group) and is then redivided within the group by the central party. Centricity is a type of complex reciprocity between the many and the one and back to the many rather than a simple reciprocity between two sides. Such complex reciprocity or pooling requires some social center as focal point for the in-and-out movement that marks centricity—in to the center and out from the center. Since centricity entails many parties (individuals and/or groups), it is a relation within a group, a replication of social unity. Consequently, centricity is a collective, group action. Since such centricity interaction takes place within a group, it is based on the social fact of groups and is rooted in the purity lines that mark off group members from group non-members, the ingroup from the outgroup. Further, since centricity is the collective action of a group and since the GSM that symbols effective collective action is power, centricity interactions will always be power interactions either alone or coupled with other GSM. The common way of describing this within-group pooling focused on some central agency is centralized control. Power on the centricity wavelength entails power centralization, normally called management with its pronouncements and programs for the group. Commitment on the centricity wavelength entails the centralization of loyalty as well as the control of commitment and of how or in what one might embed his or her emotions; this is what pledges of allegiance and forms of socialization dealing with group allegiance are about. Influence on the centricity end of the scale involves controlling the cultural story of the group, the common sets of meanings used to produce and assess evidence and thus to interpret human living. Centricity story control emerges in myth, shared social stories (cf. Doty 1980). Finally, inducement on the centricity wavelength involves controlling goods and services conceived as goods and is called redistribution. Thus management, allegiance, myth, and redistribution are all ways of expressing the to-the-center-and-out-from-the-center movement of centricity in terms of the GSM. As for agglomeration and the GSM, agglomerated power is totalitarianism, agglomerated commitment is resocialization, agglomerated influence is propaganda, and agglomerated inducement is rationing. Table 2 below summarizes the categories presented in the foregoing discussion.

TABLE 2. GSM and the Flow of the Action

GSM	when shared *reciprocity*	when controlled *centricity*	when monopolized *agglomeration*
Power	consensus	management	totalitarianism
Commitment	commitment	allegiance	resocialization
Influence	conversation	myth	propaganda
Inducement	consumption	redistribution	rationing

The main points of the discussion are that GSM are used in social interactions and that these interactions fall along a range marked, as a rule, by reciprocity and centricity. It now remains to consider both reciprocity and centricity in greater detail and then to fit both within the grid/group matrix. The value of this analysis for New Testament study consists in the capacity of the resulting model to clarify the dimensions of interaction portrayed in the texts. If the dimensions of interaction are culturally specific, and it seems that they are, then for each interaction described in the New Testament the reader might ask: what is the flow of the interaction, reciprocal or centric? Which GSM are involved? Given the reciprocal and/or centric flow along with the specific GSM, what would be the script specific meaning of the interaction, that is, what would the interaction mean to persons of that culture? In this way, the analysis should help the attentive Bible reader understand the meaning conveyed through the text in terms of the social structures of the first-century Mediterranean world. The first question then is: what are the usual types of reciprocity interactions? (The discussion that follows is heavily indebted to Sahlins 1972: 185–275.)

RECIPROCITY

Reciprocity typically involves the action and reaction of two sides or two distinct social interests. The meaning embodied and realized in vice versa reciprocity derives from the purpose of the interaction shared by one or both of the interacting sides. Thus reciprocity interchanges can run from (A) disinterested concern for the other party through (B) mutuality in a balanced and symmetrical way to (C) pure self-interest to the disadvantage of the other party. The range of reciprocity interchanges can be expressed in terms of its extremes and midpoint.

FIGURE 5. Reciprocity Scale

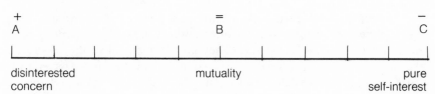

Generalized Reciprocity (A)

Of the two distinct social interests involved in reciprocity, generalized reciprocity refers to interactions that are focused immediately on the social interests of the other party. They are thus "altruistic" since focused on another. To facilitate the interests of the other, power and its commands are withheld from the other or directed to some third party on the other's behalf. Or, similarly, commitment and its requests are withheld from the other or directed to some third party on the other's behalf. Or influence and its information are freely and readily given to the other or on the other's behalf, as are inducement and its goods and services. In generalized reciprocity assistance is given without specification of some return obligation in terms of time, quantity, or quality. However, the expectation of some returned assistance is always implied but left indefinite and open-ended. Some common forms of interaction that have the structure of generalized reciprocity include hospitality, gifts, and various types of assistance given to kin and friends as well as to other people, regardless of their social location, from whom some returned assistance might always be requested at some future date. Perhaps the clearest example of such generalized reciprocity in the U.S. is that of parents toward their children. Generalized reciprocity does not keep score or keep tabs in terms of time, quantity, or quality of returned assistance due but stays open-ended and indefinite. Consequently, this is a weak reciprocity in the sense that the obligation to reciprocate is left vague, indeterminate, and unspecified. Because of the focus on the interests of the other party, social relations with the other party determine the flow of assistance. Due to this feature generalized reciprocity focuses mainly on the GSM of commitment and blends in with the other GSM insofar as they are coupled with commitment, for example, commitment plus power, commitment plus inducement, and commitment plus influence. Hence in terms of the GSM generalized reciprocity builds a store of commitment and the indefinitely expected return of assistance is rooted in obligations of commitment.

Balanced Reciprocity (B)

Given the two distinct social interests involved in reciprocity, balanced reciprocity refers to social interactions which are focused on both social interests at the same time. They are symmetrical in the sense that the immediate focus is on equivalent reciprocity in the customary equivalent form and without delay. This entails a balanced vice versa exchange, a tit-for-tat movement—a command for a command (power), a request for a request (commitment), information for information (influence), or some goods and services for other goods and services (inducement)—in equivalent terms. Obviously in developed systems of exchange GSM can be substituted for an equivalent in another GSM—information for a command, goods for loyalty, or a command for information. In balanced reciprocity the parties interact with each other as distinct social interests, concerned with more or less precise reckoning aimed at some return for the GSM given. This return is expected within some short, well-defined, and determined time. Some common forms of interaction that have the structure of balanced reciprocity include buying and selling of goods and services, paying fees for tuition, payment to professionals, peace and trade agreements, and barter or goods exchange. Balanced reciprocity keeps score in terms of time, quantity, or quality of returned GSM in a way that seeks a quick conclusion to the highly specified interaction. Thus in balanced interaction focus is not on social relations but mainly on the interaction or exchange itself. Any exchange stipulating a return of commensurate worth or equivalent usefulness within a narrow and limited time period is balanced reciprocity. Because the focus here is on each party obtaining equivalent or commensurate worth or usefulness from the interchange, it is the *interchange* that determines social relations rather than vice versa as in generalized reciprocity. Once the interchange is over social relations remain much as they were before the interaction, unless the interacting partners insert some elements of generalized reciprocity during the interchange. For example, one can become friends with one's physician, teacher, or dentist during the course of dealing with them even though they are paid for services rendered. Even after the services are completed, one may continue a friendship of the generalized reciprocity sort. Thus an interchange of balanced reciprocity may prove an occasion for developing a generalized reciprocity relationship. On the other hand, it may also prove an occasion for a negative reciprocity experience.

Negative Reciprocity (C)

Of the two distinct social interests involved in reciprocity negative reciprocity refers to interactions that are focused immediately on the social interests of the self and/or extended self (one's group). Negative reciprocity, then, is "egocentric" since focused on "ego" or extended "ego." Negative reciprocity is a vice versa movement in which one party attempts to get something from another without really reciprocating at all, hence for nothing and with impunity. The focus of the interaction in negative reciprocity is solely the social interests of the self, individual and/or extended. This entails maximizing one's own interests at the interacting partner's expense, that is, profiteering. Some common forms of interaction that have the structure of negative reciprocity are lying, cheating, theft, robbery, overcharging, substituting shoddy goods (as in "bait and switch"), chicanery, and all the varieties of appropriation and seizure of another's GSM. Thus negative reciprocity includes a range of lop-sided interactions from various, simple

rip-offs to outright robbery. Consequently, in negative reciprocity social relations are quite out of the focus; the relationship is most impersonal in that
it is oriented to the self (and extended self) alone with no consideration for
the social interests of the other interacting partner who, in the process, is reduced to the status of an object or a thing with a nature different from that
of "ego." Negative reciprocity precludes any ongoing, meaningful, human,
social relationship of the other reciprocal varieties.

The type of reciprocity structure considered appropriate in a given
vice versa interchange generally depends upon the social context of the situation in which the interaction takes place. In general, the following variables
determine the context of a situation:

(1) the purpose of the interaction: to obtain something vitally necessary,
normally necessary, or really unnecessary;
(2) the persons interacting: members of a kinship group, a fictive kinship
group, a broader polity with various ranks and statuses, or outgroups;
(3) the type of GSM used in the interaction: some are appropriate for
superior-subordinate relationships (e.g., power), some for first-last
(commitment), greater-lesser (inducement), or profound-shallow (influence) relationships, and some for equals;
(4) the place and the time of the interaction: private or public—within the
space of the community or on its periphery—and during "business"
hours or during "free" time.

The interpretation of language in any linguistic interchange depends
heavily upon the context of a situation for significant pieces of meaning. As
a matter of fact, language as interpersonal communication can only be interpreted within the context of a situation (cf. Halliday 1978). The variables
listed above constitute this context. However, here it suffices to note that interaction in the vice versa movement of reciprocity is at bottom itself a form
of communication, a type of conversation in which GSM are used instead of
or along with language. Just as language can be interpreted only within the
context of a situation, so too the meaning of the GSM in interaction depends upon a given context. The importance of the context of a situation for
interpreting such reciprocity exchanges might be seen from the following
sector analysis model adopted from Sahlins (1972). The model uses only two
of the variables—the persons interacting replicated in the space of the interaction (fig. 6, p. 105).

Notice that the model points to variations in reciprocity based on the
quality of persons in the interaction and the place of the interaction. Set out
in this way, these variables reveal a latent norm which defines degrees of
commitment and the care and concern that commitment symbols. The
model implies a definition of "who are my kin, who are my neighbors, and
who are neither kin nor neighbors." Obviously such a norm defining kin and

FIGURE 6. Sectoral Analysis of Reciprocity

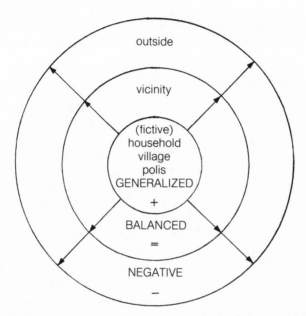

neighbor is crucial and basic for the application of social standards of all sorts: etiquette; moral and legal dos and don'ts; and customs of all types. In this perspective a given action in itself is not so much good taste or bad taste (etiquette), or simply good or bad (moral), or legal or illegal. Such judgments depend upon who the interacting partners are. What is wrong within the heart of one's family or community (e.g., killing or profiteering) may be the object of praise at the outer rim of the social circle (e.g., where killing is considered socially useful, as in war, or where profiteering is considered praiseworthy business practice such as what the market will bear).

To see further how the model might work, take the norms of reciprocity listed in the Ten Commandments in Exod. 20:2–17 and Deut. 5:6–21 and apply them to the model. To whom does the "thou" refer, and who are the presumed interacting partners—fellow Israelites, fellow Middle Easterners, fellow human beings? Perhaps in the context of ancient Israel the interacting partners are simply the adult male members of Israel bound together in reciprocal relations due to a common covenant bond with the God of Israel (cf. Gottwald 1979).

It should be quite apparent that not all social interactions are of the reciprocal sort. Given the complexity of social arrangements, a large number of human social interactions are often of the centricity type; for example, taxes go to a central government (federal, state, local) and come out again in the form of paved roads, various welfare payments, salaries, and grants. How does reciprocity, the vice versa movement of distinct social interests, become centricity, the movement of GSM to some center and out again?

RECIPROCITY BECOMES CENTRICITY

Centricity refers to any type of pooling toward some social center (person or group) with an eventual redivision of the items pooled within the group. Centricity looks to *the group*, a collectivity with more or less clear boundaries that mark it off as a closed group, such as a family or a city. What is typical of such closed groups is that some of their members (e.g., parents in a family) engage in generalized reciprocity with a number of individuals (e.g., the individual children in a family). Similarly, in a closed group such as an isolated village some village inhabitants will engage in generalized reciprocity with a number of others in the village. Generalized reciprocity, as noted previously, defers return of assistance given to some unspecified time and in no fixed amount or quality. Hence, should the person who has engaged in generalized reciprocity with a range of individuals call for return of assistance given for the sake of a goal of value to the whole community, the results would be rather distinctive. For the store of open-ended debts built up by generalized reciprocity would now flow to the person or group in the social center and flow out again for the good of the collectivity. The situation is something like a father's asking all the children in a family to give him all the money they might have saved so that he might be able to make a house payment which benefits all.

What would a person at the social center of such centricity interactions be called? In a collectivity such as a family or a small, isolated village which is a set of families such a person might be called a "head" or even a "leader." Thus one can speak of the head of the family, a village head, or a "leader." Reciprocity aimed at some focal figure, an individual or small group, is a centralized form of organization consisting of a range of reciprocities usually in some ranked order of priorities. Such a ranked order of reciprocity transactions would form a structure consisting of the focal figure's dues and obligations. The dues entail the figure's rights, who owed what to the central figure as a debt to be called up at some time, while the obligations consist of what the central figure is expected to do for those who need the figure's generalized reciprocity. In a group such a focal figure is nearly always the central recipient who calls on dues and the bestower of favors who grants generalized reciprocity requests. However, such focal figures or heads are of two types. To use rather modern technical terms, the two types are the manager and the leader (McGregor 1976; Lassey 1976).

Managers

A focal figure may get that role by ascription. It is ascribed to the figure because of lineage (birth), because institutional arrangements require a given person or group to play the focal figure role (custom), or because some superior power puts the focal figure into that role (law). This is the manager role, regardless of the titles given to those who occupy such roles in the range of the world's cultures—king, priest, father, lord, bank president, or vice-president of corporation X. Managers get their following by ascription as well; followers are placed below or behind the manager either because of birth or custom or because some superior power put the manager over the following (law). Thus the manager's central or focal position is rooted in the rights that ascription entails—the traditional, customary, or legal dues and obligations of the managerial role.

Leaders

A focal figure may get that role by achievement. The role is acquired by some person because of what he or she has done on behalf of his or her following. Normally the following is due to some generalized reciprocity initiative (e.g., generosity, heroic deed, loyalty in the face of opposition, or freely offering vital information) that serves as a starter mechanism building up a following in generalized reciprocity. Thus leadership depends upon an achievement on behalf of the group that finds itself in need of some quality, activity, or object at a given time and place. In other words, leadership is not a quality of the individual but a role dependent upon the presence of a number of variables. Centricity based upon a focal role deriving from achievement normally dissolves with the demise of the pivotal leader, and centricity based upon achievement, that is, leadership centricity, simply remains generalized reciprocity, often multiple generalized reciprocity. Such leadership-focused reciprocity normally never develops into any stable centricity structure unless it is somehow transformed.

How then do stable centricity structures emerge? Stable centricity structures are managerial structures. Consequently, for leadership-focused reciprocity to develop into a stable centricity structure, the leader must become a manager in some way. This aspect might be compared with Weber's routinization of charisma; however, charisma is not necessary for leadership, as amply demonstrated by B. Schwartz (1983). The manager's role is an ascribed one; it derives from lineage, custom, or law and thus is an office in some stable institutional structure. If the social scale of managerial centricity is extensive, with a large body of followers (e.g., citizens, fictive kin), and is broadly spread and rather specialized in individual social roles, the result is a measure of centricity approximating both the classical bureaucratic structures of antiquity—the Roman Empire's "family of Caesar" during the period of Christian origins (cf. Weaver 1972; Millar 1977) or the subsequent empire centered in Constantinople (cf. D. Miller 1969)—and, in more complex form, the bureaucratic structures of contemporary political, economic, educational, and religious institutions.

To see the relevance of the theoretical model developed thus far, consider the following questions: was Jesus as depicted in the Gospels a leader or a manager? What does the dispersal of his followers at the crucifixion indicate about his role? How did Jesus build up a fund of generalized reciprocity so as to warrant a following? Was Paul a leader or a manager? What of the role of bishop as set forth in the Pastoral Epistles? Jesus asked that alms be given to the poor, as did Judaism in general, but what reciprocity is entailed in such almsgiving? Acts 2:44–47 is a summary that describes one form of almsgiving—from the individual who has to another in need—but Acts 4:32–37 describes almsgiving directed to a central figure who then disburses the alms to the needy; what change in reciprocity structure has intervened? There are, of course, many more such questions that might be put to the New Testament in terms of the model as presented thus far, but the model is not yet complete.

The foregoing explanation attempts to describe the way in which centricity emerges from generalized reciprocity specifically by means of the central or focal role of the leader or manager. However, centricity can equally emerge from negative reciprocity. As previously noted, negative reciprocity is a vice versa movement in which one party attempts to get something from another without any return, hence for nothing and with impunity. Imagine some central personage, whether manager, leader, or small group, acting in negative fashion with a whole range of people. What does such a central personage do in effect? He or she forces (GSM of power) the ones he or she interacts with to make him or her a focal point, a center for the various GSM which he or she might then redistribute within his or her own group. For some concrete examples, think of "protection rackets" or simply conquest empires, for example, the Roman Empire or the emperor and his bureaucracy. The emperor was a leader turned manager for his people, his fellow Romans. Rome's conquest added a whole block of non-citizens to the social community, a block of subjects. Such conquest is a form of negative reciprocity that finally ends up as a centricity form with the flow of GSM to a center for redistribution. However, the taxes and tolls taken from subject peoples without the intention of distributing them within those groups remain a form of negative reciprocity embedded in centricity.

Thus both generalized reciprocity and negative reciprocity may lead to centricity (this should refute the position taken by Diamond 1973 who believes only negative reciprocity leads to centricity). Balanced reciprocity, on the other hand, would not develop to centricity since it does not allow any interacting partner to accumulate GSM so as to become a focal center.

CENTRICITY

Reciprocity, then, becomes centricity with the emergence of some focal center (individual or group). Centricity always bears upon the collectivity, and effective collective action always requires power of some sort. With a fund of generalized reciprocity at its disposal the focal center stabilizes and fixes the center-periphery relationship by means of the GSM of power for effective collective action.

Centricity structures are to be found in a whole range of concrete interactions wherever redistribution or redivision takes place in closed groups: cooperative food production; collective political action; and collective religious, educational, or economic activity. Thus pooling and redistribution mark the movement of the GSM in collective, centric interactions. The typical centricity structure is the extended household characteristic of many strong group societies. The products of collective effort are pooled mainly because strong group households are closed systems, a within-relation that requires and entails a division of labor. The principle is that the products of collective effort are pooled, and this principle applies not just to the strong group households but to any complex group that develops about some task within closed structures. At both the narrower level, such as the extended household, and the broader level, such as the polity or body of citizens (a replication of the extended household), the principle remains that goods collectively procured are distributed throughout the collectivity or in its behalf. However, the mode of distribution and redivision depends upon the special contributions to collective endeavors indicated by a person's ascribed rank or status. This principle holds in the family, in the distribution of taxes among Roman citizenry in the first century, and in salary scales in modern corporations.

Thus the GSM of power, whether wielded directly as in strong group societies or by representation as in weak group, is normally realized in centricity structures. Structures then express both the power wielder's right to call on the GSM of the underlying population—their wealth, influence, and commitment—for the sake of collective goals and the power wielder's obligations to use the gathered GSM for the benefit of the whole community. The power wielder does this by supporting a range of activities that might benefit the closed group: subsidizing political, religious, educational, and familial personnel; social pageantry; war; underwriting, supporting, regulating, and promoting craft production and trade; the construction of public buildings and of religious, political, educational, and familial projects; redistributing diverse local products; helping and supporting the community during shortages; and supporting community guests like embassies. The organized exercise of the rights and obligations of a focal wielder of power is centricity.

Generally speaking, centricity covers a range of types marked by two poles: (1) logistic centricity that focuses mainly on the GSM of inducement and power; it is realized in the practical, logistic redistribution of collective goods and services to sustain the community or the community effort in some collective, concrete sense; and (2) alternatively or often simultaneously, symbolic centricity that focuses mostly on the GSM of commitment and influence; it is realized in the use of goods and services to express fellowship, loyalty, conviction, and/or compliance with regard to the central wielder of power, thus supporting and sustaining the complex power structure in a social sense.

Whatever the practical benefits to members of the group, centricity with its pooling and redistribution generates the perception of societal unity (in strong group, with uniformity; in weak group, without uniformity). Centricity likewise replicates the social structure with its rank order and presupposes centralized organization of social order and social action.

CENTRICITY BECOMES AGGLOMERATION

A focal figure is capable of amassing generalized or negative reciprocity within a closed group. Depending on the quality of the group, whether working by ascription or achievement, that focal figure is able to acquire the GSM of power in highly deflated form. In this way reciprocity will become centricity. The centricity thus acquired can be stabilized and structured by means of lineage, custom, or law and can be focused on a manager. However, centricity deriving from situations of collective need or crisis requires the focal figure of the leader. When the crisis and the leader pass away, the group either falls back to previous modes of reciprocity or transforms the leader role into a more enduring managerial role, and thus the centricity structure abides.

What happens when the managerial centricity structure itself must deal with a crisis engulfing the collectivity? The usual reaction is for the managerial elite to advance and consolidate their power. All the available GSM are assembled into the hands of the governing elite to ensure their community's survival in time of war or social crisis. Should the crisis pass, the managerial elite find themselves in possession of the power, inducement, influence, and commitment of the collectivity. This heavy concentration of GSM within one social unit is called agglomeration. Obviously elites in such a situation have two main options: to return to the pre-crisis situation of centricity or to maintain the post-crisis situation of agglomeration. It would seem that most complex societies of extremely strong group and high grid opt for agglomeration, for example, the U.S.S.R., China, the Vatican today, and the Roman Empire that controlled the first-century Mediterranean world during New Testament times.

Agglomeration looks to total control on behalf of the elite who wield the GSM of power. It seeks to control commitment, influence, inducement, and power, normally by means of bureaucracies at the service of the central focal power, whether an individual or group. As a result, a rather broad social gap develops between the elite minority—including the ruler, leading advisers, personal retainers, court officials, heads of bureaucracies and armies, and aristocracy—and the non-elite majority—urban groups of artisans, merchants and traders, peasantry, and slaves (cf. Eisenstadt 1963).

Figure 7 below sums up the total range of interchanges considered in this chapter. In the following chapter the structural dimensions of a society determined by these interchanges will be fleshed out.

FIGURE 7. Range of Social Interchanges

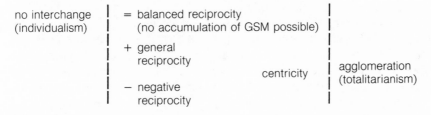

6.

Channeling the Flow of the Action

INTRODUCTION: VALUES, INSTITUTIONS, NORMS

In the previous chapter the possible directions of the flow of social interaction were considered. In those social arrangements called society this flow is not at all haphazard or capricious. Rather, human beings generally share and live up to expectations about the general direction of the flow of action, expectations usually realized in a given collectivity. The ordinary name for the general direction of the flow of action, a direction socially expected and usually pursued in the group, is *value*. The quality of a value largely depends upon the dimensions of the goals, ends, or purposes embodied by the value. Thus a core value would refer to the general target, goal, end, or purpose that holds an entire society together in its varied and manifold interactions. For example, in the U.S. the general core value is instrumental activism (cf. Parsons 1958: 199–200; Williams 1970: 452–502). Instrumental activism is the goal or target that directs the U.S. mainstream population, in general and individually, to attempt actively to master and control the environment as a main concern. This attempt at mastering the environment encompasses all the concrete and concretely experienced situations in which a person might find himself or herself. This environment is perceived as external to the society and to the individual considered as the replication of the social body. This core value is often articulated, expressed, and explained in more specific values or norms in order to give meaning to the activity of the group and to mark off the group from other groups. Such an articulation of the group's core value is called an *ideology*. Given the U.S. core value of instrumental activism, the ideological expression of this value might be called technologism, the belief that pragmatic control of the environment is *the* defining characteristic of a meaningful human existence. Thus what is typical of the flow of human interaction in the U.S. is the active mastery and control of the environment—nature, time, space, other individuals, and other societies. While core values mark off the ends or goals of a society, there are more specific societal values, replicating the core values, that look to more limited pieces of behavior. For example, the U.S. general value of instrumental activism is replicated in the specific values of "democracy" which facilitates individual instrumental mastery. Such "democracy" implies free enterprise, equal opportunity, individual self-determination, and individual franchise. Other replications of instrumental activism include individualism, pragmatism, idealism, sincerity, future orientation, humanitarianism, and voluntarism, to name a significant few. All of these values are specifically U.S. values that in fact replicate the core value of instrumental mastery, helping the *individual* "make it" in the weak group/high grid U.S. mainstream. The main point to be noted here, however, is that the core value and its replications in a spectrum of specific values direct and channel social interaction in a given society.

Obviously not all past and present societies hold to instrumental activism as a core value. For example, modern, non-Mediterranean West Europeans share a core value that might be called autonomous controllism. Autonomous controllism is the goal or target that directs the mainstream of these Europeans in general and individually. It looks to the attempt to exercise power over people—whether through property, through posts in the bureaucracy, through having one's own business, employees, or servants, or via the patriarchal family structure, wives, and children—while not having direct power exercised over oneself (cf. Hobsbawm 1971: 37). The attempt to keep control of one's own existence and above all not to be controlled by others serves as implicit agenda in all that individual persons and collectivities might do in their strong group and, generally, high grid situation.

On the other hand, to move further back in time and to cite some examples from the New Testament period, Roman society was held together by a core value we might call past-directed activism. Past-directed activism is the goal or target that directed Romans in general and individually actively to live up to and at least to match the deeds of their ancestors, the founders of Roman society ("founder" in Latin is "auctor," "growth giver"). Romans were taught to live with the burden of the past on their shoulders. Whatever was best or whatever was noblest and true was already lived out and achieved by the ancestors of a given Roman generation. Thus the individual and the society as a whole in this strong group script could only live up to the greatness of the past. By commonly held presupposition, this past could never really be equalled or surpassed. The greatness of the past was replicated and symboled in the elders of society, the people who, as they grew older, visibly moved closer to the great past. The elders were *maiores natu,* greater by birth and proximity to the truly great ones. The typical Roman ideological articulation of this value was *auctoritas* (often poorly translated as "authority"). The word means "authorization by the past," by the glorious tradition. Interestingly enough, *auctoritas* could not be translated into Greek adequately; hence the social reality it expressed is not to be found in the New Testament. Consequently, while Roman citizens might have a political voice, their decisions had to be "authorized by the past" by being submitted for the consent of the senatorial elders who bore the great burden of the past for the populace. Thus in the Roman system anything that was demonstrably old was automatically good and certainly better than anything present that did not repeat the past. Any course of action in the present had to match expectations set by the glorious past and be justified in terms of models deriving from the past (Arendt 1958; cf. the earlier data in Stavely 1982).

The motley, subject Greek population of the period shared a different core value. The Hellenistic core value might be called personal limitlessness. Personal limitlessness was the goal and target that directed various Hellenistic societies and individuals to discover effective ways to overcome human finitude and limitation especially by means of virtual or actual forms of deification. The Greek tradition of the divine and half-divine, the heroes, produced a plethora of such persons in the Hellenistic world (cf. Schilling 1980). Hellenistic philosophy in its varied dimensions would offer a significant ideological expression of this core value.

Finally there was the subject Jewish population of Palestine held by a contrasting core value. This value might be called interpersonal contentment. Interpersonal contentment is the goal or target that directed the Jewish population as a whole and individually to acquiesce in human finitude and limitation and yet to strive to achieve a genuinely human existence, finite and free. Thus while Romans sought to live up to the expectations of their ancestors and called upon ancestral divinities to help them in this endeavor and while Hellenists sought to be filled with the infinity of God, Jews sought only the enabling help of God to become what they were meant to be—limited, finite, free human beings. In Judaism Torah study and Torah practice are the ideological expressions of the Jewish core value (Fennell 1977).

If societal core values direct the flow of social interaction in a very general way, how do such values get harnessed to specific goals or situations such as adaptation to the environment, solidarity, or collective action? If a core value might be compared to something like the energy of a tornado, how is that energy channeled to meet specific tasks? The means used to focus core values on something specific is a process called institutionalization. The outcome of the process is a social structure for applying values to specific tasks. This structure is called a social *institution.*

In this discussion, then, an institution is a value structure, a definite yet broadly abstract pattern that serves as a means or vehicle for the social realization of some value. Institutions give specific shape to general core values. By means of institutions core values are replicated in a spectrum of specific values that channel the flow of social interaction toward specific ends.

Consequently, a society consists of individuals who perceive themselves to be mutually bound by means of emotionally anchored commitments to pursue and support certain directions in the flow of social interaction as well as to pursue and support certain types of actions. Commitments to certain directions in the flow of social interaction result in values becoming normative, while commitments to certain types of actions cause social structures to become obligatory, normally because of the values they bear and realize.

By and large, core values and their replications find their institutional realization in norms known as standards, customs, and laws. Standards, customs, and laws all encode, embody, and/or express values; they direct the flow of social interaction. Such norms are clearly crucial since, for social interaction to take place at all in any effective and meaningful way, interacting partners require some way to hold each other and to be held by common, shared values. Such common norms hold together the individuals that form a given society. Being held together by norms is what makes social interaction social. Now norms, as mentioned above, include standards, customs, and laws; how do these differ from each other? The usefulness of this question for New Testament study emerges in questions such as: What precisely held Jesus and his wandering group of followers together? What were Jesus' arguments with his hostile interlocutors about when they referred to the Torah? What was Paul driving at when he insisted that "we are free from the law"? Why did not Paul base any of his ethical directives on law, either Mosaic, Hellenistic, Roman, or otherwise? What is going on regarding the flow of social interaction and community formation with all the New Testament references to law, commandments, and the like?

What then are standard, custom, and law? How do they channel the flow of action? The discussion that follows will demonstrate that these types of norms are all about reciprocity and centricity, the important topics of the previous chapter (the discussion that follows is based on Selznick et al. 1968; Bohannan 1973; cf. Malina 1981a).

STANDARD

A standard is a common value encoded as a norm. As an encoded common value, a standard guides some dimension of social interaction and implies a binding obligation which is regarded as a right by one party and acknowledged as a duty by another. Effective and meaningful social interaction requires that the interacting parties have the ability to hold each other to some common values; otherwise chaos and nonsense result.

To imagine how standards arise, consider some situation in which human beings from various cultural backgrounds are for some reason or other thrown together and must interact. Survivors of an international plane crash or shipwreck can serve as an example. The norms each has from his or her previous enculturation would not be adequate since the other party does not know them and will not follow them. What do persons do in such situations, then? They will throw the various GSM at each other in some random, unsystematized way as determined by previous experience in similar situations. By focusing on power, inducement, commitment, or influence directed to the other, the interacting partner initiating the interchange implies that he or she can always apply the sanctions entailed in the GSM if the interaction does not go his or her way. If others will not listen to a command (GSM power), they will be physically coerced (sanction). Now by complying with the GSM the other partner to the interchange implies that the initiating partner has some right in this instance to obtain results from the interaction. Should the unorganized group acknowledge that the GSM wielder in fact has the right in a given case to get the results he or she seeks in a given interaction, then the GSM wielder would be said to have *authority*. Authority, in this instance, is the socially acknowledged right to oblige another. In this perspective, then, authority produces standards.

This simple authority that produces standards in rather unstructured, random, spontaneous situations might be defined as the socially accepted, approved, and achieved right to issue binding obligations on members of a collectivity. Further, the ways in which persons achieve this right to issue standards (simple authority) are the four GSM of social interaction. They are the primary means or ways of establishing rights. The corresponding duty of interacting partners to adhere to the standards set by the person with simple authority derives from the sanctions that power, commitment, inducement, and influence entail in case of non-compliance or compliance.

Social interactions that produce standards are themselves rather random, unsystematized, often non-recurring, and rare in human experience. Standards would arise nowadays, for the most part, in novel and unexpected situations such as the example previously cited—organizing a group of survivors after a plane crash or shipwreck into a brand new organization with goals previously never attempted by any other group in society. Such situations are rare in a society that is established, institutionalized, and well-directed by various sets of previously known norms shared by the collectivity. While all know what standards are, the standards that are in fact followed have already been put together into structures called institutions. Such sets of institutionalized standards are called custom.

CUSTOM

Custom is an institutionalized set of standards. If an institution can be defined as an abstract structure, model, pattern, or concept that serves as a means for the realization of some value, then institutions give shape to general values by focusing them on broadly specified, differentiated ends such as collective effectiveness, solidarity, integrity, and adaptation. Institutions then give structural shape to values, thus marking off and highlighting values for more specific contexts or areas of social action. Consequently, custom refers to standards that have been given some structural shape and directed to some specific area of human interaction.

Custom is an institutionalized set of standards consisting of a body of obligations regarded as right by one party and acknowledged as duty by another. Custom is kept in force by the specific processes of *reciprocity* along with the publicity inherent in a given basic structure or institution of a society. It is significant to note that it is reciprocity that maintains custom. Moreover, as an institutionalized set of standards, custom inheres in the basic institution itself. The norms spelling out the roles and interactions that make up an institution are in fact custom itself. For example, consider an institution that realizes the value of solidarity, such as kinship or, more concretely, a single U.S. family. Note how a more or less fixed set of standards—custom—dictates, directs, and structures the roles in the family such as father, mother, older/younger brother/sister, the rights and obligations inherent in these roles such as to respect parents or to see to children's needs, and the interactions along which the role-realizations flow such as parents with power, children with influence, and all with commitment to each other. Standards inhere only in a given interaction; after the interaction is complete, the standard vanishes unless the interaction is repeated in the same way. If people implicitly or explicitly come to agree that a given interaction must be repeated in the same way, then standard can become custom. Custom, however, inheres in the institution itself (put less abstractly, custom inheres in politics, economics, education, kinship, and religion, at least in complex Western social systems). Furthermore, while customs fix, stabilize, and structure sets of standards which are incipiently random and unsystematized, yet in any society customs are generally clear and well-known, at least implicitly, to all who are committed to participating in the institutions of a given society. All "natives" can tell foreign behavior when they see it.

If standards are produced and maintained by simple authority—the right to issue standards based on the GSM one wields—then what produces and maintains custom? Custom is produced and maintained by legitimate authority. Legitimate authority is GSM-based, simple authority which is validated by some principle other than the simple authority itself. In other words, what makes the legitimate authority behind custom legitimate is legitimation. Legitimation rests upon some common, broadly encompassing norm recognized by members of a society. This norm constrains those members to conform to the wishes of a person or group, which is considered superior and which thereby becomes a legitimate authority, and to acknowledge the subordinate status of the rest of the collectivity. Some examples of legitimating, broadly encompassing norms include the will of God, hereditary succession or lineage, kinship, seniority, election by all the members of a group, election by only the devoted elite, election by only the propertied elite, ownership, and special competence.

Legitimate authority entails not merely tolerant approval but active confirmation and promotion of social patterns of behavior in terms of common values, whether preexisting social patterns or those that emerge in a collectivity in the course of social interaction. Consequently, legitimate authority is an *ascribed* right to obligate others, which is acknowledged by other members of a collectivity and sanctioned by some higher order norm. It is the form of authority that is maintained by custom and that produces custom. This form of authority ranges from personal or traditional authority to impersonal or rational authority. Personal legitimate authority inheres in the person, that is, flows from circumstances that befall a person and are not under the individual's control; such circumstances include birth, age, sex, physical size, and the status of one's family. These features are culturally interpreted as directly related to one's capacity to exercise authority. Examples of personal legitimate authority would be hereditary rulership, hereditary priesthood, rights of the firstborn, and aristocratic control of the polity due to inherited power, commitment, influence, or inducement. Impersonal legitimate authority is acquired by a person by means of some skill or competence deemed pertinent and useful to the realization of the ends of the institution in which authority is embedded. Such authority is occupational, being bound up with some job, task, or office, and it ceases with their termination or completion. For example, most U.S. elective and bureaucratic positions are of this sort.

In sum, personal legitimate authority inheres in the person; the legitimated person automatically has the office or task. Impersonal legitimate authority inheres in the office or task; the officeholder automatically has legitimate authority. These forms of legitimate authority are two ends of a scale, as it were. In the middle they may be mixed as when an office depends on an examination (impersonal) which is open only to aristocrats, males, or whites (personal).

Along with personal and impersonal legitimate authority there is a third form that belongs in this discussion, namely, the authority that normally emerges in both low grid quadrants of the grid/group model. This authority derives from the successful criticism and dislocation of the higher order norms which legitimate the authority prevailing in a given society. It ought to be called reputational authority because it is rooted in a person's ability to influence a change in the broadly encompassing norms that constrain recognition of legitimate authority. Reputational authority is often called "charismatic" authority, but that is misleading since very non-charismatic persons have acquired and wielded it (cf. B. Schwartz 1983; on charisma as a social science category, cf. esp. Miyahara 1983; Malina 1984). This authority emerges from a person's effective ability to convince members of a given society no longer to recognize some higher order norm as binding. For example, if in a given society officeholders occupy their position because of divine will, a reputational authority will successfully demonstrate to the collectivity that divine will is not at issue at all, but force, chicanery, collusion, conspiracy, or some other principle. Most often, radical transformations of society derive from such reputational authority.

In sum, reputational authority unseats the higher order norms which stabilize and fix custom, and thus it calls existing custom into question. As a result, custom may disintegrate into free-floating, unsystematized standards again, only to be institutionalized once more into new customs. Consideration of reputational authority in the context of personal and impersonal legitimate authority can be very useful for New Testament study. One of the basic questions at issue in Jesus' interaction with his opponents and followers is the quality of his authority. The same is true of Paul. These points will be considered at the close of this chapter, but here that third type of norm mentioned above must be treated, namely, law. What is it?

LAW

Law results when one social institution subsumes and sanctions the custom of another. Law is a doubly institutionalized set of standards or a reinstitutionalized custom. Custom refers to standards that have been given structural shape and thereby focused upon some specific area of human interactions. For example, the standards of human mating and nurturing of offspring take on structural shape and direction in the custom that constitutes kinship or the family institution. In the U.S. custom directs that parents are to be monogamous, to see to their offspring by training and instructing them in the values and norms of the society, and to exercise effective control over them until they attain responsible maturity and repeat the parenting process themselves. Now what if the customary political institution, in this case the U.S. government or a state government, while pursuing its goal of effective collective action, should determine that parents *must* be monogamous under pain of death, a sanction of the GSM of power; or that offspring *must* learn societal values and norms in public schools under pain of fine, another power sanction; or that male offspring *must* serve in the armed forces at age eighteen under pain of imprisonment, another power sanction? What would all this do to the customary family? Clearly the customs that constitute the kinship institution are subsumed by the political institution, and the sanctions peculiar to that institution are brought to bear on customs which work on the basis of a different set of sanctions. For in the kinship institution the main sanction is commitment, usually realized in love, care, and concern or in their withdrawal. In this way the customs that constitute some primary institution are reinstitutionalized by some other institution, notably the political.

Law, then, is a body of binding obligations, regarded as a right by one party and acknowledged as a duty by another, which has been doubly institutionalized. In both ancient and modern complex, bureaucratic societies the institution that reinstitutionalizes custom is the political. Consequently, the political institution or, more concretely, government keeps the custom of the other differentiated institutions in force by means of its own sanctions so that society can function in an orderly manner on the basis of the norms thus maintained. For a number of reasons law tends to suppress custom as found in other institutions, that is, custom tends to become legalized, and morality rooted in custom becomes equated with legality. Further, rules of law tend to become the domain of experts in the reinstitutionalizing arena (in the U.S., lawyers), and rules of law lodged in the political institution can become "out of phase" with the perceived customary rights and duties of non-political institutions. This "out of phase" quality of law can be either retarding or propelling in its effect on perceived customary rights. For example, if the kinship institution requires divorce and remarriage in order to attain its ends and realize its values, the political institution can retard such customary development by prohibiting divorce or prohibiting remarriage after divorce. Or, vice versa, the political institution can insist on divorce as an option when the customs of the extant kinship institution totally reject divorce; in this way the political institution can take the lead in altering custom and hence in changing other social institutions.

While standards are produced and maintained by simple authority and while customs are produced and maintained by legitimate authority, law is produced and maintained by legal authority. Legal authority is the authority dimension of the political institution, embracing and subsuming the legitimate authority of the other social institutions constituting society and reauthorizing the customs of those institutions as legal or lawful. Moreover, just as legitimate authority is validated by means of a legitimating norm of some higher order, so legal authority is validated by means of explicit reasons that explain, clarify, and defend the binding directives issued by legal authority. Such explicit reasons look to the intrinsic merit of those directives (laws) in terms of the culturally specific and socially acknowledged values inherent in the directive. These culturally specific and socially acknowledged values are, of course, the society's core values and their replication. For example, the U.S. Supreme Court ruled that a married woman can have an abortion without the knowledge or consent of her husband, whether he desires to have the child or not (*Planned Parenthood of Missouri v Danforth* 428 U.S. 52 [1976]). Such a ruling will have to be rooted in and explained by U.S. values which are culturally specific and socially acknowledged. In this case the wife's rights derive from the core value of instrumental mastery of the environment. This value, of course, pertains to the society as a whole as well as to the individual replicating the social body in weak group/high grid fashion. Here the fetus is in the mother's womb, an environment to be controlled in individualistic fashion according to the prevailing cultural script. Thus the individual, female, married U.S. citizen has the legal right to decide on an abortion irrespective of the custom that would have the wife and husband mutually embedded in the kinship institution.

Legal reasoning, then, will be shaped by the core values that hold a society together. What this means is that legal authority is political authority legitimated by no other higher order principle than the intrinsic reasons generated by societal core values. As noted above, legal authority gives rise to a domain of experts in the rules of law, both procedural and substantive. Such legal professionals are experts in the assessment of authoritativeness because law is the outcome of the order or social structure institutionalized as political, and the political institution can effectively obligate. The assessments made by the legal professionals consist in formulating or criticizing the reasons upon which the obligatory nature of claims, decisions, policies, and actions rest and not in formulating or criticizing any higher order, legitimating norms. Unlike standards and customs, law is relatively well-structured, systematized, and explicit in its structural relations.

HOW CUSTOM BECOMES LAW

If custom is maintained in a society by processes of reciprocity, how is law maintained? How does law derive from custom? In a society with law the doubly institutionalizing structure (the political system) tends to resolve disputes that arise in the other institutions of society. Family fights over inheritance get settled in law courts. In that case, what is the direction of the flow of interaction? Is it a reciprocal flow within an institution or a centric movement to some center and back? If custom is kept in force by reciprocity, then it seems that law is kept in force by centricity. Law arises when the political institution of a society becomes the focal center for reauthorizing the customs of the other institutions in that society. Obviously this reauthorization may occur either over the objections of the other institutions or with their cooperation. The relationship between reciprocity and centricity sketched in the previous chapter is most pertinent to understanding the centric quality of law.

Customs of generalized reciprocity developing into centricity by means of managerial focal roles lead to the emergence of law with the cooperation of the doubly institutionalized institutions. An example of this in the Bible is afforded by the emergence of clan law in Yahwistic Israel (cf. Gottwald 1979). On the other hand, customs of negative reciprocity toward adjacent groups in a position of geographical immobility and impotence, such as might exist due to having lost a war and being subsequently occupied or due to colonization, lead to the assimilation of oppressed collectivities into the lowest social rungs of the assimilating group (e.g., Israeli law imposed on West Bank Palestinians who are supposed to be under Jordanian law or Roman law imposed on conquered, first-century peoples with their own customs). The resulting centricity that such assimilation entails leads to the emergence of law over the objections and opposition of other institutions. The discussion thus far is summarized in the diagram below (fig. 8).

FIGURE 8. From Custom to Law

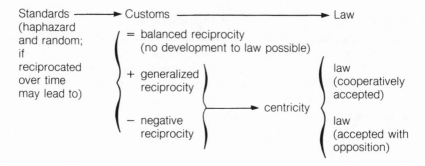

GRID/GROUP AND NORMS: AN INTRODUCTION

The discussion up to this point has dealt with reciprocity and centricity, rather broad dimensions of the flow of social interaction, as well as with standards, customs, and laws, the prevalent modes of channeling this flow. These categories must now be appropriately fitted into the larger grid/group matrix so as to make cross-cultural interpretation possible and useful. Since this essay seeks to demonstrate how the New Testament writings might be understood in terms of their underlying cultural scripts, the most direct way to this goal is to lay out a model in which both the interpreter(s) and the first-century Mediterranean persons responsible for and depicted in the documents might be clearly located and compared.

Applying the Model: Some Presuppositions

To utilize the model, a few presuppositions have to be restated. First of all, the flow of social interaction is determined by ends, purposes, or goals called values. Values, of course, fit along the grid axis of the grid/group model. Moreover, the norms expressed as standards, customs, and laws are structural means for the realization of the values which they encode and articulate. Culture refers to the ends or directions of action in a society; social structure refers to the means, the institutions, that enable and facilitate the realization of the ends by which a society is held together and which it espouses. How then do the parts of society, represented by its institutions, relate to the whole, represented by cultural goals? To respond to this question in terms of grid and group, high grid refers to equilibrium or balance in the total societal system, a system in which cultural ends and goals (values) and structural means are integrated and smoothly interwoven. High grid people will generally share and internalize the group's common goals. At the psychological level, presumably, these goals will become part of the individual's need-structure controlled by the need to realize cultural core values in order to develop a sense of self-worth. Hence high grid persons, individualistic and dyadic personalities, will accept as meaningful and make use of the prevailing structural means for the realization of the prevailing cultural goals in their lives.

The Problem of Low Grid

Low grid, on the other hand, refers to disequilibrium or imbalance in the total societal system. Low grid occurs when the expected balance between cultural ends and institutional means is not and cannot be realized. In such situations people accept the goals of the culture but reject, remain ignorant of, or cannot use legitimate structural means (strong group); or they reject, are ignorant of, or develop alternative cultural ends (weak group). Depending on the degree of drop in grid, a greater or lesser degree of normlessness can be said to exist. Such normlessness means that values and experience simply do not match in social experience; normlessness exists when dominant cultural goals and/or legitimate, normative structural means do not regulate the conduct of people in a given social system.

Strong group/low grid refers, then, to the situation in which people accept cultural goals because they are maintained by the strong group but reject, remain ignorant of, or cannot use the normative means to attain these goals. Groups may arise offering alternative means to accepted goals. They then become counterstructures or strong group/low grid factions (for information on such factions, cf. Schmidt et al. 1977). Such groups are sometimes inaccurately called "countercultures" or "subcultures." Be that as it may, so long as the problem is with means and not with the goals of the social system, alternative structures emerge as solutions. In strong group/low grid normative means generally do not regulate the conduct of people in the various segments of the social system.

Weak group/low grid refers to the situation in which people individualistically reject, are ignorant of, or develop alternative cultural goals or ends. Clusters of individuals may arise in this situation to offer alternative ends while experimenting in structures which might realize those ends. Such groups are true countercultures because they offer alternative ends or goals. In weak group/low grid dominant cultural goals generally do not direct the conduct of individuals who might still be in various segments of the prevailing social system.

Consequently low grid describes a situation in which institutionalized means are unequally available to members of a society. This situation becomes one of normlessness for some segments of the population and sets in motion efforts to adapt to or cope with the perceived split between cultural goals and structural means. What modes of adaptation to such a situation might be forthcoming? Merton (1968: 194) offers a model of adaptation to normlessness or anomie which can be readily inserted into Douglas' grid/group model to the benefit of both models. Merton's scheme describing options in the low grid situation depicted thus far is presented in table 3 below.

TABLE 3. Modes of Adaptation to Anomie (*Adapted from Merton 1968: 194*)

Modes of Adaptation	Cultural Ends	Institutionalized Means
I. Conformity	+	+
II. Innovation	+	−
III. Ritualism	−	+
IV. Retreatism	−	−
V. Rebellion	±	±

+ = acceptance of prevailing values/means
− = rejection of prevailing values/means
± = rejection of prevailing values/means
   and substitution of new values/means

High grid, of course, implies a form of adaptation that is the opposite of normlessness or anomie (Merton's I. Conformity). The more widespread and publicly acknowledged the culturally defined success goals and the more equally available the culturally legitimated structural means for realizing them, the less the potential for anomie and the higher the rate of conforming behavior in the society. Strong group looks to conforming dyadic personalities in conforming groups; weak group looks to conforming individuals. High grid, then, means no normlessness or anomie while low grid points to its presence, but adaptation to anomie in low grid, the remaining four modes listed in Merton's scheme, will depend upon the group variable as follows.

Weak Group/Low Grid

Weak group/low grid is marked by the rejection of cultural goals or ends. The main forms of adaptation would be (III), (IV), and (V) of Merton's model, in the following ways:

Ritualism in weak group would be the acceptance of structural means with slavish conformity to them, but with rejection of success goals. This allays status anxiety when structural means are used for competitive efforts for success. People adopting this mode of adaptation "stick to the system" but reject its goals, such as, perhaps, the people who joined Rev. Jones' (of infamous Jonestown in Guyana) group as it initially took shape in San Francisco.

Retreatism in weak group would be the rejection both of cultural values and goals and of structural means. The result is that the individual apathetically exists within the social system but is not involved with anything or anyone, for example, the recluse or hermit.

Rebellion in weak group would be the rejection of both means and ends but with efforts to substitute new means and ends. Rebellious behavior is most likely to occur where the frustrations and perceived deprivations over the failure to realize goals through legitimate channels increase and where groups exist which formulate *ideology* capable of channeling deprivations with new means and ends. What is required is some articulation of the norms and values shared by persons undergoing the deprivation experience, that is, an explicit ideology but one keyed individualistically. Such articulations may take the form of songs, movies, poetry, novels, or gossip. In weak group the focus of the ideology will be on new ends or goals, on the cultural component of the social system. The result is an *anticulture* or a set of values set in opposition to the values held in the broader society from which weak group/low grid individuals derive.

Strong Group/Low Grid

The *strong group/low grid* scheme of things is marked by a rejection of the structural means or paths to goals, a rejection of the system of structures controlling or marking relations among people in a society. The main forms of adaptation would be (II), (IV), and (V) of Merton's model, as follows:

Innovation in strong group involves the search for and the development of new means, new structures, and new forms of grouping to realize the success goals of the society. Since the goals are still held by the members of the society, resentment over the fact that access to these goals is closed may accompany such innovations. If such "innovative" strong group/low grid groups are embedded in larger strong group/high grid societies, such as first-century Jewish and Greek groups embedded in the Roman Empire, then such innovations would be considered "illegitimate" by the strong group/ high grid groups. For New Testament study it seems that both Jesus and Paul with their respective groups fit into this category.

Retreatism in the strong group mode is a rejection both of cultural values and goals and of existing structural means. Here groups rather than individuals exist apathetically within the social system, uninvolved in the larger society and awaiting some transformation. It appears that first-century millenarian or apocalyptic groups were of this sort.

Rebellion, as previously mentioned, is marked by both rejection of prevalent means and ends and the effort to substitute new means and ends. In a strong group setting the emphasis is on ideologies that articulate new means, that is, on the structural component of the social system. The outcome would be a competing counterstructure or alternative structure. Examples of this in the New Testament period are the rise of the synagogue as an alternative to Temple worship in Judaism, the split of Christian Jewish groups from Judaism, the Qumran community, and the Jewish rebellion sparked by Zealots. Figure 9 on pp. 128–129 situates these aspects of adaptation to anomie on the grid/group model.

LAW IN TERMS OF GRID AND GROUP

Norms, whether they be standards, customs, or laws, are produced and maintained by authority. Authority in this context refers to the ability to hold others to norms. The quality of authority in a given group depends upon the shared cultural rating of the one binding and the one bound. In weak group systems focus is on persons assessed individualistically (in the sense of "individual" previously defined). Such weak group systems presuppose that the individual is the proper locus of authority. The interactional dimensions of the individual, of course, are replicated in the concrete, individual human body; that is, the human body is treated as inviolably private unless certain contracts have been entered into, such as marriage or the implicit contracts of medical treatment. On the other hand, strong group systems focus on the social body, on the dyadic individual as embedded in and as representative of the group. Thus the social body is perceived as inviolably private unless certain contracts such as treaties have been entered into. Obviously priorities relative to specific social roles are perceived and rated differently in each group dimension. However, the main point here is that weak group gives priority to the individual and the individual body while strong group gives priority to the group and the social body.

Furthermore, high grid means that there is a close phasing between existing norms and social experience and values. Persons adhering to societal norms experience social integration. They find that life makes sense even in its broader dimensions, such as the sense of it all, its origins, and its future. On the other hand, low grid implies distant phasing between norms and experience. Experience proves that following extant norms can only lead to social catastrophe or social indignation. If these features are now placed in their respective quadrants of the grid and group model, the cultural scripts offer the following expectations:

(1) In strong group/high grid the legal institution appropriately and adequately reflects the custom that it reinstitutionalizes. Law and life in the other social institutions are in phase. Law preserves society and focuses upon the inviolable privacy of the social body.

(2) In strong group/low grid the legal institution meant to preserve society is ineffective to the task. New, often negative, social realities have intervened into the social body, warranting change and the rejection of law in favor of custom. Conflicts typically deal with the transformation of custom so as to meet the changing situation. Anarchic (i.e., non-legal) modes of preserving competing groups or factions are favored.

(3) In weak group/high grid the legal institution is expected to shape the custom that it reinstitutionalizes; this is technology replicated in the legal institution. Law and life in the other institutions are in phase. Law focuses upon the inviolable privacy of the individual body and is meant to mold society. Such a script, of course, favors the proliferation of lawyers since their task is focused on authoritativeness as applying to the individual body—many individuals require many lawyers. On the other hand, strong group/high grid scripts would have far fewer lawyers since lawyers there deal with authoritativeness vis-à-vis social bodies and since there are far fewer of those than there are individuals.

(4) In weak group/low grid, while the legal institution is meant to mold society, it is ineffective to the task. New social experiences, new and often negative knowledge and insights, have intervened into the individual body. These warrant change and the rejection of law and the custom it reinstitutionalizes in favor of standards. Conflicts deal with the transformation and creation of standards to meet the perceived changing situation. Anarchic (i.e., non-legal) modes of shaping society are favored.

All the foregoing elements have been appropriately situated in figure 9 on pp. 128–129.

FIGURE 9. Social Norms in Grid and Group

Weak Group/High Grid   **HIGH**

Law and Legal Authority (Example: U.S.)
- Cultural ends and institutional means are in phase.
- No anomie exists; there is a high degree of social conformity.
- The legal institution appropriately shapes the custom that it reinstitutionalizes. Law *molds* society and focuses upon the inviolable privacy of the individual body.

WEAK GROUP

Characteristics of weak group collectivities (high and low grid)
- all goods are unlimited
- adequate causality
- generalized symbolic media of social interaction:
  superiors: influence and wealth
  subordinates: power and commitment
- style of law/custom/standard: compensatory—obligation
  conciliatory—harmony
- individualistic personality: the individual body is inviolable

Standard and Simple Authority (Example: new group in first fervor)
- Cultural ends and institutional means are out of phase.
- Responses to anomie range from ritualism to retreatism to rebellion.
- While the legal institution is meant to mold society, it is ineffective to the task. New, often negative, social experiences have intervened into the individual body (knowledge, experiences, insights) warranting change and the rejection of law and the customs that law reinstitutionalizes in favor of new standards.
- Conflicts deal with transformation of standards to meet changing situations.
- Anarchic (i.e., non-legal) modes of molding groups are favored.

Weak Group/Low Grid   **LOW**

Group: refers here to the dimension of the interacting agents in an authority interaction.
- *Strong group:* focuses upon the social body; the social body is inviolably private unless certain contracts like treaty have been entered into.
- *Weak group:* focuses upon the individual body; the individual is inviolably private unless certain contracts like marriage have been entered into.

Law and Legal Authority (Example: Roman citizens in Roman Empire) —
Cultural ends and institutional means are in phase.
- No anomie exists; there is a high degree of social conformity.
- The legal institution appropriately reflects the custom that it reinstitu-
tionalizes. Law *preserves* society and focuses upon the inviolable
privacy of the social body.

Characteristics of strong group collectivities (high and low grid)
- all goods are limited
- personal causality
- generalized symbolic media of social interaction:
superiors: power and commitment
subordinates: influence and wealth
- style of law/custom: penal—prohibition
therapeutic—normality
- dyadic personality: the group body is inviolable

STRONG GROUP

Custom and Legitimate Authority
(Example: Conquered peoples and non-elites in the Roman empire)
- Cultural ends and institutional means are out of phase
- Responses to anomie range from innovation to retreatism to
rebellion.
- While the legal institution is meant to preserve society, it is ineffec-
tive to the task. New, often negative, social realities have intervened
into the social body, warranting change and the rejection of law in
favor of custom.
- Conflicts deal with the transformation of custom to meet changing
situations and hence are about legitimate authority.
- Anarchic (i.e., non-legal) modes of group preservation are favored.

Grid: refers here to the degree of phasing or overlap between law/custom and so-
ciety/institutions.
—*High grid:* means there is close phasing between law and societal experiences
and values. Following the law leads to societal integration.
—*Low grid:* means distant phasing between law and society, societal experiences
and values. Following the law can only lead to social catastrophe and social dis-
integration, resulting in social indignation.

STYLES OF NORMS

Be they standards, customs, or laws, norms come in different styles because of the GSM they embody. Discussion in chapter 4 indicated that the GSM have correlative sanctions. Non-compliance with power is sanctioned by coercion; non-compliance with commitment is sanctioned by commitment activation in terms of underscoring the questionable worth of the human involved. These are negative sanctions since compliance with the GSM leads to the non-application of the sanctions. On the other hand, inducement sanctions its intended effectiveness with goods and services, and influence does so with persuasive information. These are positive sanctions since compliance entails positive benefits. A consideration of the various styles of norms reveals that they too can be chunked into four highly abstract, irreducible categories: penal; therapeutic; compensatory; and conciliatory (from Black 1976: 4–6).

Penal norms derive from power, therapeutic norms derive from commitment, compensatory norms derive from inducement, and conciliatory norms derive from influence. Norm styles are basically styles of social control determined by the GSM encoded by the norm. Table 4 from Black (1976: p. 5, to which the GSM have been added) lists some traits characteristic of the styles of norms.

TABLE 4. Styles of Norms

Style:	Penal	Therapeutic	Compensatory	Conciliatory
Standard:	Prohibition	Normality	Obligation	Harmony
Problem:	Guilt	Need	Debt	Conflict
Initiation of Case:	Group	Deviant	Victim	Disputants
Identity of Deviant:	Offender	Victim	Debtor	Disputant
Solution:	Punishment	Help	Payment	Resolution
GSM:	Power	Commitment	Inducement	Influence

Black notes that penal and compensatory styles of social control are accusatory, fitting a win-or-lose, all-or-nothing type of social interaction. On the other hand, the therapeutic and conciliatory are remedial styles, methods of social repair and preventative maintenance, which look to what is necessary to ameliorate an actual or potential negative situation.

To determine which norm styles fit strong group and which fit weak group will require a brief consideration of the GSM in grid and group. As previously noted, strong group societies have superiors wielding power and commitment while weak group societies have their leading persons wielding influence and inducement. Consequently, strong group societies would emphasize penal and therapeutic styles of custom and law while weak group societies would favor conciliatory and compensatory styles. The penal style of strong group underscores prohibition and punishment based on power while the therapeutic style looks to the restoration of normality by means of assistance based on commitment. On the other side, the compensatory style of weak group focuses on quantified obligation in terms of payment of some goods and/or services based on inducement, and the conciliatory style aims at harmony in terms of dispute resolution. The application of each style in the respective quadrants probably depends upon whether the flow of action is reciprocal or centric. In the case of reciprocity strong group therapeutic and weak group conciliatory styles prevail, while in the centric instance strong group penal and weak group compensatory styles prevail. Again these styles of norms have been duly located in figure 9 on pp. 128–129, which thus summarizes and schematizes the whole chapter.

APPLYING THE MODEL: ST. PAUL AND SOCIAL NORMS

Perhaps at this point it would be appropriate to ask whether the models presented thus far can in fact clarify New Testament questions, notably those involving the role of Torah (God's directives for people). Consider the case of Paul the Apostle and the "Law" (Greek: *nomos*). To begin with, the word *nomos* is quite frequent in his letters to the Galatians and the Romans, letters closely related to each other in time and concern about "the Law." Otherwise the word is rather rare in the authentic Pauline writings (nine times in 1 Cor., twice in Phil., absent from 1 Thess. and 2 Cor.). The word is equally rare in the deutero-Pauline writings (once in Eph., twice in 1 Tim., and absent from 2 Thess., Col., 2 Tim., and Titus). Consequently, to make sense out of the explanation and application that follow, it will be extremely useful to have read through Paul's letters to the Galatians and the Romans (conveniently presented in Pilch 1983 with a brief and useful commentary).

If the information provided by these letters relative to Paul, his audience, and the use of the term "the Law" were to be set within the models developed thus far, what testable observations and conclusions might be drawn? For those unfamiliar with Paul, perhaps a little background information is in order. First of all, by his own admission Paul was a first-century Pharisaic Jew (Phil. 3:4–6; Gal. 1:13–14; 2:14–21). In the first-century Hellenistic world, Pharisaic Judaism fitted into the strong group/low grid quadrant of social scripts, as its great concern for purity, for boundaries, indicates. This would mean that members of Pharisaic groups were dyadic personalities, very much concerned about group boundaries. For Pharisees this meant purity rules; for Paul it was a question of Christian restructured purity rules determining who is in Christ and who is not. As strong group/low grid persons, they were aware of some negative influence pervading the various primary and secondary collectivities to which they belonged. For Pharisees negative influence could be seen in Hellenistic values, Sadducee attitudes to Torah, and Roman occupation; for Paul it consisted in *hamartia*, the condition of Sin (with a capital "S") revealed by the continued presence of sinful actions, sins. They were terribly conscious of living in a rather distorted and unjust cosmos.

As far as can be verified, Paul never thought of his primary dyadic social location as anything other than Jewish; he talked of himself as a Jew "in Christ." He shared the typically Jewish core values of interpersonal contentment, the acquiescence in human finitude and human limitation, and the hope of achieving a genuinely human existence. He expected the traditional God of his forefathers to provide help in facilitating the realization of the core value: to become and be what he is as God's creation, a finite and free human being. The typical Jewish articulation of this core value is *shālôm*, the presence of everything necessary for an adequately meaningful human existence realizing the core value. Paul found this *shālôm* or peace "in Christ." For Paul, as a Pharisaic Jew, and for Pharisaic Jews in general, the replication of the core value took the form of studying and practicing Torah.

The Hebrew word *tôrâh* means instruction, the giving of directives. In Jewish tradition the term refers to the directives given by God to the Hebrew people in order to facilitate the realization of the group's core value. During the period of Israelite monarchy (strong group/high grid), God's Torah was law in the previously defined sense of the term. With the Babylonian Exile of 587–538 B.C. and the subsequent restoration and resettlement of the people in the territory of Palestine called Judaea, those occupying the place (Judaeans = Jews) turned once more to Torah. By the time of Hellenistic and subsequent Roman dominance, however, Torah was no longer the law of the land. There was no political institution to reinstitutionalize the customs it articulated. The conquered populace of Judaea experienced a drop in grid. Torah functioned as custom which was legitimated by God. Thus, during the period before and after the turn of the era, arguments about Torah dealt with the interpretations of these legitimated customs. To follow the previous models, these customs rested upon the legitimating authority of "the God of the Fathers" of Israel and of those impersonal legitimate authorities authorized to interpret them, the scribes. Given the strong group/low grid cultural script, there were, of course, competing groups, factions, or "schools" of interpretation (for types of groups in Paul's society, cf. Meeks 1983: 74–84; on faction formation in this quadrant, cf. Schmidt et al. 1977).

About the third century B.C., the Hebrew (and Aramaic) Torah was translated into Greek. This version is known as the Septuagint, meaning "seventy," named for the legendary seventy translators who did the version; hence it is abbreviated as LXX. It was the Hellenistic Jewish translators of the LXX who rendered the Hebrew word *tôrâh* with the Greek *nomos*. *Nomos* in Greek means a rule or norm. The Latin word *lex*, used to translate *nomos*, basically means law, and this shifts the word *tôrâh* to a much more specific field of meaning; generally it is with the Latin field of meaning that most readers of Paul read his letters, since Paul's *nomos* is regularly translated "law" in the English versions. Thus when *tôrâh* refers to those sections of the Hebrew normative writings that spell out rules or norms then *tôrâh* and *nomos* cover the same field or stand for the same semantic conceptual prototype. But since the LXX uses *nomos* for *tôrâh* nearly all the time, even in those parts of the Torah that do not at all deal with rules or norms, the LXX practice thus gives "a misleading legalistic tone to much of the Old Testament" (Dodd 1954: 41). With this background, readers of Paul subsequently think he is opposing a legalistic ideology with his rejection of the "law," that is, the ideology of Judaism. But this is not exactly the case, as the foregoing models should suggest.

What then is Paul's point about *nomos* or *tôrâh*? In order to understand Paul's contention at the level of social analysis attempted here, it is important to recall that the first-century Hellenistic world recognized only two formally differentiated social institutions, namely, politics and kinship. Religion, education, and economics existed in substantive, non-formal ways. They were embedded in one or the other of the formal social institutions. What persons in the U.S. would call private religious practice was certainly obligatory in strong group societies, both high and low grid, because it was part of the kinship institution in which everyone lived. On the other hand, public participation in religion was a political piece of behavior, considered obligatory for strong group/high grid societies such as Romans and elite Roman citizens. But in strong group/low grid societies such as the ethnic groups conquered by Rome, which found themselves in this quadrant for the most part, public participation in religion was optional, sporadic, and non-obligatory. The reason for this was that "public" religion was part of the political institution and it specifically obliged those who sat at the tops of the hierarchies of the various sets and subsets of government in the Roman Empire.

Furthermore, a person in the social role that Paul adopted, according to his own letters and according to Acts, would have been characterized as a philosopher by Greeks and Romans or as a scribe by Jews. Given his Jewish background within the common strong group/low grid setting, Paul's concern was not with public, political, optional, substantive religion. Rather, it was with obligatory religion in the private sphere embedded in kinship networks and strong group/low grid voluntary associations. These associations were called *collegia* by the Romans and $h^a b\hat{u}r\hat{o}th$ by the Jews. They were basically fictive kinship groups, often part of fictive kinship networks. Consequently, Paul's concerns were not with the whole of society but with groups and group formations replicating the values of kinship institutions.

Why this concern with fictive kinship groups? Paul tells us that within his Jewish, Hellenistic, strong group/low grid social world he had an experience that drove him into a rather recently formed Torah group focused on the figure of Jesus of Nazareth (Gal. 1:11–24). This group believed Jesus was raised by the God of Israel after dying an utterly shameful and degrading death, a death accursed by the Torah itself (Deut, 21:23). After a time of exposure to the structures mediating the values of this new group, Paul undertakes the role of the traditional Jewish strong group/low grid leader, the prophet (Gal. 1:15–17). The Christian term for this role, Paul intimates, was "apostle," indicating one traveling or wandering on the road with the purpose of setting up new groups.

In a Jewish context the task of the leader known as prophet was to make known and articulate the specific will of God in and for some here-and-now situation so as to influence and persuade the members of the group (not outsiders) to adopt a given perspective or follow a given line of conduct that would be in conformity with God's good pleasure. The goal is to please God and simultaneously realize the culture's core value. What characterizes Paul's implementation of this leadership role, at least insofar as his letters attest, is his ability to articulate the problems faced by the group, such as the strong group/low grid problem of pervading negative influence which Paul calls "Sin," to set out a culturally plausible and realistic solution to those problems, to fend off possible objections, and thus to win commitment or emotional anchorage from group members to the new sets of symbols that he presents.

In attempting to understand Paul's attitude toward and reaction to Torah and *nomos* in general (unless it is Roman *nomos*), the first thing the model of social norms allows one to see is that Paul is not really talking about law at all, at least not in the weak group/high grid sense in which mainstream U.S. persons use the word. Given Paul's social location, "law" for Paul must mean custom, especially normative Jewish custom. His basic argument is that the divine will that legitimated the custom enshrined concretely in the Torah has been withdrawn, as Jesus' death and resurrection prove. Hence the binding and revealed customs of Judaism are no longer binding because they are no longer legitimated by God. At most, the Torah contains standards, but standards valid, good, noble, and useful only in and for the past. This past set of standards is no longer normative or obligatory. Rather, Torah presents a normative story of the past, a sacred Scripture that clarifies very well how God's people got to their present situation but offers no obligatory or normative rules for the present and the future. As a form of social control from God and pleasing to God, the Torah no longer binds. In fact it has been abrogated by God. This is the burden of Paul's argument in various forms.

Consequently, as Meeks (1972: 443) points out:

> The question of norms, How can I know what I ought to do? is much less likely to receive a clear and helpful answer from Paul. One of the intriguing things about his responses to practical ethical dilemmas in his congregations is the diversity of norms and guides that he employs. He appeals to catechetical rules of thumb—some with a long history in popular Greek morality—to "nature"; to the practical harmony and "building up" of the congregation; to his own life-style, depicted as analogous to the death and resurrection of Christ; to a rather general notions of "freedom." But one thing he never does: he never uses "the law," either the Torah of Moses or any Hellenistic substitute for it, to lay down regulations for the Christian community. What stands behind every Pauline admonition—and they are many and manifold!—is the requirement that the Christian be "transformed by the renewal of your mind" in order to "test what is the will of God."

In terms of the model in this chapter, Paul clearly intended to articulate ways in which Christians living "in Christ" might develop their incipient standards into a set of Christian customs, both customs of generalized reciprocity (e.g., Rom. 13:8–10; 2 Cor. 6:1–10; Gal. 5:16–26; Phil. 4:8–9) and customs of balanced reciprocity (e.g., Rom. 15:1–6; 1 Cor. 9:1–14; 2 Cor. 2:5–11; 8:8–15; 9:1–15). What legitimates the new customs is the God of Israel now perceived in a new activity on behalf of the people, raising Jesus from the dead. The God of Israel now has the name "him that raised from the dead Jesus our Lord" (Rom. 4:24 *et passim*). Jesus is perceived as God's Messiah, dyadic (not personal or individualistic) Lord and redeemer, who saves God's people from the strong group/low grid negative influence Paul calls Sin. Torah custom is no longer legitimated since Torah custom has no bearing at all on the resurrection of Jesus. As a matter of fact, by Torah norms God would have rejected Jesus (Gal. 3:13–14). However, God's raising Jesus indicates that God now legitimates the customs of those "in Christ," while those "in Israel" no longer have a God-legitimated Torah; God no longer holds this people to those standards. Then what about Jews adhering to Torah? Torah history indicates that Israel is God's elect, and this remains certain. But given the new situation Israel ought to be subsumed under the new election of all "in Christ" and to be maintained by the new standards. Yet some in Israel do not see this, mainly so that non-Jews might enter the new competing group first; then Israel will follow (Rom. 9–11).

Thus, just as Torah, God's instruction taken as a whole including its customs (which were God's decrees, declarations of right, and legal decisions), was laid down by Moses and legitimated by God, so now, since the legitimation has been removed, a new set of customs deriving from the directives of God perceived by those "in Christ" by means of God's spirit will ultimately develop and is being developed "in Christ." In sum, to understand Paul and the law, the first thing to do is to refrain from reading the word "law" as law is commonly understood in the U.S. Perhaps it would be best for the non-Greek-reading student of Paul to read the word "law" as norm or rule in the very general sense given above, that is, as a statement of value. Then, in terms of the accompanying text of Paul's letter, the reader might decide which dimension of norm is involved: standard; custom; or law.

Along with this clarification of Paul's view of the "law," the models in this chapter allow for some further conclusions about Paul and his groups. His letters reveal that he varies the GSM he uses to have effect on his audience. For example, what he asks of the communities that he himself had founded is the activation of commitment to God in Christ and to Paul's gospel (Gal.; 1 and 2 Cor.) along with the acceptance of influence. But in his letter to the community which he himself did not found, Romans, his chosen medium of interaction is influence. Furthermore, by seeking to dislocate the higher order norms legitimating Torah customs, Paul shows himself to be a reputational legitimate authority, that is, a dislocator of previous legitimation. His authority is achieved, and hence he is a leader by achievement, not a manager by ascription. Consequently, he can have no successors, only fellow workers who may or may not be leaders or managers, all depending on the quality of the norms of their groups and the problems to be faced.

What is Paul's attitude toward his social superiors? It is interesting to note how he differentiates between wielders of power and wielders of commitment. To begin with, in his consideration of the wielders of power, Paul distinguishes two forms of power at work in the social experience of the Mediterranean populations. One form is focused in and derives from a single collectivity, Rome, while the other permeates Mediterranean society as a whole. The former power is the readily and politically experienced, perceptible power of the Roman government and the Roman presence: Roman law and the customs sanctioned by the law, such as slavery, citizenship, marriage, and taxation. Paul encourages recognition of and compliance with the authority of those wielding this political power and the demands of its laws (Rom. 13:1–7; cf. below). However, the latter form of power, the power that pervades all groups and collectivities known in the Mediterranean world, is a negative and hostile power which Paul sees permeating strong group/low grid society as a whole. As noted previously, Paul calls that power *hamartia*, Sin in the singular. In Paul's writings this word does not refer to sinful actions; for that he uses words such as sins, transgressions, and trespasses, or he names a particular line of deviant behavior. Such actions are simply symptomatic of the general condition labeled "Sin." Sin, then, is the name that Paul gives to the negative, coercive force that permeates the porous boundaries of group structures. Strong group/low grid normally involves a perception of some such permeating negative force. Through a process of stereotypical, "sociological" thinking common to dyadic personality (cf. Malina 1979; 1981b), coupled with concrete historical experiences of persons and events, Paul deduces the specific shape of this negative force and gives it a name. Note that Sin for Paul functions in terms of power and its replication in law in the proper sense. Sin rules as ultimate, implicit power in the social world (Rom. 6:12, 14) and functions as lawgiver subjecting human beings through its *nomos* (like Roman *lex* in Rom. 7:23, 25; 8:2). Sin works with the same power a slave dealer has, a perfectly legal situation in Roman law (Rom. 6:16, 19; 7:14, 24; 8:15). Finally, sin is much like the power over humans that sickness is, specifically the first-century malady known as demonic possession (Rom. 7:8–24). Paul thus uses three well-known experiences of power from his social world (empire, slavery, demon possession) to describe the nature of the evil permeating his strong group/low grid world (cf. Schottroff 1979).

It was "in Christ" that he came to see this new reality in a focused way (Rom. 1–3), and it is by shifting one's group loyalty and by putting one's commitment "in Christ" that a person can escape the power of this permeating evil. Thus, while the power of social superiors ought be complied with, the power of Sin must be opposed and diffused. This is so because all is under the power of God "in Christ." The customs that Paul urges upon his communities, as noted above, basically point to mutual commitment of the group members, "the body of Christ," with no one exercising power in the group apart from Christ. Hence recognition of the power of God "in Christ" has as its outcome the mutual subjection of group members to each other in terms of commitment, not power. The emotional anchorage "in Christ" that Paul calls "faith" leads to the general and balanced reciprocity that Paul calls "love," the forms of reciprocity characteristic of group members who are all equal "in Christ." But they are not equal in the larger society in which they live. The following line of thought might illustrate what this entails.

Paul's response to the anomie of strong group/low grid existence indicates that he ought to be considered an innovator (not a retreater or a rebel). He offers new means for realizing accepted goals, the goals of Judaism, "in Christ." The social body meant to embody and realize these new means—the "body of Christ," that is, Paul's communities or churches—is now to be inviolable "in

Christ." It is to this end that he urges them to develop customs of generalized and balanced reciprocity, legitimated by the higher order norm of God's spirit. In this regard there is something curious to observe for, while Christians develop new means or new structures, Paul insists that not any and every means and structure ought to be employed. In line with the distinction made between institutional power and commitment wielding superiors, it seems that Paul nuances his argument along the lines of whether the means or structures fall within the power realm (i.e., political system) or within the commitment realm (i.e., kinship). In Paul's view, it seems, the means, structures, and institutions that fall within the power system of the Hellenistic world are to stay the same for Christians: social status (1 Cor. 7:17, 20, 24), slavery (1 Cor. 7:21), the ascribed, subservient role of women (1 Cor. 11:2–16; 14:33b–36), and roles based on sex and ethnic origin (Rom. 10:12; 1 Cor. 12:13; Gal. 3:28) are not important. *Therefore* his communities should not change or bother about those structures; they should not be actively concerned about them and need not destroy them. Rather, they ought simply to leave them as they are (for subsequent Christian history, cf. Coyle 1981 relative to marriage and family; and de Ste. Croix 1975 relative to slavery). This is an obvious strong group perspective, mirroring equally the lack of interest in the political institution and those substantive institutions embedded in it. On the other hand, means, structures, and institutions falling within the commitment system must be actively rejected: circumcision; following Torah customs; and eating food offered for the dead in Graeco-Roman funeral rites (1 Cor. 8–10). Commitment is owed to God in Christ, and emotional anchorage along with behavior expressive of such anchorage must be focused centripetally within "the body of Christ," the faction consisting of those "in Christ."

Finally, as the model predicts, a consideration of the styles of developing norms attested to in Paul's letters reveals that those styles are penal or therapeutic. The penal, prohibitory aspect is clear in the suggested treatment of deviants: they are to be shunned (Rom. 16:17–20a; 2 Cor. 6:14–7:1) or expelled from the group (1 Cor. 5:1–5). The therapeutic aspect is manifested in the thrust of Paul's developing norms. Since the focus of these norms is the implementation of the core value of *shālôm* (peace), the outcome of their practice ought to be normalcy, the way God intended human interrelations to be.

Such then are the dimensions of law in Paul in the light of the models developed in this book. While not all possible conclusions have been drawn from the models relative to the writings of Paul, those that have been set out should suffice to situate Paul and his audiences relative to contemporary American Christians in some broad and general ways. Also they should enable the contemporary reader of Paul's letters rather easily to understand the range of meanings attached to the word "law" in those letters.

7.

Facilitating the Flow of the Action: Rites and Their Agents

INTRODUCTION

In chapter 4 social interaction was compared to a field game in which social interaction takes place on a field marked off by the various features of the cultural script. On the field thus marked off a number of games take place simultaneously, and these are games regulated by the respective generalized symbolic media of social interaction—power games and commitment games, inducement games and influence games. The GSM set off and maintain the flow of the action. This action is then channeled in reciprocity and centricity forms by means of norms: standards; customs; and laws. To move the comparison a step further, during the course of any game there are various occasions for a "time-out": because a player or group of players is hurt, dazed, confused; or for the sake of substitution, when some player is ready to take the place of another in a new role; or in order to mark the regular flow of the game, such as by quarters or halftimes so that all players get the opportunity to rest and evaluate their play. In all instances of time-outs, whether irregular such as for hurt players or for substitutions or regular such as quarter and halftime breaks, there are certain persons whose role it is to call the time-out and/or direct activity during such sessions. This chapter will focus on the time-out sessions and those who call the time-outs or direct activity during them.

TIME-OUT ACTIVITIES:
RITES—RITUALS AND CEREMONIES

In the normal flow of social interaction, time-out periods are periods when *rites* take place. There are two general types of such social time-outs. The first is the irregular break in the action, called *ritual*; the second is the regular break in the action, called *ceremony*. The persons who determine, call for, and then preside over irregular breaks in the action are *professionals* who direct rituals, for example, physicians, dentists, or clergy. The persons who call for and preside over the regular breaks in the action are *officials* who direct ceremonies, for example, a father/mother presiding over family meal, a clergyperson presiding over weekly church service, or a politician presiding over a national holiday gathering. The difference between rituals and ceremonies, then, is something like the difference between irregular and regular time-outs in a game (cf. Farwell 1976 from whom the division of rites into rituals and ceremonies derives).

Rituals are irregular time-outs. Just as irregular time-outs in a game are determined by situations or conditions that affect individual players or groups of players and cannot be predicted ahead of time except statistically, so too rituals occur when situations or conditions that affect individuals or groups arise calling for a halt in the action. Such rituals have as their purpose either to help a sidelined player to get back into the action or to allow for substitution in which a player or group of players is able to take on some new and better role in the game. Rituals that meet the first type of purpose, to help a sidelined player get into the action again, are called rituals of status reversal, such as being declared well by a physician and let out of a hospital or being declared innocent by a judge. Rituals that look to the second type of purpose, allowing players to take on new and better roles, are called rituals of status transformation, such as college/professional school graduation, marriage, ordination of the clergy, or installation in public office.

Ceremonies, on the other hand, are regular time-outs called for by the very quality of the social structure, irrespective of the condition of the players. Ceremonies can be readily predicted since they are marked on a calendar and set by the norms of society to indicate regular intervals in the life of the social group. Ceremonies do not depend upon the conditions that might befall individuals or groups in the game, but rather they occur as predetermined by the social structure which sets the regular rules of the game.

Ceremonies

As mentioned above, the core values of a group become implemented and focused upon specific areas of life by means of the social structures called social institutions. Such institutions are patterned arrangements of sets of rights and obligations called roles, of relationships among roles called statuses, and of successive statuses or status sequences which are generally well-recognized and regularly at work in a given society. Among such institutions readily recognized in the U.S. are kinship, politics, economics, education, and religion. Such institutions keep people apart by defining differences; for example, my family is not yours, my political party differs from that of other persons, and my economic activity such as occupation and salary differs from yours. Furthermore, such institutions, individually and together, constrain action, with the GSM being the symbolic means for constraining action within and between institutions.

Time-outs can be set up for the purpose of confirming the social institutions that structure the dimensions of communal living, in order to bolster the respective statuses of persons in those institutions and thereby effectively demonstrate the solidarity among all those persons who together realize and give concrete shape to the institution. Social interactions during such time-out periods are *ceremonies*. Examples of ceremonies include: the celebration of birthdays and wedding anniversaries within the family, always on a regular, predefined date; the celebration of a national day as well as participation in the political process on election day, generally occurring on a regular, predefined date; the worship days of institutionalized religion on regular, predefined days; and the celebration of the economic institution on regular, predefined paydays and dividend days. All these are examples of ceremonies confirming the social institution involved and demonstrating the individual person's solidarity with the institution. Such ceremonies are more or less embedded in and are part and parcel of the institution. Rooted in some historical situation from the past, ceremonies look to the present celebration time and mark present solidarity in the group concretizing the institution. Thus as a rule ceremonies celebrate belonging and mark a time-out to enable persons to evaluate their place in the belonging dimensions of their life. (Too many investigators make no distinction between regular ceremonies and irregular rituals; cf. Kideckel 1983 and the whole of that issue of *Anthropological Quarterly* for a perspective on political rites.)

Rituals

On the other hand, there are those irregular time-outs that take place when a person or group needs them or is ready for them. These take place *between* social structures in order to mark the transition or transformation of some person or group from one state to another or from one set of duties and obligations to another. Such interactions express individual or group transition into or out of the flow of social interaction in terms of the same or new social roles. Social interactions during such time-out periods are *ritual*. For example, healing interactions focused on the transition from the sick state to the healthy state, legal interactions focused on the transformation from the accused state to the acquitted state, and educational interactions focused on the transformation from a state of incompetence to one of competence are all rituals of the status reversal type, looking to a reversal of the present situation in which a person or group finds itself sick, accused, or incompetent. Such status reversal rituals are cyclical or oscillating in that they can recur. A recovered person can become sick again, an acquitted person can be accused of something else again, and a person competent in one area can find himself or herself incompetent in another. Such rituals differ from rituals of status transformation, which are like substitutions in a game to a new and better position.

Rituals of status transformation are those rituals that mark a transition in some irreversible way, frequently following the biologically rooted and culturally noted stages of human personal and social development, for example, birth rituals assimilating new members into the group, rituals marking the transition from childhood to adulthood, marriage rituals, and rituals marking accession to kingship or some other irreversible status. Good examples of irreversibility in such rituals of status transformation are parenthood rituals, since the one parenting a child is irreversibly father or mother, at least in U.S. perceptions, and rituals marking adulthood, since one attaining adulthood simply cannot revert to biological childhood.

Ceremonies and Rituals Compared

It is worth noting that, while rituals are those irregular time-outs that befall persons or groups when they need or are ready for them, yet they are always forms of crossing the lines that constitute the purity system of the group. Ceremonies, on the other hand, do not so much entail significant line crossings as they mark the recurring pauses in the action in a regular, predictable way. Ceremonies focus on the stability of the lines that continue to mark off the group in some clear and distinct way, even if the lines are porous at times. In terms of spatial images, ceremonies focus on the inside, that is, on immanence, inwardness, or the within dimension of a social and individual body. Conversely, ritual focuses on the beyond, that is, on transcendence and transformation, or it focuses on transition to something else beyond the normal human limits, whether vertical, horizontal, depth, or mass, and hence beyond the individual and social body.

Nearly every complex society has people who fill the roles of coach/manager and referee/umpire in the game of social interaction. The coach/manager is the expert who often calls the irregular time-outs and then directs activity during that time; the referee/umpire is the one in charge of determining the regular time-outs. The coach/manager is the expert whose task it is to help people in ritual transitions; the referee/umpire is the official in charge of the proceedings. What are the dimensions of the social roles of persons who function like a coach/manager or referee/umpire in the flow of social interaction experienced in human society? For New Testament study, the answers to this question bear specifically upon the social roles embodied by Jesus, by his apostles, by St. Paul, and by their adversaries and opponents in their dealings with people at social boundaries. Who were the experts, the officials, the social professionals, the social appointees, and what might such social positions mean in ritual and ceremonial behavior?

LIMIT-BREAKING AGENTS

Complex societies usually have roles filled by persons whose task it is to see people through various ritual processes. People undergoing a ritual do so because they find themselves in situations that they would like to leave, to get behind, and to get beyond or transcend. Persons in such situations find themselves hemmed about by limitations and boundaries such as those marking off the sick from the well, the child from the adult, or the unmarried from the married. For social interaction to take place in a meaningful way for such people, they have to move from where they are to some other social location beyond the personal and social limits that hold them in. In order to get beyond or transcend the socially imposed and culturally defined limits of the human condition, persons have recourse to limit-breaking agents who can take them over the limits in some socially accepted and satisfying way.

In U.S. cultural experience people point to negative constraining limits when they talk of sickness, death, meaninglessness, boredom, or anxiety. To shed the constraints and get beyond the limits means to experience new or renewed health, meaning, love, joy, and life. In terms of the GSM, Americans would like to have adequate shares of energy (health) to use the power they have, of meaning (influence) to use the influence that is theirs, of love and care (commitment) to activate the commitments they control, and of goods and services (inducement) to utilize the wealth they have. In this society with its core value of instrumental activism, individual power is crucial, and Americans generally are willing to part with huge amounts of the GSM of inducement in order to remove obstacles in the way of their individual exercise of power. The main obstacle, of course, is pain and what it signals, powerlessness. The pain involved is both physical and social. Physical pain is the province of physicians, dentists, and other professionals who care for the sick, while social pain is the province of lawyers and other professionals who care for the potential or actual social deviant. Since ignorance does not directly cause pain, payment given in exchange for instruction to allay ignorance is often considered a questionable deal. After all, the meanings most often provided by educational and religious institutions are of a broad, general, worldview sort which cannot be immediately converted into the instrumental mastery that power brings. The point behind all these examples, then, is that even in American society people have recourse to limit breakers who take them across the lines either to reverse or to transform their social standing. Even in the U.S. social standing is not exclusively a matter of inducement ability, that is, wealth.

Limit Breakers and Their Competence

From where do such limit breakers derive their competence? If a person were sick or in trouble with the law or the customs that formed social institutions, to whom would he or she turn for help? What would one look for in a limit-breaking agent, a ritual specialist who might bring a person across the line so that he or she might experience transformation and/or be able to return to the group of "normals" once again? Jesus of Nazareth certainly functioned as healer (GSM of power) and teacher (GSM of influence); if he were to function as such in a contemporary U.S. community, would his competence be recognized? How do people in weak group/high grid assess competence? How is such evaluation made in the other quadrants of the grid/group model? Once again, the quadrants of the model have to be considered in sequence, and the ensuing discussion will be summarized in a diagram at the close of the chapter.

To begin with, the question here concerns the competence required of those to whom people have recourse in order to reverse or transcend the constraints of human experience that thwart them in the pursuit of goals, normally some replications of the core values of the society. *Competence* in this context is a person's ability to wield one or more of the GSM, along with recognition of this ability by members of the group. This recognition of ability derives from some implicit or explicit norm. As pointed out previously such norms of assessment run along a range from standard through custom to law. Competence is a social right. Rights are of little value unless other persons in a society recognize their obligation to allow a person to use his or her rights. Also, competence is a recognized ability, but abilities are useless unless persons in a society allow one to use the ability. That which moves persons to recognize, acknowledge, and comply with a right—what makes persons fulfill their obligations—is authority. For competence to surface and function effectively in a society, it must somehow be embedded in or endowed with authority. Given the three types of authority noted above—simple authority producing and maintaining standards, legitimate authority doing the same for custom, and legal authority doing the same for law—it would follow that there are three types of competence: standard-based, customary, and legal competence. With these distinctions in tow it should now be possible to posit the types of competence that would emerge in each of the grid/group quadrants and, therefore, the types of limit-breaking agents or ritual experts proper to each.

Strong Group/High Grid Limit Breakers

Strong group/high grid limit-breaking agents derive their competence from filling legal limit-breaking roles such as healing, teaching, forecasting, and counseling. These roles were once customary limit-breaking roles now doubly institutionalized into offices rooted in law. Given the fact that strong group/high grid "superiors" control society by means of the GSM of power and commitment, the legal competence of this quadrant is specified by the commands of the power wielders and spelled out in some power-sanctioned law. Thus an illegal practitioner would automatically be considered incompetent simply because of the illegality. That practitioner, if not of the same social status as the controllers of power and commitment, would be eradicated, annihilated, or killed either physically or symbolically; if of the same social status, an illegal practitioner would simply be exiled, shunned, or set out of the well-fixed boundaries of the social group. The reason for this is that strong group/high grid is rooted in a social structure that is primarily vertical and is based on power and on higher and lower statuses. Lower status illegals can be sanctioned with the sanctions of power/commitment, while equal status illegals can only be sanctioned with the sanctions of influence/inducement since they have equal power/commitment. Both types of illegals are effectively deprived of the wherewithal to maintain their status and hence are placed outside the group.

Strong group/high grid competence then is based upon law and is a form of legalized, legal or power-endorsed, competence. The legal institution appropriately reflects the customary roles of competence that it reinstitutionalizes. Since law here preserves society and focuses upon the inviolable privacy of the social body, any limit breaker perceived to threaten the integrity of the social body is simply eliminated. Examples of such legal competence would be teaching and healing as well as research and legal occupations in the U.S.S.R., China, Germany, Switzerland, and the Vatican. The granting of degrees licensing competence is controlled by centricity forms typical of strong group/high grid. Illegal practitioners, those who move outside the pale of legislated practice, are eradicated either physically (the Soviet Union, China) or symbolically (Germany, Switzerland, the Vatican). In this way those societies attempt to maintain clean and clear purity lines.

Strong Group/Low Grid Limit Breakers

Strong group/low grid limit-breaking agents derive their competence from occupying customary limit-breaking roles, now doubly institutionalized into offices rooted in law, just as in strong group/high grid. Only here purity lines are porous. Hence along with legal competence one finds an extremely large proportion of illegal competence that is difficult to control. While legal competence in this quadrant is specified by the commands of power wielders and spelled out in some power-sanctioned law, inflated power makes it difficult for the power wielders to apply the sanctions. Given the porous purity boundaries, intruding illegal competence is frequently and readily recognized as legitimate (hence as valid customary form) by persons wielding influence and inducement, who at times form groups or factions about persons with legitimate (and illegal) competence. As an example of this, note the groups of people wielding influence and inducement that clustered about Jesus who possessed legitimate but illegal authority.

Since, in strong group/low grid, network groups count for more than some hierarchically shaped, integrated society, they show the most concern for their porous boundaries. Incompetence is rated in terms of legitimacy and custom, not legality and law, and the incompetent are the illegitimate, those with no sanctioning higher order norms to back their behavior. Such incompetents are normally simply ejected from the group—excommunicated, expelled, shunned, and ostracized.

As a result, strong group/low grid allows for two sets of limit-breaking agents often in conflict with each other. One set is endowed with legal competence based on the inflated power and commitment of the political institution, while the other set wields legitimate competence based on the equally inflated influence and inducement of the various non-political institutions of the society. Arguments and competition between representatives of the two sets focus on the legitimacy and the legality of each; those with legal competence point to the illegality of their challengers, while those with legitimate competence admit the legality of their opponents and yet question their legitimacy in terms of higher order norms. Ultimately the argument breaks down into one of legitimate authority, of higher order norms, and this is typical of strong group/low grid. To give a New Testament example, the priestly Sadducees would have legal competence while their critics, the scribes of the Pharisees, would have legitimate competence. Moreover, the sketch of legitimate authority in the previous chapter indicated that this form of authority might likewise be acquired by the person who successfully dislocates the higher order norms legitimating it; this authority was labeled as reputational legitimate authority. It seems that this is the type of authority that Jesus of Nazareth has in the Synoptic Gospels.

In sum, strong group/low grid settings evidence the following: one set of persons with legal authority; another set with legitimate authority often viewed as illegal; and, at times, a third set with reputational authority challenging the legitimacy of the legitimate and legal sets while, of course, disregarding the legality of the latter. Emphasis is placed here on the range of distinctions in strong group/low grid because of its importance for New Testament analysis. Figure 10 on p. 147 sets out the types of limit-breaking agents that can emerge in strong group/low grid. The examples in the dia-

FIGURE 10. Limit-breaking Agents: Strong Group/Low Grid

GSM:	(client dependent) Illegal Competence (Legitimate)		(office dependent) Legal Competence
Influence (knowledge and reputation)	mantics and their-mancies, astrologers, diviners	reputational prophet	official priests, oraclists, philosophers, diviners, prophets
Power (force and enforcement)	sorcerers, witches	reputational healer	emperor, priests, bureaucrats, army, physician-philosophers
Inducement (social position, goods, services)	traders, pseudo-rhetors	reputational social climber	imperial household, aristocracy (by birth)
Commitment (activator of commitment)	group leaders	reputational leader	empire head, city head, family head

Weak Group/Low Grid intrusions
into Strong Group/Low Grid society
rooted in Interpersonal Competence (client dependent)
Reputation Primary
Usual legitimation and legality secondary

gram derive from the perceptions of conquered peoples of the first-century Mediterranean world, the societies of Jesus and of Paul.

In the model the role of reputational legitimate authority derives from and is rooted in weak group/low grid in some way. Consequently, the existence of reputational legitimate authority and its successful challenge to the higher order norms legitimating personal/impersonal legitimate authority depend upon some weak group/low grid experiences of persons in the society. Since such experiences and consequent perceptions are not continually forthcoming in any predictable way, there is no need to postulate the existence of reputational authority in every strong group/low grid society. But, when it does emerge, radical change in social structure and sometimes in values can occur.

Weak Group/High Grid Limit Breakers

Weak group/high grid limit-breaking agents derive their competence from admittance into customary limit-breaking roles such as healing, teaching, research, and law which are now doubly institutionalized into professions or services certified by law. Given the fact that weak group/high grid superiors control society by means of the GSM of influence and inducement, the legal competence of this quadrant would be specified by certification (cf. Collins 1979). A certificate or diploma provides credentials which symbol the GSM of influence sanctioned by power. Certification is controlled by the wielders of influence/inducement, and its procedures are spelled out in terms of a socially shared model of meaning rooted in the society's core values and made to serve as touchstone for what is factual or not and for what is reasonable or not. This, of course, is the very stuff of the GSM of influence. In this quadrant an illegal practitioner is the uncertified practitioner. This is the practitioner who has not been certified for mastering the model of meaning required either by those wielding influence/inducement and currently practicing according to that model or, more rarely, by those who once accepted that model of meaning but now reject it in practice. Hence what persons in weak group/high grid look for in their limit-breaking agents is not legal competence, as in strong group/high grid, but legally certified competence. An uncertified practitioner would automatically be considered incompetent because uncertified. Withdrawal of certification means withdrawal of the social acknowledgment of competence. Such an evaluation requires the sanction of the GSM of influence; that is, reasons and facts must be produced, and those unwarrantedly claiming competence are exposed and branded as incompetent for life.

Weak group/high grid competence, then, is based upon certified ability assessed in terms of the GSM of influence wielded by professional groups. In weak group/high grid modes of legalization, power is located in the population at large which invests it in individuals who generally already wield broad influence and great inducement. Influence and inducement are then joined with the power deriving from the group, resulting in significant conjunctions of power and influence and of power and inducement. Professional groups function much like power-wielding individuals in that they also invest their power in those with greater inducement and influence, for example, in governmental officeholders, corporate heads, the very wealthy, and members of research institutions, who are then expected to pay heed to the influence and, at times, the inducement of such professional groups (cf. Wrong 1976). This results in the legal institution's being suitably attuned to the goals of influence-wielding professional groups and in their reinstitution-alizing the customs of those groups. Simply put, weak group/high grid limit-breaking agents require that their ability be certified by appropriate and specialized professional groups wielding influence. The validation and bind-ingness of those certifying professional groups are then sanctioned by the political institution. The political institution, here a legal one, molds society and focuses upon the inviolable privacy of the individual body. Should influence-wielding, professional groups certify a person who subsequently proves incompetent in dealing with a member of the society, the legal institution can step in to deal with the individual practitioner and the individual societal member, with the professional group on the sidelines as autonomous certifying body. Since law in weak group/high grid molds society and seeks to maintain the privacy of the individual, any limit breaker perceived to threaten the integrity of the individual can be declared incompetent by law and can have certification removed. Examples of such certified competence, as noted above, include teaching, sick-care, research, and legal occupations in the U.S. Here the granting of degrees that certify competence is controlled by autonomous, influence-wielding groups such as universities, the American Bar Association, or the American Medical Association and not by the central government as in strong group/high grid. Incompetent practitioners, those who move outside the pale of customary practice which is legally sanctioned, are exposed and branded as incompetent. In this way the individual influence-wielding agencies and not the society at large maintain clean and clear pragmatic purity lines, and the social body of influence-wielding professionals replicates the weak group/high grid norms focused on the individual.

Weak Group/Low Grid Limit Breakers

Weak group/low grid limit-breaking agents derive their competence from the recognition accorded by other members of the collectivities in this quadrant. This recognition acknowledges that the limit breaker in fact embodies the values which given clusters of individuals might be holding from time to time. What counts is recognition from wielders of power and commitment in this quadrant, that is, from individual followers. This recognition enables the limit-breaking agent to exercise his or her influence rather effectively but only so long as his or her followers perceive the embodiment of their values and goals in the limit breaker. This is an interpersonal competence which lasts only as long as followers can utilize the limit breaker as a mirror of their aspirations. Should the followers refocus their aspirations, the limit-breaking agent is simply abandoned as interpersonally incompetent. Again, competence here is the ability to embody the values and goals of some following in highly individualistic fashion.

Since weak group/low grid forms a rather highly unstable quadrant that straddles crisscrossing directions down from weak group/high grid or across from strong group/low grid, it would seem that the fortunes of limit breakers and their acknowledged competence depend on whether the agent and his or her following can move to the adjacent quadrants. A successful move in this case means perduring acknowledgment of competence, while an unsuccessful move means abandonment. What would a move in either direction, then, require of the limit breaker? A move up the grid to weak group/ high grid would entail some certification procedure deriving from an influence-wielding, professional group recognized by law. This move is, in fact, often perceived as an unwarranted intrusion into the pragmatic purity lines of existing limit-breaking agents and their professional groups. It will therefore call for litigation in terms of weak group/high grid laws which seem to maintain the inviolability of the individual/group body. For example, weak group/low grid limit breakers such as chiropractors seek to have their certification procedures legalized in the face of opposition from the American Medical Association. The weak group/low grid limit breakers in the circles of Ron Hubbard and the Church of Scientology and of the Rev. Moon and the Unification Church seek to have their certification procedures recognized in the face of opposition from already established church organizations and their influence-wielding professionals. The point is that, since weak group/high grid limit-breaking agents are perceived to have competence rooted in ability due to certification by wielders of the GSM of influence/inducement, limit breakers emerging from weak group/low grid into this quadrant will have to develop similar forms of certification if their limit-breaking roles are to endure.

On the other hand, a lateral move from weak group/low grid into strong group/low grid entails some displacement of existing legitimate authority, either personal or impersonal. The role that successfully displaces legitimate authority is the reputational legitimate authority (often unwarrantedly called charismatic authority; cf. B. Schwartz 1983; though at times with warrant; cf. Miyahara 1983). Such reputational legitimate authority counters the higher order norms legitimating the limit breakers then in vogue in a given strong group/low grid society or group. It is important to note that, in the perception of persons in the weak group/low grid quadrant, those serving as limit breakers are seen to possess interpersonal competence, while in the perception of persons in strong group/low grid these same persons are said to have reputational legitimate authority. Thus, depending on the quadrant and cultural scripts of one's following, the role of the limit breaker will be interpreted quite differently. This is rather important for New Testament study since Jesus, Paul, and the wandering prophets of early Christianity would readily be perceived in terms of one or the other role depending on the cultural scripts of their following. For example, for the churches of Matthew, Mark, and Luke, Jesus apparently was a reputational legitimate authority who successfully challenged the higher order norms legitimating the Jewish, Torah-based authorities of the day. On the other hand, the group represented by John's Gospel presents Jesus as someone with interpersonal competence who uses his influence to gain the commitment of his followers in highly individualistic fashion, as befits weak group/low grid (cf. Malina 1985). The wandering prophets of early Christianity seem to have been weak group/low grid persons of interpersonal competence moving into strong group/low grid communities. These communities would focus on the influence (meaning, arguments, style of life) of these wandering prophets to test whether they warranted the reputation required of them to function legitimately. Paul too seems to have been subject to some such procedure; his arguments on the legitimacy of his limit-breaking role are precisely arguments about the sources of his legitimation.

Figure 11 on p. 152 summarizes the discussion of limit-breaking agents up to this point. Note that limit-breaking agents are not to be confined to "religion," since the limits with which such agents deal during the time-outs of life include all that persons perceive as important for a meaningful life, such as meaning, health, security, and love. To validate this point, consider the types of behavior deemed to be appropriate in the U.S. within those physical spaces dedicated to replicating significant ultimate boundaries: churches dealing with meaning; hospitals dealing with health; or banks dealing with security. Note how personal (i.e., individualistic) problems are dealt with quietly and privately between the limit breaker and the client, note how publicity or shouting is considered out of place, and note how there is really no active role for children in these places except as appendages to their parents or other adults who have to deal with the important matters transacted in these sacred places.

FIGURE 11. Limit-breaking Agents in Grid and Group

The cultural-script locus of agents to whom people have recourse in order to transcend limits of human experience (i.e., the "metaphysically unnecessary"—negatively: sickness, death, meaninglessness, adversity, etc.; positively: health, meaning, love, joy, life, etc.).

HIGH GRID

Weak Group/High Grid   **Strong Group/High Grid**

Certified Competence   Legislated (Enforced) Competence

Competence derives essentially   Competence derives essentially
from *ability*, as *certified*   from *office*, as specified by
by the wielders of the GSM   the *commands* of the wielders of
of Influence/Inducement.   the GSM of Power/Commitment.

The incompetent, once exposed,   The incompetent (illegal practitioners)
are branded as such (for life?).   are eradicated, annihilated.

WEAK GROUP {

  Operative GSM: Operative GSM:
    Influence/Inducement   Power/Commitment

  Reactive GSM: Reactive GSM:
    Power/Commitment   Influence/Inducement

} STRONG GROUP

Interpersonal Competence   Infiltrated Legislated
                                            (Enforced) Competence

Competence derives from personal   Competence derives essentially from
embodiment of communitas values   *office*, as *directed* by wielders of the
(interpersonal *ability*), as *recognized* GSM of Power/Commitment, but *along*
by wielders of Power/Commitment,   *with* intruding illegal competence,
i.e., followers, clients.   as *chosen* by wielders of Influence/
                                            Inducement, i.e., followers, clients.

The incompetent   The incompetent
are simply abandoned.   are expelled or excommunicated.

Weak Group/Low Grid   **Strong Group/Low Grid**

LOW GRID

Finally, note how the limit breakers officiating at the rituals which take place in these sacred places are expected to be certified competents who are capable of wielding influence and/or inducement in society at large. In the weak group/high grid U.S. mainstream, limit breakers and their rituals are sought out mainly for status reversal: to find overarching meaning, recover health, or regain security after these are lost or confused in the flow of living. However, in the U.S. weak group/high grid script many of the specific limit-breaking agents also serve as officials in ceremonies which mark regulated, predictable intervals in the flow of time. For example, attendance at church every Sunday, a visit to a physician or dentist for an annual checkup, and the use of the services of a bank for monthly savings or check cashing are all ceremonies focusing on solidarity with the societal institutions of religion, kinship, and economics. In this case persons chosen for ritual interaction are often the same as those officiating at ceremonies. However, such is not the case in all the quadrants of the grid/group model.

In strong group/high grid, since competence is rooted in office (as in weak group/high grid but for different reasons), limit-breaking agents who direct rituals and officials who preside at ceremonies often belong to the same rank. On the other hand, in strong group/low grid there is a divergence from the unified strong group/high grid limit-breaker roles; official limit breakers are often called into question and challenged. Here, while officeholders and their ceremonies are highly regarded, a range of limit breakers deriving from smaller competing network groups coexists with the officials and is perceived by officials as infiltrating the boundaries of legislated competence. This can be clearly seen in Mark 1:42–44 where the healed "leper" has to go to a priest; Jesus heals as reputational legitimate authority, yet the individual must go to the official priest for the ritual of acceptance into the community. Hence in strong group/low grid, officials are to be found alongside unofficial limit breakers. The officials preside over ceremonies and can direct rituals, but it seems the groups making up strong group/low grid societies have their favorite unofficial limit breakers and use them in the typical spirit of "nothing ventured, nothing gained."

Finally, weak group/low grid would have no officials at all. It is a quadrant in which law and even custom are simply not at work. Rather, every ceremony is a ritual meant to lead to some limit breaking, to transcendence, or to some "high." Should the expected limit-breaking or transcendental experience not materialize, the limit breaker and his or her interpersonal competence are relinquished as the inhabitants of this quadrant continue their quest for new antimodes of living which might satisfy their goal of an adequately meaningful, human existence.

LIMIT-BREAKING AGENTS AND THEIR GROUPS:
SOME REPLICATIONS

The foregoing consideration of limit-breaking agents and their ritual roles and of officials and their ceremonial roles was focused on the roles normally played by individuals in interchanges that facilitate the flow of social interactions. If the concrete individual person replicates the social body and if the social body imparts and incorporates the values and norms mirrored in the individual body, what social body can be said to stand behind the various limit-breaking and official roles that have just been considered?

To continue with the sports comparison, if a limit-breaking agent is something like the manager/coach who functions during the time-outs to facilitate the flow of the game for the players, then what kinds of team styles require what kinds of coaches? Obviously baseball, basketball, football, and soccer teams require different kinds of coaches in that different qualifications are demanded of coaches and players alike. In the analogy developed here, the different types of teams and coaches varying from game to game would refer to the different types of social institutions and the games they represent. Here, however, the question has to do with team styles reflected in coaching styles and vice versa. Even in the same game coaching styles and styles of play can be varied. For there are styles of cooperation, of selfishness, of one outstanding player per team with the other players contributing to the high scorer or star, and of spreading the points around with no single outstanding player at all. Team styles are frequently reflected in and replicated by limit breakers and officials. Now what types of team style emerge in the various scripts?

From all that has been presented thus far, it would follow that the styles of social interaction within each quadrant depend upon the styles of control predominant in each. Strong group/high grid would consist of pyramidally arranged statuses controlled by legal authority at every higher stratum. Strong group/low grid would consist of competing network groups with porous boundaries, each group being controlled by some legitimate authority. Weak group/high grid would consist of interconnected swarms of competing individuals of varying measurable endowments, clustering into competitive groups about some controlling competent authority to which the individual voluntarily submits for as long as necessary and pragmatically useful. Finally, weak group/low grid would consist of scatterings of individuals and clusters pursuing rather autistic ends, at times focused about a leader perceived to have interpersonal competence, thus aiding the individuals in their liminal condition to maintain the emotional peaks that they seek. In sum, the style of strong group/high grid is legal, that of strong group/low grid is legitimate, that of weak group/high grid is voluntaristic, and that of weak group/low grid is liminal. However, the liminal style of the weak group/low grid is not a perduring style; the quadrant is a transitional one, as previously indicated. The prevailing styles characteristic of the perduring societal forms of the other three quadrants are the styles reflected in the legal and customary norms which embody the statuses and roles making up the social structure.

Male and Female: Two Aspects of Human Societies

One might ask whether even in the perduring quadrants there might be social forms in which persons could "let their hair down" and relate to others in ways not determined by socially structured roles and statuses which differentiate individuals and groups. Are there weak group/low grid intervals or oases available to people in the other quadrants? Are there ways in which people in these quadrants might relate to each other on the basis of a common, shared humanity (typical of weak group/low grid) instead of some well-defined social persona, for example, on the basis of socially generated roles and statuses?

Victor Turner (1969: 177) has observed:

> All human societies implicitly or explicitly refer to two contrasting social models. One . . . is of society as a structure of jural, political, and economic positions, offices, statuses, and roles, in which the individual is only ambiguously grasped behind the social persona. The other is of society as a communitas of concrete idiosyncratic individuals, who, though differing in physical and mental endowment, are nevertheless regarded as equal in terms of shared humanity. The first model is of a differentiated, culturally structured, segmented, and often hierarchical system of institutionalized positions. The second presents society as an undifferentiated, homogeneous whole, in which individuals confront one another integrally, and not as "segmentalized" into statuses and roles.

In other words, societies generally will have two salient aspects to them, the one expressing the society as a complex structure of distinct, individual parts, the other expressing the society as a homogeneous totality. The first aspect focuses upon the person in terms of what he or she does by way of social functions and social roles; the other aspect deals with the person in terms of who he or she is as a person, personhood being something accepted in and for itself. To see what this means to some extent, consider the self-descriptive information Americans must typically furnish on forms for school registration, bank loans, and insurance claims. What kind of person do such forms describe? Then, consider how those same Americans define themselves within the family, to grandparents, to aunts and uncles and cousins. The first set of definitions looks to what a person does, a person's social location in terms of statuses and roles. The other set of definitions derives from who a person is, the person being accepted simply because the person is who he or she is. Another example of the presence of the two contrasting models might be the following. How does the typical U.S. citizen explain himself or herself to another American, and how would that same typical U.S. citizen explain himself or herself to a native of another country while visiting or living in that country? The explanation given a fellow American will tend to be differentiated and evaluated in terms of ethnic and local origins, social functions, and mutually appreciated statuses. When mainstream U.S. persons meet each other for the first time, they tend to demonstrate to each other how mutually different they are. The second set of explanations, to a "foreigner" in a foreign country, will tend to be in terms of a homogeneous totality, the "ideal American," set in comparison to some non-U.S. cultural type.

These two contrasting social models seem to be replications of bisexual humanity used as metaphors for the social body. Just as human individuals are either male or female, and this is quite apparent in the individual body, so too the social body has male and female sides to it, not biologically of course but in terms of replicating social roles. As a rule, the individual body replicates the social body, but the individual body happens to be male or female, and each replicates the social body both as a totality (the person) and in rather gender-specific ways (as male or female person). If this is so, then the social body has a total aspect to it as well as male and female aspects. This can be seen in a number of strong group societies in which the patrilineal side is the structured, segmented side, the repository of rights and obligations (a male side), while members of the matrilineal side deal with each other in non-structured and non-jural terms (a female side; "jural" here means on the basis of legal and legitimate rights and obligations).

Describing the Tallensi of Ghana, Fortes wrote (1949: 32):

> The dominant line of descent confers the overtly significant attributes of social personality—jural status, rights of inheritance and succession to property and office, political allegiance, ritual privileges and obligations; and the submerged line [constituted by matrifiliation] confers certain spiritual characteristics. Among the Tallensi it is easy to see that this is a reflex of the fact that the bond of uterine descent is maintained as a purely personal bond. It does not subserve common interests of a material, jural or ritual kind; it unites individuals only by ties of mutual interest and concern not unlike those that prevail between close collateral kin in our culture. While it constitutes one of the factors that counterpoise the exclusiveness of the agnatic line, it does not create corporate groups competing with the agnatic lineage and clan. Carrying only a spiritual attribute, the uterine tie cannot determine the jural and politico-ritual solidarity of the patrilineal lineage.

Turner (1969: 114) comments on this as follows:

Here we have the opposition patrilineal/matrilineal, which has the functions dominant/submerged. The patrilineal tie is associated with property, office, political allegiance, exclusiveness, and, it may be added, particularistic and segmentary interests. It is the "structural" link par excellence. The uterine tie is associated with spiritual characteristics, mutual interests and concerns, and collaterality. It is counterpoised to exclusiveness, which presumably means that it makes for inclusiveness and does not serve material interests. In brief, matrilaterality represents, in the dimension of kinship, the notion of communitas.

Ends Values and Means Values

Perhaps the simplest way of paraphrasing what Fortes and Turner are talking about is to say that every society has ends and means aspects to it. There are certain values in the ideology of a society that look to the service of others (means values) and certain values that look to the ones being served (ends values). Thus certain values are ends values, and certain values are means values. Consider the strong group world of the New Testament. The Hellenistic world was clearly patriarchal and patrilineal on its dominant, exposed side. The main social bodies—the empire and the cities and various ethnic groups in the empire—are all conceived of in terms of ends values. For these are all social bodies that exist in and for themselves, much like the Hellenistic male. Hence both the individual and the social body are characterized by such ends values as a sense of independence, leadership, task orientation, outward orientation, assertiveness, self-discipline, impassivity, activity, objectivity, analytic-mindedness, courage, unsentimentality, rationality, self-sufficiency, confidence, and emotional control. All these are male ends values in a patriarchal system, the dominant, jural side of the Hellenistic world.

What of the corresponding means values such as dependence, non-aggression, non-competitiveness, inner orientation, interpersonal orientation, sensitivity, nurturance, subjectivity, intuitiveness, yieldingness, receptivity, and supportiveness? As means values, values directed to the maintenance of another or for the sake of another, they shape the female side, the underside of Hellenistic society. The strong group societies of New Testament times, as noted above, consisted of only two clearly differentiated social institutions: politics and kinship. In terms of the ends-means analysis begun here, it would seem that both major social institutions had dominant, jural, segmented ends values on their dominant side (the emperor, the emperor's household as bureaucracy in the political institution, the male head of the family in kinship) along with submerged, non-jural, non-segmented means values on the other side (the emperor's household as household offering others access to the emperor, the female side of the family in kinship). In this society religion, education, and economics were embedded in these two institutions, with the range of religious expression following the aspects of the institutions in which they were realized.

This means that in the non-monotheistic traditions of the period, there will be deities to provide general overarching meaning for the total polity and to show concern for effective collective action and the common good along with deities concerned with the naturing and nurturing of individual kinship groups. Within each institution some of the deities will embody ends values—showing that they exist in and for themselves, for example, Zeus, Jupiter, and their councils for the polity and ancestor spirits for the kinship group—while other deities will embody means values—showing that they exist for another and to facilitate the functioning of the other, for example, the goddesses Victoria, Pax, and Fortuna for the polity and the fertility, healing, and good-fortune household deities (the Roman lares and penates) for the kinship group. Obviously with the religious institution embedded in the political (and kinship) institution, there could be no "separation of church and state." As a matter of fact, with such a social arrangement in which the gods embody ends values which are identified with the common good of the polity, it would not be amiss to insist that such systems were basically a diffused form of theocracy. The traditional gods of Rome and the ancestors of the kinship groups ultimately authorized and controlled the fate of the Roman people and their empire.

Ends/Means in Judaism and Christianity

However, in the monotheistic tradition of Judaism the situation is somewhat different since monotheism allows for no deity to embody means values. The traditional God of the Jews, Yahweh, embodied ends values both in the traditional polity and its temple cult and in the kinship groups of Jewish society. Who or what, then, embodied the means values in the monotheistic religion of Judaism, itself embedded in Jewish political and kinship institutions? It appears that the means values were embodied in the social roles and statuses which comprised the structures of Jewish political and kinship institutions. Thus if Yahweh were the sole and only end in the political institution, then the ruler and the bureaucracy would be the effective means to the end, an arrangement resulting in a highly emphatic form of theocracy. Similarly, if Yahweh were the sole and only end in the kinship institution, then the family group would be the effective means to that end, again an arrangement resulting in a highly pronounced "religious" family. In the first-century Mediterranean world, then, Judaism would have been perceived as quite unique in that it had no deities embodying means values. The

Jews themselves embodied means values in relation to their deity. Consequently, for Jewish political and kinship groups to claim to be ends in themselves would be a form of apostasy from Yahweh, a form of rebellion incompatible with the perceived "God of the Fathers." Hence the jural and segmented dominant side of Jewish society looked to the ends values embodied by Yahweh, while the non-jural, non-segmented means values belonged to the submerged side embodied in Yahweh's people in their typically Mediterranean social forms. In this way the individual Jewish male could relate to God with female qualities (means values) in both political and kinship institutions and still serve God as male. Judaism thus reveals an embedded religious institution that offers its male adherents a type of social-psychological integration and allows them expression of the total range of human values, male and female. This means that Jewish institutions were largely, if not exclusively, male focused. The problem for females was: how can women as cultural means become ends and still remain female selves? The problem, of course, was simply and selectively unattended to.

The foregoing considerations are important for understanding emerging Christianity since the movement set upon its way by Jesus of Nazareth was essentially a Jewish movement. As a Jewish movement, it embodied means values, with the God of Judaism embodying ends values. Note that the titles for God used by Jesus derived from the political and kinship institutions of the day. "The kingdom of heaven," referring to God's rule, was political, while "Father" was a kinship term. Of these two, as Paul attests, the kinship titles emerged as normative in the early Christian groups founded in various first-century Mediterranean cities. These early Christian groups were called *ekklēsiai* (translated: churches), a word referring to the assemblies of the male citizenry of a Hellenistic city, thus perhaps mirroring the dominant and jural side of the Graeco-Roman cities. The Christian churches or gatherings embodied the non-jural, submerged side of society as well as its means values. Furthermore, the fictive kinship terminology used of church members indicates that the Christian *ekklēsiai* were a non-jural form of the kinship institution–Christians are "brothers and sisters" who worship God, the "Father" of Jesus.

As the submerged side of a dominant patrilineal society, the Christian churches united individuals by personal bonds of commitment (GSM of commitment in kinship groups) and hence by mutual ties of concern and care. As fictive kinship groups, the churches were likewise the locus of embedded religion, sharing a set of overarching meanings. As submerged-side social arrangements, the churches were not in competition with the dominant jural and politico-ritual structures of the Roman Empire. Members of the Christian group would not have seen themselves as undermining the jural and politico-ritual solidarity of the dominant society since they formed fictive kinship associations committed to the mutual interests of members and held by means values. Thus the roles and statuses in the groups described by Paul are not positions of power (GSM of power used by strong group superiors, both political and familial) but positions of commitment activation, focuses of loyalty, care, and concern. Perhaps those who became prominent in Christian network groups derived their prominence from leader-centricity forms emerging from generalized reciprocity, as was the case with Paul.

In sum, the early Mediterranean Christian groups, viewed in relation to society at large, formed social bodies which realized means values as church wedded to ends aspects in society at large. The same was true of a given church's position relative to God. God embodies ends values and therefore is viewed as typically and traditionally male. In Jewish tradition God's people embodied means values and hence is typically and traditionally female (although, in Hebrew, the people "Israel" is a he, not a she, male and not female; cf. Schmitt 1983). Thus males subject to God serve means roles, a feature admirably pointed up by the biblical analogies for God-men relations in terms of marriage and divorce. On the other hand, the new Christian datum postulates Jesus as Messiah intervening between the church as a collectivity and God. It is therefore quite understandable that Jesus as Messiah takes on both ends and means values, thus replicating the union of God and the church. For Jesus is eventually understood as God-man: God, hence end, and man, hence means. At this level of symbolic replication, Jesus-as-man points to Jesus-as-means on behalf of humans; if Jesus were not human (as later Docetists and Gnostics held) then there would be neither means to God available to humankind nor means for God to be effective on humanity's behalf. Yet it is Jesus-as-God, hence as end, to whom the church-as-means relates. If Jesus were not God, hence end, there would be no way to account for the existence of the Christian church as means, a fictive kinship group deriving from the reputational legitimate authority of Jesus who became reputational legitimate authority by God's raising him from the dead. The raising of Jesus becomes, for Christians, the higher order norm legitimating both Jesus' personal authority and the emerging customs of the Christian factions. Leadership and subsequent management in these factions take the form of male roles in the non-dominant, non-jural side of society, much like the mother's brothers in the example previously cited from Fortes. In other words, Christian leaders who founded churches as well as the leaders or managers who succeeded those founders (either bishops or a group of elders called presbyters or the Christian body as a whole or a combination of the three) basically did not wield power within the group. Rather the predominant GSM at their disposal was commitment activation or loyalty, revealed in the care and concern typical of maternal uncles in dominant patriarchal and patrilineal societies. Thus early Christianity was marked by *maternal-uncle-archy* or "emarchy" rather than by patriarchy (Fiorenza 1983 offers a gynecocentric analysis of early Christianity that fully ignores such cross-cultural anthropological information; for alternate models with data that are applicable here, cf. Countryman 1981). Such male leaders, then, embodied ends values in non-jural style on behalf of the group. The style of emerging custom in the group was, for the most part, therapeutic. Penal sanctions were applied only to defend the porous boundaries of the group. Figure 12 should clarify this discussion.

FIGURE 12. Ends (male) and Means (female) Replications in the Church

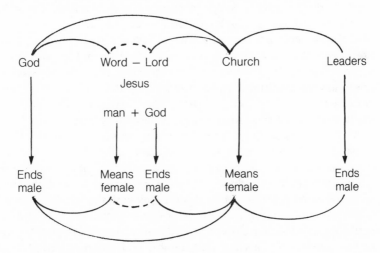

MODELS OF THE CHURCH IN GRID AND GROUP

Since the general purpose of this book is to provide a set of models for understanding the New Testament, especially in comparison with general, U.S. cultural presuppositions, it should be of value here to examine briefly how the Christian church-as-means would fare (and has fared) as the Christian movement made its way into the respective grid and group quadrants. To set up the model, the conclusions spelled out in the preceding chapter will have to be used, notably the model of interpreting social norms (fig. 9, pp. 128–129).

On the group axis strong group points to the inviolable privacy of the social body. In this social body, according to the Jewish and subsequent Christian tradition, God is end—the bearer of end values—while the group and the dyadic personalities that comprise the group are means—the bearers of means values vis-à-vis God. With God as end, church management and/

or leadership would replicate that role and hence would be male, symbolizing ends values. On the weak group side of the model individualism requires the individual to be end—to be bearer of ends values—with God as means to the individual's ends. God thus is a junior partner or a means to be called upon when and if necessary, but who otherwise will remain reticent. With God as means, church management and/or leadership is replicated in either males or females, and this for two reasons. The first is that individualism endows individual persons with simultaneous means and end values; the single person must express both aspects since the individual, not the group, is the social focus. And secondly, with God as bearer of means values, individual males and females can likewise replicate means values, just as they regularly do in the other competency-based, limit-breaking roles which serve the ends of other individuals in the broader society.

On the grid axis high grid with its law and legal authority endows the prevailing religious institution with jural standing; in high grid the religious institution becomes a dominant side institution, with its management/leadership having jural standing. In strong group this jural standing follows the dominant jural mode, that is, historically it was patriarchal and paternalistic. In weak group this jural standing is based on competency and its certifications. Conversely, in low grid with its customs and standards as well as its questioning of legitimacy the situation is more complex. At its outset Christianity was a strong group/low grid movement with non-jural standing, providing for male centeredness and male integration as described above. In time, Christian churches attained jural rank with the strong group/high grid assimilation that began with Emperor Constantine. Yet that grid/group location did not last, since drops in grid marked various periods of the history of Christianity. Perhaps the most notable grid-dropping period for contemporary Christian self-understanding was the Reformation. Those Christian churches in new low grid situations after a period of high grid experience found themselves among competitive groups with their legitimacy questioned and the authority of their legitimate management/leadership readily called into question or simply ignored. Any period of proliferating "reforming" churches points to strong group/low grid intrusions into larger strong group/high grid churches. "Reforming" churches are the emergence of competing non-jural Christian forms. It follows from the grid/group model that jural churches in low grid situations would lose their male membership since the inflated ends values cannot provide the integration that non-jural churches can in such circumstances. Consequently, non-jural churches will fare better in periods of inflated GSM than churches insisting on their rights.

In summarizing this means and ends analysis of God and the religious institution in the Christian tradition, the following points are noteworthy:

(1) In strong group/high grid God, symboling the overarching order of existence in personal terms, is almighty, a political center, a monarch. The church is a means to God as end, jurally. The managers of the church, the clergy, replicate God's end role jurally; they function in patriarchal and paternalistic modes, wielding the GSM of power and commitment. Jurally, the church is means, and hence is female in its imagery and articulation of functions; the church is a "she." Since only institutions have rights in this quadrant, the dyadic personality will find meaning, safety, and security within the institution.

(2) In strong group/low grid God, symboling the overarching order of existence in personal terms, takes on ambivalent shape. In a church dropping from high grid, God is still the almighty, a monarch, but in a confused and seemingly uncontrolled universe. God fails to exercise monarchy as it might be used. The church is meant to be a means to God as end, jurally, but social experience makes this quite difficult to perceive. If it is believed, its implementation has to await another time and place such as the future or the hereafter. Jural clergy who manage the church find their patriarchal and paternalistic modes inflated, questioned, or ignored by males (embodying ends values themselves), but the modes are accessible to females (embodying means values) who find their culturally confused situation replicated by the church under the management of the jural clergy. Since only institutions have rights, the dyadic personality embodying ends values will seek meaning, safety, and security in non-jural forms of associative, fictive kinship groups, while dyadic personalities embodying means values will look for the same in the inflated jural church. However, since the female is embedded in the male, should the male insist, the female too will move into the non-jural group.

On the other hand, in a church emerging in low grid as a competing faction to existing groups, God would be chiefly a Father, the Merciful in a confused and seemingly uncontrolled universe. The church as a non-jural, fictive kinship group is a means to God as end, and social experience makes this perception quite ascertainable in the non-jural dimensions of experience (the jural being inflated and in disarray). Non-jural clergy, males, find their avuncular modes of wielding loyalties rather successful even if competing factions call loyalties into question. Such non-jural, fictive kinship groups offer meaning, safety, and security to their membership by providing ready integration to males and ancillary roles for females.

(3) In weak group/high grid God, symboling the overarching order of existence in traditional personal terms, takes on the role of an ultimate limit-breaking agent. God facilitates and enables the individual to attain his or her ends. Here both the church and God are means to the individual's ends. The religious institution is given jural status, but it is depersonalized and im-

personalized; that is, the church is no longer a "she" but simply an "it" ranked among the other social institutions whose task it is to facilitate and enable living for the individual. Individual rights often supersede those of institutions; hence the individual is free to use institutions as he or she sees fit within significant limits. Clergy in this cultural context replicate God's means role and act as limit-breaking agents facilitating the individual's quest for meaning, safety, and security, but only so long as the individual has need of his or her services. Because they are means, clergy in this quadrant, just as the limit-breaking agents of other institutions (e.g., physicians, lawyers, teachers, or dentists), can be male or female.

(4) In weak group/low grid God takes on the role of a symbol of the overarching order of existence perceived by individuals in this quadrant as freer or liberator from the norms and values of the quadrants from which the individuals have come. God is a "trip," a "high," or a means to attaining and maintaining effervescence, spontaneity, and an emotional, steady state of euphoria. The church, the cluster of individuals in weak group/low grid groups, is a means to the individual's ends, much as God is. The church, of course, is a non-jural entity here, a fictive kinship group with great emotional anchorage so long as the emotional euphoria lasts. Only individuals count; hence movement from group to group upon loss of ebullience is normal. In this quadrant the group leaders or clergy are non-jural individuals with interpersonal competence, serving as emotional anchorage for group members and facilitating the goals of those individuals. The clergy role here is based on reputational legitimate authority, on the ability to challenge successfully the higher order norms that legitimate the authority of clergy in the churches of the other quadrants. Such successful challenge by the reputational legitimate authority thus further facilitates the clergy's intended function as means for individualistic ends.

These then are the features of God and Christian church in terms of grid and group. Figure 13 on p. 165 sums them up. To be more serviceable, it has to be used in conjunction with figure 1 (pp. 14–15), the main grid and group model, and with figure 9 (pp. 128–129), the model of social norms. When combined in this way, these models should prove to be useful tools for situating and understanding the implicit scripts followed by both the U.S. mainstream Bible reader (weak group/high grid) and the New Testament writers and their audiences (strong group/low grid, except for John's Gospel which is weak group/low grid).

FIGURE 13. Ends and Means Analysis and God
in the Christian Perspective

HIGH GRID
Religious Institution Jural

Weak Group/High Grid

God, the Enabler, the Facilitator

Church and God are Means to/for
Ego as End, jurally

Clergy = functional, to facilitate
church/God for the individual

Church is "it" jurally

Individuals have rights

WEAK GROUP { Individualist Ego is End
God is Means

Strong Group/High Grid

God, the Almighty, the King

Church is Means to
God as End, jurally

Clergy = patriarchal,
paternalistic

Church is "she" jurally

Only institutions and collectivities
have rights (dyadic personality)

God is End } STRONG GROUP
Dyadic Ego is Means

Low grid if from high grid:

God, the Almighty, the King in
uncontrolled universe

Church is Means to God as End,
jurally

Clergy = patriarchal, paternalistic,
inflated

Church is "she" jurally

If native to this quadrant:

God, the Trip, the Ego-Liberator

Church and God are Means to/for
Ego as End, non-jurally

Clergy = reputational authority, interpersonal competence as
Means for individualistic Ends

Church is "he/she" androgyne
non-jurally

Only individuals have rights

God, the Father, the Merciful

Church is Means to God as End,
non-jurally

Clergy = avuncular
(maternal uncle
analogy)

Church is "she" non-jurally

Only institutions and collectivities
have rights (dyadic personality)

Weak Group/Low Grid

Strong Group/Low Grid

Religious Institution Jural/Non-Jural
LOW GRID

8.

Telling About the Flow of the Action: Historians and Their Cultural Scripts

INTRODUCTION: ABOUT DISCOURSE

Even if one were only dimly aware of what happens after a game is over in the world of sports, one would certainly know that what sports fans do at that point is talk about the game. The sports pages in newspapers witness to the social salience of such talk. People who did not attend the game either in person or through simultaneous media usually have to be told about the game. Of course there is a difference between talking about the game with some fellow observer or participant in the action and telling about the game to someone who was not there. Yet in both cases people speak about the game, and such speech consisting of more than a sentence is called discourse. People not only discourse about games in sports but also about the flow of action in their everyday lives. People express their feelings, opinions, attitudes, observations, and thoughts in discourse. The complex mental and emotional structures of the social world and a person's participation in that social world are encoded and transmitted to others in discourse. Discourse, either talking or telling, always entails some intent on the part of the speaker to change the mental and behavioral state of the hearer. Speakers want to inform, ask, request, command, convince, recall, thank, or greet their hearers by discourse. Knowledge of the internal states and actions of others derives from such discourse. Reaction to what is heard is therefore highly conditioned by the experience of previous discourses and the modes of listening and interpreting such experience yields. Any system of social interaction between humans is based upon socially shared knowledge and appreciation of previous discourse. Nearly all historical, mythical, and scientific knowledge derives from the socially acquired and shared appreciation of discourse and not from inductive, empirical experience. So too do all the conventions, values, and norms regulating any society (cf. Van Dijk 1972: 332–333).

If this is indeed the case, then an understanding of those aspects of society called norms and values should benefit greatly from an explicit knowledge of the structures of discourse which mediate historical, mythical, and scientific knowledge. From the viewpoint of a speaker's purpose, there are four types of discourse: argumentation (to prove); exposition (to talk); narration (to tell); and description (to show). Argumentation has as its purpose to convince another by producing evidence that establishes the truth or untruth of a case; this form of discourse is often combined with exposition. Exposition seeks to explain the nature of an object, idea, or theme (as this book does). Narration looks to recounting an event or series of events; this form is often combined with description. Finally, description pictures a scene or setting or an interaction in a scene or setting.

This chapter deals with telling about the flow of the action and hence with narration and the outcome of narration, a narrative. A narrative is a story told for its own sake (e.g., literature, oral or written), a story told for some other reason (e.g., history, oral or written), or a story told partly for its own sake and partly for some other reason (e.g., historical fiction, oral or written). This chapter will consider the stories historians tell. "Historian" here refers to anyone telling a story for some social reason. Hence the historian may be any person telling about the flow of the action in his or her life or a professional historian telling about the flow of the action in a given segment of time, in a given social location, or in the life of a given individual or group. In the New Testament the Gospels and Acts are instances of such stories told by historians, narratives that tell; the other New Testament writings normally have other forms of discourse yet often with narrative interspersed (e.g., Gal. 1; 1 Cor. 15; 2 Peter). What follows now is a model of historical narrative, a model of how historians go about their task of telling stories for the sake of something else. Data from this model will then be coupled with the respective quadrants of the grid and group model to demonstrate how the work of the historian does in fact tell for the sake of something else and to indicate what this something else might be in terms of cultural scripts. The description offered here, of what goes into a historical work, is entirely indebted to Hayden White (1973) and his model of metahistory, a description of what the process of creating a historical work entails (for an assessment of White's work, cf. the articles by Golob, Kelner, Mandelbaum, Nelson, and Struever, in a 1980 *History and Theory Beiheft* devoted to White). If the description presented here comes to sound somewhat abstract, it may be useful to keep some historical narrative in mind as the explanation develops, for example, one of the Gospels.

HOW HISTORIANS TELL STORIES

Just as most other members of their society, historians too are mainly interested in the present, in the flow of the action that surrounds them and affects them. Their concern is to explain this present in terms of how and why the present is the way it is. To find some explanation they look to the past, specifically in terms of the way the past has impact on the present. To clarify this point, consider the table of contents of any college world history textbook. To whom is ancient history ancient, the middle ages in the middle, the modern period modern? People in the first-century Mediterranean world did not believe they were ancients living ancient history. The demarcation and naming of historical periods is the work of people in the present who define the past in terms of its impact on the present. Such evaluations of the importance of the past are determined more by the contemporary cultural scripts of the historian, that is, the social, rather than by any objective or "scientific" criteria, and this seems to hold as well for those telling about the flow of the action in antiquity as it does for contemporary historians.

Historians then and now begin with some unprocessed record or field of activities from the past with the purpose of making that record or flow of action more comprehensible in the present to some audience of a particular kind. Storytellers tell their stories to somebody, and that somebody is a contemporary of the storyteller. The first two steps in the task of telling about the flow of the action are to select and to arrange data from the unprocessed record of the past. In this way the historical work or story serves to mediate among the unprocessed historical record (the historical field or the flow of the action from past to present), other historical works if there are any, and an audience in the present. For example, Mark's Gospel mediates between the unprocessed historical record and an audience in his present (the Markan community), while Luke clearly serves to mediate among the unprocessed historical record, other historical works (read Luke 1:1–4), and an audience in the present (the Lukan community). Now the primary steps the historian takes in composing his or her work are chronicle and story.

Chronicle

Chronicle refers to the arrangement of aspects of the flow of past action in some temporal order. The historian sifts through the flow of past action and focuses upon some aspects considered to be of importance. These are perceived as events of significance, and the first step is to arrange such events in the time sequence of their occurrence. It would seem from all that has been presented in this book so far that the historian's perception and evaluation of those aspects of the flow of past action, which are to be rated as significant events and as discerned relationships among events, depend upon the cultural script of the historian and his or her immediate audience. Thus even the very first step in drawing up a historical work, the seemingly uncomplicated step of arranging events in the temporal order of their occurence, is a culturally specific activity. Once events have been sorted out in some time sequence, the next step is to tell a story with those events, to tell about the flow of the action in the past with a view to the present.

Story

Story refers to the process of transforming the chronicled information into a meaningful flow of action. Storytelling turns the data of chronicle into a process of happening, a process conceived as having a beginning, middle, and end, much like the historian's perception of the flow of the action in the present. Thus the historian turns chronicle into story by choosing, arranging, and classifying some events in the chronicle as beginning elements, others as concluding elements, and still others as transitional elements. Depending on the type of story, the same element can be a beginning element, a transitional element, or a concluding element. For example, the ascension of Jesus is a concluding element in Luke's Gospel but a beginning element in Acts.

Like every other human being who tells about the flow of some action, the historian too has to pick and choose. For example, to give a detailed and total description of all that Jesus said and did in the course of his one-year ministry (Matthew, Mark, and Luke) or three-year ministry (John) would take approximately a year or three years, respectively. Persons telling of the flow of the action have to be selective, to bring forward those events which best fit the type of story one wants to tell. The historian constructs the story by including some events and excluding others, by stressing some and subordinating others. This procedure of selection, exclusion, emphasis, and de-emphasis is carried out in the way it is because of the historian's intention or purpose of telling a story of a particular kind. Now the kind of story one tells is determined by the plot. Hence in gathering materials for story from chronicle the historian is guided by plot. For the historian necessarily and continually emplots his or her story throughout the whole research or recall procedure.

Mode of Emplotment

Mode of Emplotment refers to the direction given to the flow of events. A plot describes the flow of the action from one state of equilibrium or balance (beginning) to another state of equilibrium or balance (conclusion) through an intervening process of disequilibrium or imbalance (middle). In all plots the first state is disturbed by something that sets the interaction under way (i.e., some GSM) resulting in disequilibrium (i.e., a reaction to the GSM); a counterelement (compliance with the GSM or its sanction) then restores the equilibrium, and the second equilibrium is somewhat like the first but never identical with it. How the second equilibrium matches the first and the extent to which it differs from it are determined by the mode of emplotment. The mode of emplotment provides the "meaning" of a story by identifying the kind of story it is. There are basically four modes of emplotment that constitute a followable story. These all respond to questions of the following type: what happened next? How did it happen? Why did things happen this way rather than that? How did it all come out in the end? The names ascribed to the four modes of emplotment are not all that important; however, following White, the names chosen derive from narrative criticism rooted in antiquity, except for "romance" which emerges in the period of the Enlightenment. The four modes of emplotment are romance, satire, comedy, and tragedy.

(1) *Romance* follows a plot line with heavy focus on the individual and the individual's heightened sense of self and self-identification. In romance this plot line takes the shape of a central character's (hero, heroine) transcendence of the world of experience, his or her victory over it, and his or her final liberation from it. The flow of the action in romance entails the drama of good over evil, of virtue over vice, of light over darkness, or of the ultimate transcendence of the individual over the world in which he or she was held back, constrained, or imprisoned. The individual succeeds in breaking the fetters of the group and can stand alone, independently. Note how well the romantic mode of emplotment fits the *weak group* pole of the group axis of the grid and group model.

(2) *Satire* is the direct opposite of romance. Here the plot line is dominated by the emphatic apprehension that the individual is ultimately a captive of the world rather than its master, that the individual simply cannot break out of the constraints of his or her social world and indeed should not. In satire this plot line is symboled by the untiring analyses of how and why human consciousness and will are always inadequate to the task of definitively overcoming the dark forces of death, the unremitting enemy of humanity. This symbolic perception is a replication of the perception that the individual apart from the group simply cannot function without being overcome. Being embedded in a group that constricts individuality marks the only mode of existence possible, since the forces of death are bound to overcome the disembedded individual. Satire, as a mode of emplotment, aptly fits the *strong group* pole of the group axis of the grid and group model.

(3) *Comedy* follows a plot line that repeatedly underscores how well societal values and human experiences match. Comedy describes the flow of action resulting in the certain, if temporary, triumph of human beings over their world, while highlighting the equally certain, if occasional, reconciliations of the forces at play in the social and physical worlds. The reconciliations that occur at the end of comedy are reconciliations of humans with humans and of humans with their world and their society. The condition of

society is represented as being purer, saner, and healthier as a result of the contest among seemingly unalterably opposed elements in the world. These elements are revealed to be harmonizable with each other in the long run and hence ultimately unified and at one with each other and all else that exists. Comedy then would readily tally with high grid perceptions; hence among the modes of emplotment comedy marks the *high grid* pole of the grid axis of the grid and group model.

(4) *Tragedy* is the opposite of comedy. The plot line of tragedy is marked by an initial contest which foreshadows a state of division among human beings more terrible than the initial contest. Ultimately, the hero/heroine (individual or group) falls, and the world which the hero/heroine inhabits shakes at the end. But such negative goings on are not regarded as totally threatening to those who survive the contests of life. The survivors gain in awareness by means of a dawning perception of the regularities governing human existence. This dawning perception is brought forth by the hero's/heroine's exertion against the world, revealing why experiences and values do not match, a revelation yielding some higher order explanatory principle. Reconciliations at the end of tragedy are somber, much like resignations to the conditions under which humans must work in the world. These conditions, in turn, are assessed to be unalterable and rooted in the very beginnings of humankind (like original sin). Tragedy implies that the human person cannot change conditions but must either work within them or look beyond himself or herself for rescue, salvation, or liberation. The dour conditions embracing human beings set the limits on what they may aspire to and legitimately aim at in their quest for meaning, security, and health in the world. Again, as a mode of emplotment, tragedy matches well the *low grid* pole of the grid axis of the grid and group model.

The value of distinguishing these four basic story forms is, of course, that they readily serve as a tool for characterizing the different kinds of explanatory effects to which a historian is limited at the level of narrative emplotment. By overlaying these story forms on the grid and group model, hence by using these story forms as grid and group variables, a given historical work can easily be situated within one of the quadrants of contrasting cultural scripts. Thus, for example, satiric comedy or satiric tragedy would be a mode of emplotment consonant with the interests of those historians working in strong group cultural quadrants. Such historians are likely to perceive behind or within the welter of events contained in the chronicle an ongoing structure of relationships, the constant recurrence of the same in the different and hence an emphasis on universal elements. In strong group/high grid (satiric comedy) these universal elements explain why experience and social values match so well and lead to such stable and certain outcomes. In strong group/low grid (satiric tragedy) universal elements serve to explain the sorry condition of humankind and to clarify why experience and social values simply never match as they might have been intended to. (As will be seen as the model develops here, the New Testament writings apart from John's Gospel are satiric tragedy, not comedy; for a contrary view, see Via 1975.)

On the other hand, romantic tragedy or romantic comedy would be modes of emplotment favored by historians working in weak group cultural quadrants. Such historians are likely to perceive the emergence of the different, the new, and the particular behind or within the flow of events contained in the chronicle. Emerging values rather than ongoing structures would hold their interests. Weak group/high grid (romantic comedy) would stress how the emerging new forces and new conditions explain why values and experiences match so well even though the processes derived from the chronicle appear at first glance either to be changeless in their essence or to be changing only in their phenomenal forms. Weak group/ low grid (romantic tragedy) would underscore how new forces and new conditions require and demand social interruptions and step-level changes, since values and experience do not match; ultimately it is the unique, the individual, and the particular that count while the universal and the changeless are illusory.

As the plot takes the historian from initial equilibrium to variable disequilibrium and back to some restored but altered equilibrium, an implicit judgment will ordinarily be made on the meaning of the whole process—the point of it all. What is the ultimate sense behind the flow of the action in this or that particular way? This dimension of the historical work—of telling about the flow of the action—is called the mode of formal argument.

Mode of Formal Argument

Mode of formal argument refers to the ways in which the meaning of something is explained in terms of some broader picture. The historian's formal argument would look to the meaning of the flow of events described in the historical narrative in terms of some "point-of-it-all" explanation. In other words, while the historian tells of the flow of events, he or she cannot avoid talking about them. Usually this talking about the meaning of events is implicit. Historical explanations, like any explanations, are bound to be based on different, non-historical presuppositions about the nature of the historical field. These presuppositions derive from the cultural scripts which control the historian in his or her telling activity. From the viewpoint of the activity of telling, cultural scripts provide the teller with different conceptions which generate the culturally specific kinds of explanations that can be used in historical analysis. Basing himself upon a model developed by Stephen Pepper (1942; 1945; and, most appropriately for history, 1967: 319–377), White distinguishes four general types of formal argument or, ultimately, four general types of culturally specific explanations used in historical analysis. Pepper's names for these four are the formist, the contextualist, the organicist, and the mechanistic.

(1) *The formist mode of argument,* according to White, aims at the identification of the unique characteristics of objects inhabiting the historical field, the unprocessed historical record. The formist considers an explanation to be complete when a given set of objects has been properly identified, when its class, general qualities, and specific attributes have been assigned, and when labels attesting to its particularity and individual uniqueness have been attached.

At this point a detour into the domain of semantic analysis may be useful, since the modes of formal argument readily lend themselves to articulation in terms of the categories of that field. Narrative descriptions of reality can be analyzed in terms of seven highly chunked categories: location; agent; act; object; agency; purpose; and outcome (White here uses Kenneth Burke 1969: 3–20; I add the category "outcome"). Briefly:

- location refers to the physical, social, and cultural scene, the when/where of the story;
- agent refers to the animate instigator of the action, the who;
- act refers to the action, state, or change of state being described, the what is going on;
- object refers to the focus of the act, the whom or what; if the object is animate it is the "patient," or if inanimate, it is simply "object";
- agency refers to the means by which action takes place, the how;
- purpose refers to the goals of the agents in the story, the why;
- outcome refers to the unintended consequences or goals achieved beyond, beside, or against the intentions of the agents, the "but."

In a consideration of the modes of formal argument, one might profitably ask, with White: which of these categories of semantic analysis are emphasized (cf. figure 14 on p. 177 for a summary)?

In the formist conception of historical explanation, the uniqueness and individualistic quality of the different agents, agencies, and acts which make up the historical "events" to be explained is central to the telling of the story and hence to historical investigation and research. On the other hand, the location, the physical and social scene or "ground" against which these central elements arise, is of peripheral importance. In analyzing the data perceived to be important facts, formists tend to be dispersive rather than integrative, offering a scattergram of information which highlights the contours of particular individual features. Formist argument does not perceive any regularities (laws or principles) in the flow of action; similarities are selectively unattended to. Rather, the flow reveals vivid representations of agents, acts, and agencies, and these are set forth in impressionistic fashion.

Note how well the formist mode of argument fits the *weak group/low grid* cultural script. The formist argument is weak group because it focuses on the individual, the particular, while totally rejecting laws or principles of history. This rejection, in turn, replicates the perception that sees no close phasing between universally held values and experience. Formist history, then, reveals how ad hoc standards arose in given interactions against the general flow of custom and law. The individual, the particular, is the focus in romantic tragedy. The best example of formist narrative in the New Testament is the Gospel of John (cf. Malina 1985; for a modern example of this mode relative to the life of Jesus, cf. J. Miller 1980; information on recent lives of Jesus used in this chapter comes from Hollenbach 1983).

(2) *The contextualist mode of argument* explains events by setting them within the context of their occurrence with the purpose of showing their functional interrelationship, how they work together to produce the effect that they do. The seven elements of location, agent, act, object, agency, purpose, and outcome are all involved, but the binding element is the functional relationship between what happens and how it happens. In this way acts and agencies and their relationship become crucial for explaining the flow of events. The agents of the flow of the action are explained, similarly, in terms of what they do and how they do it—their acts and agencies. The result is a still-life picture peopled with pragmatic personalities.

In analyzing data contextualists produce their facts from the historical field by identifying the threads that link "events" of the past to their present and future, a feed-forward procedure. The result is a description of trends, tendencies, or general profiles of periods, eras, and epochs in terms of specific efficient causes, that is, in terms of effects derived from acts and agencies. Contextualists are not much interested in first causes, the ultimate explanation of it all, nor in final causes, the ultimate purpose of it all, nor in material causes, the stuff out of which the action flows in particularistic and concrete detail. As a result, the explanation offered by contextualists appears somewhat timeless, a cut across the grain of time, a mixture of formist (weak group/low grid) and organicist (strong group/high grid cf. below) explanation. The focus is on individual events and their relationship to some immediate context.

The contextualist mode of argument seems to be typically *weak group/ high grid*. White sees it as a mixture of formist and organicist modes, and he is undoubtedly correct. The formist element is the weak group aspect, while the organicist element, as will be seen, is the high grid aspect. Contextualist argument is weak group in that it focuses on individual events, looking at the pragmatic effects of acts and agencies to explain individual events. Ready examples of this mode of argument can be found in U.S. news magazines and their accounts of events. This is technologism applied to telling about the flow of the action. It is high grid because it presumes it can describe trends, tendencies, and the general profile of a period as well as point to links between the past and the present and future. There is some continuity or relationship clearly presupposing some phasing between cultural values and experience. The presumption that individual events do indeed have close relationship to their contexts, that events do not and cannot transcend their immediate contexts, is a typical weak group/high grid perception; the individual event in immediate context is the focus of romantic comedy, as previously noted.

There are, of course, no contextualist narratives in the New Testament. Such narratives can be found in works on New Testament history by persons writing in terms of the U.S. mainstream (e.g., Hollenbach's essays on the historical Jesus, 1979; 1981; 1982; 1984; and M. Smith 1978). As a matter of fact, if one were to write a history of early Christianity in terms of the models presented in this book, the result would be a contextualist narrative since the whole grid and group approach developed here argues for the overwhelming significance of context, cultural and social.

(3) *The organicist mode of argument* is rooted in the presupposition that all of reality is similar to a great biological organism in which individual elements act with purpose in their own domain and thus contribute to the slowly emerging and inevitable purpose of the whole. Thus organicist narrative attempts to depict the particulars found in the unprocessed historical field as components of synthetic, biological-like processes in which the presumed function of the whole cosmic process is replicated in microcosmic form in the individual segments of the cosmic process (cf. Van Parijs 1981 for this mode in the social sciences). For example, consider the mode of argument presented by Carl Sagan (1980) in his television series, *Cosmos*, or his book by the same name. Sagan tells a story of the flow of the action in the organicist mode of argument. Individual identities are components of processes which aggregate into wholes that are greater than or qualitatively different from the sum of their parts. Even though an organicist story deals with the past, the story is always focused on the end, the goal, the terminus of history. Hence focus is trained upon the purpose of the process, generally expressed in terms of principles, ideas, or cosmic laws of universal application, with emphasis on similarities that recur in inevitable fashion. For this perspective there are indeed purposive laws built into the historical process, "natural" laws, so to speak. These purposive laws and their expression in the principles or recurrent ideas of history guarantee human freedom in attaining goals since the human being

simply replicates the goal-attaining quality of the whole process anyway. If the historical process is goal oriented, so are human beings who are therefore responsible agents. In analyzing data from the historical field organicists produce facts that fall together into an integral, whole picture of the principles or recurrent ideas that they began with. All facts can be reduced to these integrating principles, ideas, or purposive laws. Of the seven elements of narrative description, purpose or goal is everything and everywhere. The scene is rather insignificant, even illusory. Thus the argument turns out to be an abstract explanation of final cause, ultimate purpose, or teleology.

The organicist mode of argument is undoubtedly *strong group/high grid*. It is strong group because the individual is simply a component and replication of the total group process, itself a piece of the cosmic process. It is high grid because values and experiences constantly match to "prove" the truth of the existence of the purposive laws governing the inevitable historical process. Strong group/high grid, as previously noted, is the universalizing quadrant regulated by law which controls the flow of the action. Global purpose or teleology is the focus of satiric comedy. Again, there are no organicist narratives in the New Testament, but they can be found in elitist ancient Roman historians (e.g., Suetonius or Tacitus, cf. Ruch 1972) and in New Testament histories that generate principles of theology (e.g., the works of Swiss and German theologians such as R. Bultmann, O. Cullmann, J. Jeremias, or E. Käsemann and the modern histories of Jesus that focus on his teaching, doctrine, or ideas alone, such as Charlesworth 1982; Harvey 1982; Meyer 1979; or Sanders 1982).

(4) *The mechanistic mode of argument*, according to White, seeks out recurrent causes that determine the outcomes of acts in the historical field. Once such recurrent causes are discovered, they are formulated in terms of laws which regulate the objects of historical study (for an example, read Brander 1983; and cf. Goldwert 1981). These historical objects are all interconnected in a part-to-part relationship something like a giant jigsaw puzzle with regularly fitting parts but with no overall plan derived from the parts. The plan is latent, implicit, below the apparent surface. In analyzing data from the historical field mechanists produce facts that fall into an integral, whole picture of the partial regularities that they began with. All facts can be reduced to such segmentary and partial regularities. Of the seven elements of narrative description mechanism is inclined to view the acts of agents within the historical field as manifestations of extrahistorical agencies; people and their actions are controlled by forces over which they really have no control. These agencies have their origins in the scene within which the action depicted in the narrative unfolds. The scene, the physical environment, and the social situation are everything. The task is both to discover the "laws" or

FIGURE 14. Semantic Analysis and Modes of Formal Argument

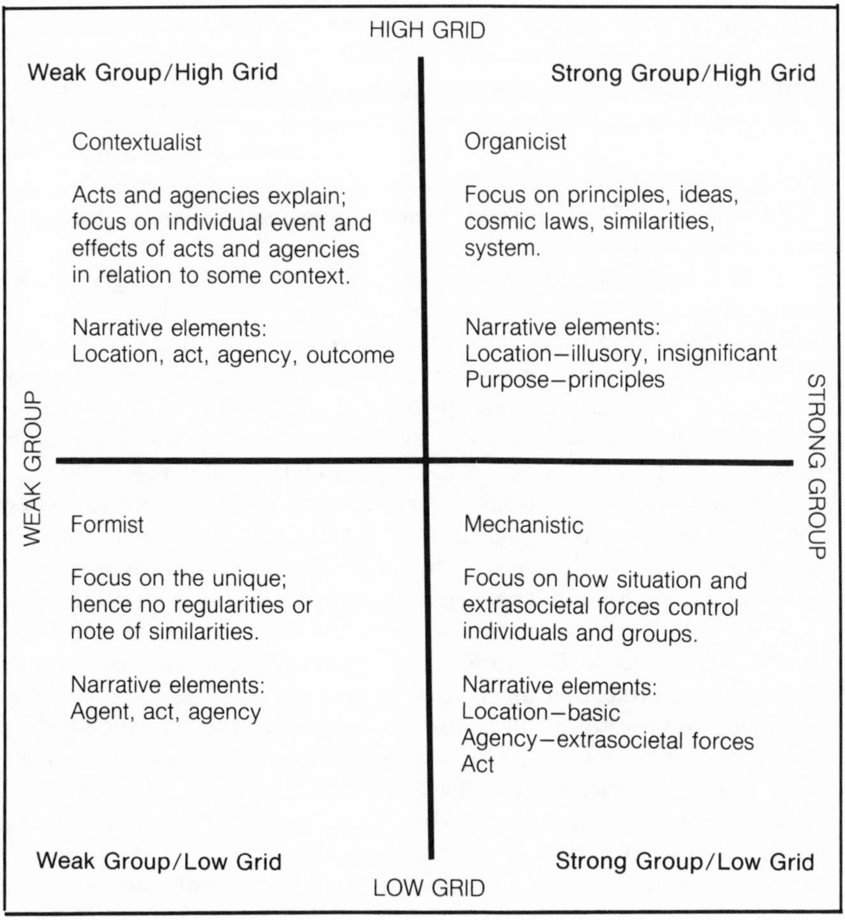

HIGH GRID

Weak Group/High Grid | **Strong Group/High Grid**

Contextualist

Acts and agencies explain;
focus on individual event and
effects of acts and agencies
in relation to some context.

Narrative elements:
Location, act, agency, outcome

Organicist

Focus on principles, ideas,
cosmic laws, similarities,
system.

Narrative elements:
Location—illusory, insignificant
Purpose—principles

WEAK GROUP | STRONG GROUP

Formist

Focus on the unique;
hence no regularities or
note of similarities.

Narrative elements:
Agent, act, agency

Mechanistic

Focus on how situation and
extrasocietal forces control
individuals and groups.

Narrative elements:
Location—basic
Agency—extrasocietal forces
Act

Weak Group/Low Grid | **Strong Group/Low Grid**

LOW GRID

NARRATIVE ELEMENTS
1. Location (where/when) = scene, physical and social
2. Agent (who) = animate instigator
3. Act (what) = action, state, change of state
4. Object (what/whom) = focus of act
   (a) personal = patient (b) impersonal = object
5. Agency (how) = by what means
6. Purpose (why) = agent's goal(s)
7. Outcome ("but") = latent effect(s)

regularities that govern action in history and that are controlled by extrahistorical agencies and, subsequently, to display those "laws." These extrahistorical agencies and their regular control of the flow of the action are clearly
constraints to human action, unconcerned as they are with human decisions,
sealing human beings in a fate beyond human control. Thus human beings
are quite restricted in their choices and abilities relative to attaining goals.
Figure 14 on p. 177 charts the elements of semantic analysis in terms of the
modes of formal argument.

The mechanistic mode of argument is a version of the organicist with
the grid down; it is *strong group/low grid*. It is strong group because the
individual is controlled by forces from above and beyond, such as the environment, social pressure, and physical limitations. It is low grid because
values and experiences simply do not match; the laws of history simply
prove human beings cannot attain the goals that they would like to attain.
Instead, the proper strategy for humankind is a fatal resignation in a
rather unjust situation. Strong group/low grid, as pointed out above, perceives the universe as unjust in its processes as far as humans are concerned; the universe is governed by forces that are constantly penetrating
the porous group boundaries, contrary to human wishes and intentions.
Extrahistorical agencies rooted in the scene are revealed in the acts of
agents, forces such as God or gods, demons and angels, and the inevitable
power of the proletariat or of world communism. In the New Testament
the Synoptic Gospels are mechanistic in this sense. The "salvation history"
approach to Christianity is of this type (cf. Boys 1980) as are some recent
lives of Jesus (Riches 1980; Wilcox 1982; and the lives of Jesus produced
by liberation theologians, e.g., Pixley 1977: 64–100). Furthermore, the perception of God immanently at work in human processes likewise seems to
fit the mechanistic mode of argument in telling about the flow of the
action.

The foregoing types of formal argument seek to discover the point of
the flow of the action. While this point is being made, the historians perform
another implicit task in their telling of the story. They tell their audience
what they should do about it, and this pertains to ideological implication.

Mode of Ideological Implication

Mode of ideological implication refers to the ideological setting of the
story. As previously defined in this book, ideology refers to the articulation
of a social group's views and values that legitimate and reinforce the present
order and practice of the group and that protect that order and practice
against competing groups. Ideology, in this sense, implies an assessment of
the world along with a set of prescriptions for taking a position in the world

and for acting upon that position. Depending on the ideology, the world will have to be changed or maintained in its current condition. The set of prescriptions that surface as the group's perspective on life is normally based on arguments perceived to derive from the world as it really is, that is, the group's cultural conception of the world. The historian, like other human beings, works within the framework imposed by a cultural script. From the perspective of that framework, he or she gets to learn the point of the flow of the action as well as what mature and responsible human beings ought to do about it. This is the ideological implication of storytelling. This dimension mirrors the moral or ethical element in the historian's assumption of a particular position—the implications that can be drawn from the study of past events for the understanding of present ones. Ultimately this is the motive force behind the historian's telling of the flow of the action at all. The mode of ideological implication points to how the storyteller's audience or readership must view the present because of the continuities with the past discovered by the historian.

The four basic ideological positions which can be derived from what historians tell their readers they ought to do about the present are the anarchist, the liberal, the conservative, and the radical (again, the terminology is from White).

(1) *Anarchist.* By way of ideological implication, anarchists conclude that the best option is to abolish society and set up a community based on fundamental humanity. The best times of humanity are in the remote past. This greatness that was in the past is achievable at any time, if only people would live their fundamental humanity. When it is achieved, humankind will find itself in an atemporal utopia. The thrust of human activity will be total social transcendence.

The anarchist view is a replication of the *weak group/low grid* script in terms of its ideological implication. The call for abolishing society, of course, means abolishing the society previously experienced and inhabited by persons in this quadrant. Since what people must strive for is to transcend any existing social situation, all physical destruction is simply a symbolic replication of the fundamental thrust to annihilate previous exclusive purity lines—lines of the sacred which reflect the definitions and limitations of society. Such destruction will inevitably lead to transcendence, an ongoing emotional peak, or the breaking of limits that might release individuals to find themselves and each other in some culturally unadulterated humanity. This is the liminality of weak group/low grid and the type of fundamental human fellowship feeling it seeks to generate. Again, in the New Testament John's Gospel is the best representative of this view (cf. Malina 1985). It is perhaps also the view of the wandering prophets of early Christianity, that is, those with reputational legitimate authority who broke with family and community to find the lost fundamental humanness of humankind as they perceived it in Jesus of Nazareth.

(2) *Liberal.* The ideological implications of the liberal position lead to the conclusion that the best option for the present is to "fine tune" existing social arrangements, to adjust them for maximum efficiency, and thereby to maximize the current social scheme. The outcome of such effort would be heightened social rhythm, harmony, and efficiency. The best times of humankind are in the remote future. People have not yet exhausted their possibilities for progress. The thrust of human activity will look to relative conformity, to congruence of social action with the demands of the present to the extent that this is possible.

The liberal view is a replication of the *weak group/high grid* script in terms of its ideological implications. The lesson of history in this quadrant is that people must come to grips with their situation quite pragmatically. Progress is inevitable, even in the present condition. All that is necessary is for individuals to have the opportunity to achieve their maximum. Those in charge of society, societal managers, must use their resources to "fine tune" the social "machine" and lubricate the works properly for peak efficiency in the present. Living the present to its utmost guarantees positive development into the future.

This view, of course, is not in the New Testament. Rather, it is the mainstream U.S. view to be found in U.S. advertising, both religious and non-religious, as well as in the many "how-to" books and programs typical of this cultural script. Not a few fundamentalist religious groups espouse these ideological implications unabashedly and without criticism and read the Bible as though its books shared this ideology. The Moral Majority is the easiest current example that comes to mind. Yet even the opponents of the concrete proposals of the Moral Majority share similar ideological implications. In this quadrant nearly all presume that if the "fine tuning" of the social sphere is carried off well then a relatively much better present is in store for all.

(3) *Conservative.* The ideological implications flowing from the conservative standpoint lead to the conclusion that humanity's best option is to enable and allow society to develop by means of its own internal forces and natural rhythms, much as plants change and develop in the unattended world of nature. Since the social body is not very unlike a slowly developing organism, the powers and regularities within the social body must be allowed to unfold and redound to the benefit of the whole. The best times of humankind are in the present, right now. Things have never been better. Hence it is clear that the thrust of social behavior will be focused on total conformity, on total congruence of social activity with the demands of the present. This is both possible and necessary.

This conservative view replicates the *strong group/high grid script*. The lesson of history in this quadrant is clear; present social conditions derive from forces immanent in the nature of things and are the best conceivable situation for society. All that is necessary is to maintain the present since it will inevitably develop and change imperceptibly and gradually in the direction of its immanently determined thrust. To allow for this natural growth, the present must be maintained at all costs. The world is just, history is a fair and impartial process, and total conformity with the present validates this view.

The conservative view represents the ideological implication of the strong group/high grid script. While it is not in the New Testament, the conservative view becomes increasingly evident in the writings of post-Constantinian clergy but especially in the works of Christian medievals. We should likewise expect such conservative lessons from history to be offered by contemporary politicians and clergy in strong group/high grid societies, for example, the Vatican, Switzerland, and elites in West Germany or Saudi Arabia. While the religious perspectives of official Soviet and Chinese spokespersons might be antiChristian, they still fall into the same vein.

(4) *Radical.* The radical standpoint generates ideological implications that lead one to conclude that the best option for humanity at present is to restructure society on some entirely new basis. History teaches that contemporary social structures are obsolete, constraining, impractical, and, above all, not representative of the genuine values developed and held by "our" people from the past to the very present. To give these genuine values the opportunity to emerge and be effective, society needs new structures and refashioned institutions. The best times of humankind are imminent, right around the corner. Hence one ought to invest his or her hopes in the immediate future when the transformation of existing structures will take place. The thrust of social behavior will look to a relative transcendence of the present.

The radical view, of course, expresses the *strong group/low grid* perception of reality. The insistence on overhauling the social structures of the present and a hope focused on the imminent, relatively near future are typical of the strong group/low grid script. The present is good in part, notably for those segments of society that espouse and preserve the genuine values of the past. However, there are segments of society which oppose those values. Existing social structures simply do not allow for the realization of those traditional values. Sporadic physical destruction of people and things symbols the high priority placed on the destruction and transformation of existing institutions which, of course, are social, non-concrete entities. Limit-breaking agents can serve as leaders to steer society out of the crisis and as guides who can point the way to transcending the present so that genuine

FIGURE 15. implications of Storytelling (History) in Grid and Group

*Mode of Emplotment—why did things happen this way rather than that? How did it all come out in the end?

<table>
<tr><td colspan="2">Weak Group/High Grid</td><td align="right">COMEDY:</td></tr>
<tr><td rowspan="6">ROMANCE: WEAK GROUP</td><td colspan="2">

*Mode of Emplotment = *Romantic Comedy:* the hero (individualistic) successfully struggles against opposing psychological, physical, or social constraints revealing the ultimate reconcilability of opposing elements in human life.

†Mode of Formal Argument = *Contextualist:* the meaning of events is to be sought in the functions of interrelated elements (efficient cause) in a specific context. There is a functional relationship among location, agent, act, object, agency, and purpose; but since the moving force (efficient cause) in an event is the agent revealed in acts produced by means of agencies, these latter three are the focal core. Result is a slice of time foregrounding individual events in their immediate, open-ended context (with no concern for first, final, or detailed material causes).

‡Mode of Ideological Implication = *Liberal:* fine tune society for maximum efficiency (convolution).
The best of times is in the remote future.

</td></tr>
<tr><td colspan="2">

Mode of Emplotment = *Romantic Tragedy:* the hero (individualistic) struggles unsuccessfully against opposing psychological, physical, or social constraints, yet the struggle reveals how success can be found beyond the constraints or by acquiescing in them.

Mode of Formal Argument = *Formist:* the meaning of events is to be sought in the unique qualities of agents, acts, and agencies described impressionistically by identifying unique and particular class, assigning distinctive attributes, and applying labels attesting to particularity.

Mode of Ideological Implication = *Anarchist:* destroy society in favor of fundamental, universal humanity (devolution).
The best of times is in the remote past that is immediately recoverable.

</td></tr>
<tr><td>Weak Group/Low Grid</td><td align="right">TRAGEDY:</td></tr>
</table>

Group—Romance: the hero, with an individualistic sense of self, moves beyond, transcends, overcomes, frees himself or herself from the varied constraints of the world of experience, of the group(s) in which he or she was part.
—Satire: the hero, most often a dyadic personality, finds himself or herself necessarily confined, constrained, and fettered by the world of experience and by the social group and ultimately cannot overcome or should not overcome these constraints.

†Mode of Formal Argument—what is the point of it all?
‡Mode of Ideological Implication—what should we do about it?

HIGH GRID   **Strong Group/High Grid**

Mode of Emplotment = *Satiric Comedy:* the hero's (dyadic personality or
  group) interactions pitted against psychological, physical, and/or social constraints result in positive outcomes demonstrating that the
  acceptance of such constraints leads to harmony, unity, reconciliation,
  life.

Mode of Formal Argument = *Organicist:* the meaning of events consists
  in how they reveal and fulfill in their own way the goal or purpose of the
  whole human social process which inevitably and ineluctably unfolds
  toward its complexified terminus, like a great, evolving, self-transform-
  ing biological organism. Events thus put forward the great purposive
  "laws" controlling the historical process.

Mode of Ideological Implication = *Conservative:* allow society to change
  of its own internal forces and natural rhythms (evolution).
  The best of times is the present.

Mode of Emplotment = *Satiric Tragedy:* the hero's (dyadic personality or
  group) interactions pitted against psychological, physical, and/or social constraints result in negative outcomes demonstrating that one
  cannot overcome one's situation of embeddedness in its manifold
  dimensions; one can learn how to accept the situation or one can seek
  and perhaps find a solution lying beyond normal human limits.

Mode of Formal Argument = *Mechanistic:* the meaning of events is to be
  sought in the latent, implicit, sub- or suprasurface (hence extrahistorical) agencies that control the acts of agents. These agencies are to be
  found in the scene or location—the physical and/or social environment
  that is governed by agencies, following predictable "laws" that in fact
  constrain agents and their acts; discovering and articulating those
  "laws" and uncovering those agencies are of primary concern.

Mode of Ideological Implication = *Radical:* restructure society in its entirety (revolution).
  The best of times is imminent, right around the corner.

LOW GRID   **Strong Group/Low Grid**

SATIRE: STRONG GROUP

Grid—Comedy: interaction among seemingly unalterably opposed elements in the
  physical/social world of (comedic conflict) results in positive outcomes, indicating a world of ultimate reconciliation, harmony, and unity.
  —Tragedy: interaction among opposed elements in the physical/social world
  of humans proves that the oppositions are quite real, deep-seated and unalterable; hence one must accept them or look beyond them.

values can be realized effectively. Such "leaders" and "guides" dominate the social scene and are dominated by it.

The radical standpoint as described here is typical of all the New Testament writings apart from the Gospel of John. The ideological implications of this standpoint can also be found in the stories told by the first Christian historians, such as Eusebius, Socrates, Sozomen, Theodoret, and Evagrius, although some of them began to move up the grid (cf. Chesnut 1977). Finally, such ideological implications can be found in all interpretations of history in strong group/low grid situations, most notably those interpretations which have in fact spawned "revolutions," whether the American, French, or Russian. All have in common the desire to restructure society in order to implement genuine traditional and human values (cf. Eisenstadt 1978).

CONCLUSION

The purpose of this chapter was to analyze the ways in which people tell about the flow of the action in their social experience, whether these people be ordinary folks or professional historians. Directly or indirectly, all storytellers inevitably tell their hearers or readers the point of it all as well as what to do about it, "it" being social life in general. The analysis was presented in successive stages in terms of a model developed by Hayden White. White's model, in turn, was fitted into Douglas' grid and group model, to the benefit of both. Figure 15 on pp. 182–183 sets out the various points made and conclusions drawn in the course of the chapter, once more within the grid and group framework.

9.

Testing the Models:
The Case of Fasting

INTRODUCTION

The last eight chapters have introduced a set of selective models deemed useful for interpreting life and its meanings in the first-century Mediterranean world as described in the New Testament writings. The task left to this final chapter will be to demonstrate the usefulness of those models again, this time by determining and defining the *meaning* of fasting in the New Testament writings. The issue of *why* persons fasted in New Testament times is rarely raised by interpreters and, when it is, it is generally answered with highly subjective, untestable reasons or with present-day ideas. For example, Wimmer writes, "In answer to the question, 'Why should I fast?', the New Testament responds, 'As a sign of your love'" (1980: 22). However, more often than not, biblical interpreters are satisfied with listing biblical and extra-biblical passages indicating *that* people fasted (e.g., Mark 1:12–13 and par. [Matt. 4:1–4; Luke 4:1–4;]; Mark 2:18–20 and par. [Matt. 9:14–17; Luke 5:33–39]; Mark 14:22–25 and par. [Matt. 26:26–29; Luke 22:14–18]; Acts 23:12–22; Q material [Matt. 11:16–19; Luke 7:31–35]; single traditions [Mark 9:29(?); Matt. 6:16–18; Luke 2:36–37; 18:9–14; Acts 9:9; 13:2–3; 14:23; Mishnah Taanith]; table 5 on pp. 186–189 presents for the reader's convenience the significant New Testament passages).

At times, these interpreters may even go a step further to determine *who* fasted or *how* people fasted in those days: from what foods, during what periods of time (notably Arbesmann 1949–51; cf. also MacCulloch 1912; Maclean 1912; Milgrom and Herr 1971; Brongers 1977; Satran 1980; the best bibliography available is that provided by Wimmer 1980; the least useful collection of information is that of Grant 1980, which lacks any interpretation). But, as a rule, the culturally specific meaning of fasting is ignored. What then is the social meaning of fasting? Why did first-century Mediterraneans practice the willful non-consumption of food and drink? Why would such behavior be sensible to their contemporaries? How did such behavior fit into some larger frame of understanding of how the world works that would legitimate such non-consumptive behavior?

TABLE 5. New Testament Passages on Fasting

THE DESERT

Matthew 4:1–4	Mark 1:12–13	Luke 4:1–4
Then Jesus was led up by the Spirit into the wilderness to be tempted by the devil. And he fasted forty days and forty nights, and afterward he was hungry.	The Spirit immediately drove him out into the wilderness. And he was in the wilderness forty days,	And Jesus, full of the Holy Spirit, returned from the Jordan, and was led by the Spirit for forty days in the wilderness, tempted by the devil. And he ate nothing in those days; and when they were ended, he was hungry.
And the tempter came and said to him, "If you are the Son of God, command these stones to become loaves of bread." But he answered, "It is written, 'Man shall not live by bread alone, but by every word that proceeds from the mouth of God.' "	tempted by Satan; and he was with the wild beasts; and the angels ministered to him.	The devil said to him, "If you are the Son of God, command this stone to become bread." And Jesus answered him, "It is written, 'Man shall not live by bread alone.' "

Deuteronomy 8:2–5 *(author's translation)*

Remember this whole passage which the LORD, your God, made you pass through these forty years in the desert, to humble you and put you to the test, to find out what was in your heart, and whether or not you have observed his commandments. / He humbled you, he made you experience hunger, then he fed you with manna, which neither you nor your fathers had ever known before, in order to make you understand that man does not live by bread alone, but by everything that comes from the mouth of the LORD. / During these forty years, your garments did not grow old, and your feet never swelled. / Therefore, remember in your heart that just as a man corrects his son, so does the LORD, your God, correct you.

Matthew 3:4	Mark 1:6
Now John wore a garment of camel's hair, and a leather girdle around his waist; and his food was locusts and wild honey.	Now John was clothed with camel's hair, and had a leather girdle around his waist, and ate locusts and wild honey.

THE BRIDEGROOM

Matthew 9: 14–15

Then the disciples of John came to him, saying, "Why do we and the Pharisees fast, but your disciples do not fast?"

And Jesus said to them, "Can the wedding guests mourn as long as the bridegroom is with them?

The days will come, when the bridegroom is taken away from them, and then they will fast.

Mark 2:18–20

Now John's disciples and the Pharisees were fasting; and people came and said to him, "Why do John's disciples and the disciples of the Pharisees fast, but your disciples do not fast?"

And Jesus said to them, "Can the wedding guests fast while the bridegroom is with them? As long as they have the bridegroom with them, they cannot fast.

The days will come, when the bridegroom is taken away from them, and then they will fast in that day.

Luke 5:33–35

And they said to him, "The disciples of John fast often and offer prayers, and so do the disciples of the Pharisees, but yours eat and drink."

And Jesus said to them, "Can you make wedding guests fast while the bridegroom is with them?

The days will come when the bridegroom is taken away from them, and then they will fast in those days."

JUDGMENT ON THIS GENERATION

Matthew 11:16–19

"But to what shall I compare this generation? It is like children sitting in the market place and calling to their playmates,

'We piped to you, and you did not dance; we wailed, and you did not mourn.'
For John came neither eating nor drinking, and they say, 'He has a demon'; /
the Son of man came eating and drinking, and they say, 'Behold a glutton and a drunkard, a friend of tax collectors and sinners!' Yet wisdom is justified by her deeds." /

Luke 7:31–35

"To what then shall I compare the men of this generation, and what are they like? / They are like children sitting in the market place and calling to one another,

'We piped to you, and you did not dance; we wailed, and you did not weep.'
For John the Baptist has come eating no bread and drinking no wine; and you say, 'He has a demon.' /
The Son of man has come eating and drinking; and you say, 'Behold, a glutton and a drunkard, a friend of tax collectors and sinners!' / Yet wisdom is justified by all her children." /

Matthew 17:21

[*excised from most critical editions*]

But this kind never comes out except by prayer and fasting.

Mark 9:29

(*exorcism technique*)

And he said to them, "This kind cannot be driven out by anything but prayer" [other MSS: and fasting].

OATH AT THE LAST SUPPER

Matthew 26:26—29	Mark 14: 22—25	Luke 22:14—18
Now as they were eating, Jesus took bread, and blessed, and broke it, and gave it to the disciples and said, "Take, eat; this is my body." / And he took a cup, and when he had given thanks he gave it to them, saying, "Drink of it, all of you; / for this is my blood of the covenant, which is poured out for many for the forgiveness of sins.	And as they were eating, he took bread, and blessed, and broke it, and gave it to them, and said, "Take; this is my body." / And he took a cup, and when he had given thanks he gave it to them, and they all drank of it. / And he said to them, "This is my blood of the covenant, which is poured out for many.	And when the hour came, he sat at table, and the apostles with him. / And he said to them, "I have earnestly desired to eat this passover with you before I suffer; / for I tell you I shall never eat it again until it is fulfilled in the kingdom of God." / And he took a cup, and when he had given thanks he said, "Take this, and divide it among yourselves;
I tell you I shall not drink again of this fruit of the vine until that day when I drink it new with you in my Father's kingdom."	Truly, I say to you, I shall not drink again of the fruit of the vine until that day when I drink it new in the kingdom of God."	for I tell you that from now on I shall not drink of the fruit of the vine until the kingdom of God comes."

OATH BY PAUL'S OPPONENTS

Acts 23:12–15

When it was day, the Jews made a plot and bound themselves by an oath neither to eat nor drink till they had killed Paul. / There were more than forty who made this conspiracy. / And they went to the chief priests and elders, and said, "We have strictly bound ourselves by an oath to taste no food until we have killed Paul. / You therefore, along with the council, give notice now to the tribune to bring him down to you, as though you were going to determine his case more exactly. And we are ready to kill him before he comes near."

THE PHARISEE AND THE TOLL COLLECTOR

Luke 18:9–14

He also told this parable to some who trusted in themselves that they were righteous and despised others; / "Two men went up into the temple to pray, one a Pharisee and the other a tax collector. / The Pharisee stood and prayed thus with himself, 'God, I thank thee that I am not like other men, extortioners, unjust, adulterers, or even like this tax collector. / I fast twice a week, I give tithes of all that I get.' But the tax collector, standing far off, would not even lift up his eyes to heaven, but beat his breast, saying, 'God, be merciful to me, a sinner!' / I tell you, this man went down to his house justified rather than the other (JB: and not the other); for every one who exalts himself will be humbled, but he who humbles himself will be exalted."

ALMSGIVING, PRAYER, AND FASTING IN SECRET

Matthew 6:1–6, 16–18

"Beware of practicing your piety before men in order to be seen by them; for then you will have no reward from your Father who is in heaven.

"Thus when you give alms, sound no trumpet before you, as the hypocrites do in the synagogues and in the streets, that they may be praised by men.

Truly, I say to you, they have their reward.

But when you give alms, do not let your left hand know what your right hand is doing, / so that your alms may be in secret;

and your Father who sees in secret will reward you.

"And when you pray, you must not be like the hypocrites; for they love to stand and pray in the synagogues and at the street corners, that they may be seen by men.

Truly, I say to you, they have their reward.

But when you pray, go into your room and shut the door and pray to your Father who is in secret;

and your Father who sees in secret will reward you."

"And when you fast, do not look dismal, like the hypocrites, for they disfigure their faces that their fasting may be seen by men.

Truly, I say to you, they have their reward.

But when you fast, anoint your head and wash your face, / that your fasting may not be seen by men but by your Father who is in secret;

and your Father who sees in secret will reward you."

OTHER TEXTS

Luke 2:36–37

And there was a prophetess, Anna, the daughter of Phanuel of the tribe of Asher; she was of a great age, having lived with her husband seven years from her virginity, / and as a widow till she was eighty-four. She did not depart from the temple, worshiping with fasting and prayer night and day.

Acts 9:9

And for three days he was without sight, and neither ate nor drank.

Acts 13:2–3

While they were worshipping the Lord and fasting, the Holy Spirit said, "Set apart for me Barnabas and Saul for the work to which I have called them." / Then after fasting and praying they laid their hands on them and sent them off.

Acts 14:23

And when they had appointed elders for them in every church, with prayer and fasting they committed them to the Lord in whom they believed.

nēstis = hungry (like *asitia*):
Mark 8:3/ /Matt. 15:32; Acts 27:33–34
nēsteia = hunger
2 Cor. 6:5; 11:27

A presupposition throughout this book has been that, while one can readily learn what people do or say about anything and how they do so, it is often far from certain whether one can so readily discern what they mean. As noted at the outset, meaning realized in language is rooted in a social system. Hence, to derive meaning in some articulate way, one must somehow have recourse to a social system, either one's own or that of one's informants. Native speakers take their social system for granted. They use language with the presumption that all with whom they interact understand "how the world works" in the same way they do. Descriptions of behavior from the natives' point of view is called *emic* description. The New Testament writings might be considered an anthropologist's field book full of emic data (both Leach 1976 and Kraft 1979 make this suggestion). The study of cultures requires some model of how the world works that might include both the world of the observer and the world of the observed in some articulate, non-impressionistic, and independently verifiable way. Descriptions deriving from such models are called *etic* descriptions. In philosophical terms the articulation of the emic in the etic mode overcomes the so-called "hermeneutical gap," the gap in understanding between people in different cultures, whether past or present. Articulate cross-cultural comparison does not allow for such a gap. The models previously described in this book should allow for the development of a workable, cross-cultural etic model to understand the whys of fasting.

Social Science Perspectives

All would agree that fasting deals with the non-consumption of food and drink. The existence of such non-consumption in various human groups can be explained variously. Perhaps the easiest and most obvious structural-functionalist explanation is that fasting periods allow for adequate distribution of provisions over a longer period and take place at times of chronic shortages anyway. Christian Lent occurred when food supplies dwindled to the extreme, ending at a time when first harvests were being brought in. The same might be true of the fast before Christmas as well as the countless other fasts that marked the Christian year in late antiquity and the Middle Ages. Conflict analysis might look at food non-consumption as a vehicle for boundary marking and conflict development and/or resolution. The control of food supplies can be made to have an effect on one's opponents, while non-consumption would serve to minimize such effects. However, such structural-functionalist and conflict analyses do not specifically address the question of the meanings realized by non-consumptive behavior, as might a symbolic approach. The explanation that follows derives from a symbolic approach.

Symbolic approaches to explaining human social behavior presuppose that the basic features of human existence are universal, at least from the observer's etic perspective. Such universal features include self, others, nature, time, space, and the All that ties them together. They also include less abstract features such as the four-dimensional quality of human experience: the vertical; the horizontal; depth perception; and quantity or mass perception. These basic features form the raw, objective stuff that individual cultures or social systems can endow with meaning and feeling in highly concrete situations. For our purposes it would seem that it is highly probable that human food/drink consumption is universal, and it is equally highly probable that human food/drink non-consumption is equally universal, at least inasmuch as people do not drink/eat every minute of the day and night. As universal human behavior, eating and drinking as well as non-eating and non-drinking provide the raw, objective stuff that individual cultures or social systems might endow with meaning and feeling. This raw, objective stuff is part and parcel of human social experience and allows for the development of "natural" symbols (Douglas 1973).

Food/Drink Consumption as Natural Symbol

A further assumption in this chapter is that consumption and non-consumption of food and drink form a piece of behavior realizing a natural symbol, consumption. As natural symbol, consumption and non-consumption can bear both general and highly specific meanings. However, the specific meanings that consumption and non-consumption might bear depend upon the manifold features of a given social system, not the least of which might be the core values giving direction to the life of a group, perceptions as to whether the core values are realizable or not, and whether individualism is normal or abnormal in the group or not (cf. fig. 16 on pp. 194–195 based on chaps. 2 and 3 above and on Douglas and Isherwood 1979; of course these features are fundamental for the formation of the grid/group matrix).

"In no society are people permitted to eat everything, everywhere, with everyone, and in all situations. Instead, the consumption of food is governed by rules and usage which cut across each other at different levels of symbolization" (Cohen 1968: 508). While Cohen's essay is concerned with food consumption and distribution, his observation is no less applicable to the use of force, of speech, and of sexual intercourse. In no society are people permitted to use these as they like, everywhere, with everyone, and in all situations. In many respects fasting, the non-consumption of food/drink, will be much like pacifism (the non-use of force), silence (the non-use of speech), and celibacy (the non-use of sexual intercourse). How these refusal behaviors function, what ties them together, and what meanings they bear are some of the more interesting questions raised by social science approaches to interpreting New Testament texts. Moreover, "when proscriptions concerning the consumption of food are attacked, it can be assumed that significant changes are taking place in the socioeconomic structure of that society" (Cohen 1968: 508; also cf. Barthes 1979). Of course, the same may be said of proscriptions concerning force, speech, and sexual relations.

Bibliography for Assessing Fasting

To return to the task at hand, however, how might one develop an interpretation of the meaning of fasting in the first-century Mediterranean world as reported in the New Testament? In the social sciences approach the first step is not to look up biblical commentaries, encyclopedias, monographs, or articles. As previously mentioned, such sources will provide the investigator with the whats and hows of fasting but with hardly any reasoned explanation of the whys of fasting in any non-ethnocentric, non-anachronistic way. Rather, the first step toward discovering the meaning of fasting is to find out what meanings people can convey with food in whatever culture about which information might be available. Here bibliographies such as those compiled by Wilson (1979) or Freedman (1981) as well as the perspectives and bibliography of Farb and Armelagos (1980) prove to be of great use. They in turn point to books and articles dealing with cross-cultural meanings conveyed by food, methods to assess such meanings now in use, and examples of food interpretations. From this information one finds that there are seven methods presently in use to assess the meaning of food (Grivetti and Pangborn 1973 list the following: environmentalism; cultural ecology; regionalism; culture-history; functionalism; quantitative approaches; clinical approaches). While each method was developed for generating a particular type of information, ultimately "diets develop in accord with cultural perception" (Grivetti and Pangborn 1973: 205; their assessment of Douglas [1966] in their 1974 article on Old Testament dietary regulations is wholly inappropriate, however; cf. also Simoons 1978). "Man's culture determines what is and is not fit to eat" (Grivetti 1978: 171). The problem is: how does culture do so and why? In any event, it would seem that it is the comparative study of culture that will yield some solution.

NON-CONSUMPTION: DISTINCTIONS AND DEFINITIONS

Such a study will have to begin with the construction of some etic model, in our case an etic model of fasting. The model is based on the fact that people practice food/drink non-consumption. Such non-consumption may be freely chosen or not freely chosen. When not freely chosen, such non-consumption leads to hunger and/or starvation (for definitions of these terms in U.S. elite perception, cf. Brooks et al. 1981); of course these non-consumption results may likewise be freely chosen. When freely chosen, then food/drink non-consumption is of two types from the viewpoint of the non-consumer's intended effects, with a third type of effect deriving from sheer social constraint. The three types are as follows.

Abstinence

One type of non-consumption is intended to have some effect on the non-consumer himself or herself. This form of non-consumption is *abstinence*. Abstinence in all its forms (e.g., dieting, asceticism, encratism) has a common characteristic, namely, the effect which non-consumption seeks is in/on the person not consuming food/drink for whatever reason. Some such reasons include purification, purgation, weight loss, vision causation, and imitation of the gods or God (cf. Arbesmann 1949–51). Since abstinence looks for effects within the non-consumer, it is not a form of social interaction although it most often is socially meaningful. In the U.S. persons who say they are dieting are readily understood, and their behavior makes sense; yet that behavior does not cause other people to act in a way either explicitly or implicitly directed by the non-consumer.

Fasting

Another type of non-consumption is in fact intended to have some effect on persons other than the one not consuming. Such non-consumption of food and drink is *fasting*. What all forms of fasting have in common is that the effect which non-consumption seeks is on persons other than the non-consumer. In this sense fasting is a form of social interaction. As a form of social interaction seeking to have effect on another, fasting is a form of communication.

Avoidance

For completeness' sake, a third form of non-consumption must be mentioned. This form falls beyond the control of the non-consumer and is instead socially commanded as the only form of consumption permitted and actually practiced. Exclusive food/drink prohibition of this sort is typical of *avoidance* as practiced in strong group/high grid (cf. fig. 16 on pp. 194–195). Such avoidance emerges as legal prohibition in strong group/high grid but as customary prohibition in strong group/low grid. It takes the form of socially sanctioned proscriptions of a range of foods/drinks which are either

FIGURE 16. Fasting and Feasting in Grid and Group

Weak Group/High Grid	**HIGH**

Considers nature as benignly amoral, to be used to foster individual achievement. Thus the edibility of food depends upon its potential to facilitate achievement, upon pragmatic criteria [e.g., "health," getting a promotion, being seen in the right restaurants, getting eating "out of the way," etc.]. There is no need to denature foods, and there is preference for short cooking time.

In eating, focus is on practicality, with emphasis on:

— *food* as medium for/in achievement orientation, to facilitate "up the ladder" movement or expression;

— *feast* as rare fare to underscore achievements (blessings) [rare in availability or mode of preparation];

— *fast* as form of communication through nonconsumption directed horizontally, to one's equals, generally to raise awareness and get power/solidarity to work for faster; also fast as form of weak group instrumental manipulation: dieting to stay in shape to compete/achieve.

Identifies its values and structures as natural (i.e., unlike the "unnatural" societies from which it emerged). Hence the edibility of food depends upon keeping foods as close to natural states as possible. Denatured food is evil, like "topside" denatured society. The "natural" division between animal and vegetative beings is used to evoke the identification of the human with animal, with plants alone allowed as food. Animals are to be neither killed nor disciplined, but to be allowed to follow their own "natural" course like humans, uninhibitedly.

In eating, focus in on contentment, with emphasis on:

— *food* as natural, i.e., grown naturally, without competition, greed, chemicals, or human labor or whatever topside society emphasizes and symbols;

— *feast* as expressive of nature's bounty, seasonal, opposed to greed/competition created by opposing quadrants;

— *fast* only as non-communicative non-consumption as a form of individualistic self-manipulation.

WEAK GROUP

Weak Group/Low Grid	**LOW**

Grid: Refers to the degree to which socially held values and individual experiences match:
—high grid means high match
—low grid means low match

Projects its social structures and values upon nature. Thus the edibility of food depends upon a part to whole analogy.

In eating, focus is on enjoyment, with emphasis on:

— *food* as class specific, both in kind and in mode of preparation;

— *feast* as stratum specific and affirming interaction;

— *fast* as a form of communication through nonconsumption directed vertically, to one's superiors, generally about structure maintenance and expressed in terms of self-humiliation.

N.B.: There is no non-communicative non-consumption in strong group/high grid since everything is done in socially determined moderation anyway.

Characterized by concern about porous social boundaries. Its boundary problems are replicated in perception of nature (e.g., no eating of carnivores which represent "them" opposed to "us" and our need to be separate from them). Thus the edibility of food depends upon kind as well as on long, complex boundary-passing processes that transform the raw [debilitating outside] into the cooked [support-giving side]. Often there is little possibility of recognizing the original food item.

In eating, focus is on danger; hence there are restrictive attitudes on food and drink, with emphasis on:

— *food* as group defining, marking off insiders from outsiders;

— *feast* as ceremony giving salience to group boundaries;

— *fast* as a form of communication through non-consumption directed both vertically to superiors and horizontally to equals, generally about problems with porous boundaries and their maintenance or collapse; also fast as a form of strong group instrumental manipulation to acquire power and/or solidary loyalty over others of use to the group.

STRONG GROUP

Group: Refers to the degree to which individuals perceive themselves embedded in primary social groups:
  —strong group at the extreme refers to total embeddedness
  —weak group at the extreme refers to total individualism

unavailable or unthinkable as food/drink. The Hindu beef prohibition as well as the Jewish and Islamic pork prohibition (cf. Diener and Robkin 1978), the Islamic alcohol prohibition, and the Pythagorean bean prohibition (cf. Lieber 1973 and Scarborough 1981/82) are instances of socially determined proscriptions; in fact these examples derive from the use of food to replicate the hierarchical boundaries of society, and thus they maintain and bolster the structures which those boundaries delimit (cf. Malina 1981b: 122–152). The avoidance of certain foods and drinks in strong group/high grid is normal structure maintenance as is the "balanced diet" in weak group/high grid.

FASTING AS COMMUNICATION

To return to the topic of fasting, food and drink non-consumption undertaken in order to have effect on others is like language in that it is a form of communication but unlike language in that its channel or medium is non-linguistic. In fasting, persons use food/drink as mediating materials for communication. Similarly, in pacifism, force is used as mediating material; in silence, utterance is used as mediating material; in celibacy, sexual cohabitation is used as mediating material. In fasting, food is used as mediating material precisely because the one fasting refuses to use food and expects some other person to understand a message in the refusal.

Definition of Communication

Communication might be defined as the process by which messages are transferred from a source to a receiver for a purpose. A source (Source) sends a message (Message) along a certain channel (Channel) to some receiving individual or group (Receiver) with some effect (Effect). Communication may take place in terms of language, apart from language, or in combination with language and some other channel. Communication in terms of language is the process by which one or more persons (Source) present another person or group (Receiver) with an oral or written utterance, a speech event (Channel), that encodes or stands for some social world object to which the utterance refers (Message) with the purpose of some reaction or outcome (Effect).

Social interaction, likewise, is the process by which one or more persons (Source) present another person or group (Receiver) with goods, services, actions, or a range of words, written and oral (Channel), that comprise symbolic experiences encoding social-world human values to which the symbol (Channel) refers (Message) with the purpose of getting results from the interaction (Effect). As in all communication, the message may be effectively received, garbled, muted, or turned to noise.

The GSM and Communication

Chapter 4 above dealt at some length with the point that social interactions with a view to some effect run along four broadly based channels: power; commitment; influence; and inducement. These channels lend themselves to being perceived quite "naturally" in terms of the four dimensions of human perception: power is a vertical dimension (cf. B. Schwartz 1981); solidarity or commitment is a horizontal dimension (cf. Needham 1973); influence is a depth dimension; and inducement is a mass or quantity dimension. These four are generalized media of social interaction (cf. Parsons 1969). They serve as four irreducible strategies for playing the game of life. They are like language in that they are means of social interaction. However, they are unlike language in that they are not employed to encode the totality of human experience as language generally is. Rather, these four media are specific to the particular subsystems that make up the human social world. For example, power is the medium specific to the system of effective collective action (politics); solidarity or commitment, to the belonging system (family, kinship, friendship, patron-client); inducement, to the adaptive system (economics); and influence, to the meaning system (religion, education). These four generalized media are in fact symbolic models. They serve mainly to symbolize intrainstitutional or interinstitutional interactions; their function is manipulative in that they seek results or effects from social interaction. In terms of the definition of communication offered above, social interaction in terms of the four generalized symbolic media means that some person (Source) embodying the symbolic medium (Channel) applies the medium (Medium/Message) with a view to altering the attitudes or behavior (Effect) of another person or group (Receiver) in a direction in which the source believes to be desirable. However, here the medium (Channel) and the message are identical, the medium is the message.

The foregoing considerations allow for the following schematization. Effective non-linguistic communicative media and messages include:
  (1) power, the vertical dimension, entailing collaboration and cooperation for effective, collective ends (linguistic dimension: command);
  (2) commitment, the horizontal dimension, entailing cohabitation marking off the belonging system (linguistic dimension: compact or covenant);
  (3) influence, the depth dimension, entailing conciliation or consent to reasons offered, developed in terms of shared meaning system (linguistic dimension: conversation or colloquium);

(4) inducement, the mass/quantity dimension, entailing consumption and compensation expressing the adaptive system (linguistic dimension: compromise).

Negative GSM

If power, commitment, influence, and inducement are generalized symbolic media of social interaction, then pacifism, celibacy, silence, and fasting mean a refusal to interact in those media, just as though a merchant refused to take U.S. currency as valid tender. Furthermore, since these media are not only means of social exchange but also institutionally specific channels of communication, then a refusal to embody the media implies a rejection of the institution in which they are rooted. For example, pacifism would be a rejection in part or in totality of the prevailing political system; celibacy, of the belonging system; silence, of the ideology generating or meaning system; and fasting, of the adaptive system. Naturally these refusals, just as the generalized symbolic media themselves, may be used in combination. There are pacifists who remain silent in the face of indignity, just as there are celibates who fast. In any event, refusal behavior can be a form of communication.

At the other end of the spectrum there are the GSM used negatively, in forms of negative reciprocity. These are mentioned here simply to point out the range of meanings GSM might convey. The effort to secure unfair advantage over another is called hustling. Hustling is using the GSM in negative reciprocity. Thus the attempt to obtain unfair advantage by means of the GSM of power is extortion, while such negative use of the GSM of inducement is bribery. Similarly, favoritism or nepotism refers to obtaining unfair advantage with the GSM of commitment. Finally, behavior that includes activities such as information leakage, unwarranted secrecy, or lying falls under the negative use of the GSM of influence to obtain unfair advantage. The negative use of the GSM, then, is quite different from the negative GSM described here. Table 6 on p. 199 lists the GSM under discussion.

FASTING AS NEGATIVE GSM

The Human Body as Channel of Communication

But why pacifism, or silence, or celibacy, or fasting? Douglas has noted how communication invariably imparts information from the social system in which it takes place and how in fact communication ultimately constitutes the social system (1971 - 1975: 87). She goes on to note that in all social systems the human body serves as the favored vehicle of communica-

TABLE 6. Negative GSM (and GSM Used Negatively)

	POWER	COMMITMENT	INFLUENCE	INDUCEMENT
Mediating } Materials }	force	sexual relations and nurturance	speech, utterance	food/drink goods
a) Freely chosen negative GSM: With intended effect on SELF	non-violence	non-marriage	non-speaking	non-eating/ non-drinking (abstinence)
With intended effect on OTHERS	pacifism	celibacy	silence	fasting
	[General effect: refusal to interact, to cross boundaries]			
With socially constrained effect	prohibited use of force (e.g., assault, battery)	forbidden degrees or age limits for sexual relations	social times/places where/when non-speaking is required	prohibited/ avoided food (e.g., dog, rat) and drink (e.g., blood, alcohol)
b) Negative GSM not freely chosen:	physical weakness	"others" form a different "species"	inability to speak/hear	starvation due to lack

Appendix:
GSM used negatively attempting to secure unfair advantage with

HUSTLING is the effort to secure unfair advantage, here with the inappropriate use of GSM, thus:

POWER	COMMITMENT	INFLUENCE	INDUCEMENT
is extortion	is favoritism, nepotism	is secrecy, lying, information control/ leakage	is bribery

tion. People use their individual physical bodies as portable roadmaps of the social body; the individual physical body replicates the social body. Furthermore, the body mediates the social situation by being the field on which a feedback interaction takes place, notably by the way bodily boundaries are regarded or disregarded. Finally, the human body is available to be given as the proper tender for some of the exchanges which constitute the social situation, as in cuddling, sexual relations, and physical labor.

If fasting is a form of communication carried out in terms of non-consumption of food/drink, then the human body is certainly the privileged vehicle of communication. Non-consumption minimally means a refusal to cross boundaries, and thus it focuses on boundaries. Silence, pacifism, and celibacy do the same. By refusing to allow any generalized symbolic media to cross bodily boundaries, humans have their bodies both express the social situation as they perceive it at any given moment and make a particular contribution to that situation. Inevitably, then, since the body is mediating the relevant social structure, it does the work of communicating by becoming both an image of the total situation as perceived and the acceptable tender in the exchanges which constitute the situation.

Messages Conveyed by Fasting

What is the message communicated by fasting? As a form of communicative non-consumption, fasting means a negation of the reciprocities that make up social interaction. As a refusal to reciprocate, fasting places the one not consuming "out of social bounds," outside of the normal limits that define social interaction. Generally speaking, then, fasting denotes the refusal to reciprocate in the area of consumption, i.e., meaningful goods exchange. Similarly, pacifism is the refusal to reciprocate in the area of meaningful power exchange; silence, in the area of meaningful, mutual influence; celibacy, in the area of meaningful solidarity or loyalty exchange. Such refusal can have positive meaning, depending on the social system, much as "silence means consent." The positive meaning depends upon the social script in which the message is conveyed. Figure 16 on pp. 194–195 offers a sketch of such a range of positive meanings. Moreover, the practice of group fasting necessarily entails the rejection of reciprocities with other groups and their members and thus further highlights group boundaries.

By choosing to refuse to interact in terms of consumption, the faster places himself or herself out of normal social bounds, as previously noted. To be out of normal social bounds is to be in a liminal state. Liminal states occur to out-of-bounds persons during periods of transition, whether ceremonial or ritual. Such transitions occur as the social expression of the hoped-for status reversal or of the request for status transformation, as noted in chapter 7 above. What then would account for the liminal state revealed and expressed by fasting, a hoped-for status reversal or a request for status transformation? It would seem that the positive refusals denote above all a message requesting status reversal and, as a rule, are directed to those who can effect a status transformation. Victor Turner notes (1969: 176–177):

> Cognitively, nothing underlines regularity so well as absurdity or paradox. Emotionally, nothing satisfies as much as extravagant or temporarily permitted illicit

behavior. Rituals of status transformation accommodate both aspects. By making the low high and the high low, they reaffirm the hierarchical principle. By making the low mimic (often to the point of caricature) the behavior of the high, and by restraining the initiatives of the proud, they underline the reasonableness of everyday culturally predictable behavior between the various estates of society. On this account, it is appropriate that rituals of status reversal are often located either at fixed points in the annual cycle or in relation to movable feasts that vary within a limited period of time, for structural regularity is here reflected in temporal order. It might be argued that rituals of status reversal are also found contingently, when calamity threatens the total community. But one can cogently reply by saying that it is precisely because the whole community is threatened that such countervailing rites are performed—because it is believed that concrete historical irregularities alter the natural balance between what are conceived to be permanent structural categories.

Turner's reference to the ability of status reversal rites to make the low high and the high low, thus reaffirming the hierarchical principle, that is, the power system, would go a long way toward explaining the meaning of fasting where the hierarchical principle is the main mode of social perception. This would work for strong group/high grid in figure 16, pp. 194–195. There fasting would be a socially meaningful act of communication directed to those in control of the faster's existence with a view to status reversal. Emphasis is on maintenance of the social structure seen as in some way shaken or collapsing (grid descending) due perhaps to drought, famine, war, epidemic, conquest, taxation, or inflation. Communicative non-consumption in this context is a form of self-humiliation. This form of fasting is typical of most of the instances cited in the Hebrew Bible (cf. Milgrom and Herr 1971; Brongers 1977) and is clearly reflected in the Hebrew synonym for fasting ($ta^{ca}n\hat{\imath}th$): "humiliation/affliction of the self." Fasting makes sense here since the one in control of the social fabric is a God conceived and modeled after analogies drawn from human personhood; God is a person and hence can be the interacting partner in communication. Fasting would make no sense in strong group/high grid India since Hindu elites view the ultimate as process, as do Buddhist elites in strong group/high grid Japan. Abstinence with a view to becoming part of the process is far more appropriate and the only sensible form of non-consumption.

NEW TESTAMENT TEXT-SEGMENTS

On the other hand, the text-segments from the New Testament come from a social script that is strong group/low grid. Emphasis here is not on hierarchy maintenance but on boundary maintenance in a social setting where self-definition derives from group affiliation. Dyadic persons seek to maintain group boundaries symbolized in the values of honor and shame in an agonistic setting (cf. Malina 1981b). Here fasting would be a form of communication directed vertically to God to see to boundary maintenance and directed horizontally to one's group members to symbolize group affiliation. What provokes the fast is the perception of status reversal—the negative estimate of the state in which the group finds itself. This negative estimate might range from a panic-provoking perception of boundary porosity to the certainty of an all-suffusing and firmly lodged evil.

Mark 2 and Parallels: No Concern for Boundary Maintenance

In the question about fasting in Mark 2:18–20, the John group and Pharisee groups are said to fast (twice a week for Pharisees according to Luke 18:9–14). Yet the Jesus group does not fast. Had they any need of boundary maintenance as did every other significant Jewish group at the time? Jesus' rejection of fasting would indicate that his movement had little concern about boundaries or evil lodged in the group; it would also indicate that the hoped-for status reversal was in some way already realized since all indications point to a strong group/low grid social location that hopes for status reversal or transformation.

Note how a similar point is made in the Q-discussion in Matthew 11:16–19 // Luke 7:31–35. Hence, exorcism, behavior typical of intense and anxious concern for boundaries, is to take place due to the effects of prayer (cf. Malina 1980) not of fasting (although the manuscript tradition indicates subsequent traditioning did not share the same view). Furthermore, in the text-segment located in the Sermon on the Mount (Matt. 6:16–18) disciples who do fast in the Matthean group are to focus on the vertical dimension of the communication only; this is the power axis directed to God for the purpose of status reversal, for having the inward and/or outward situation altered by means of God's power should God so deign. The horizontal aspect of boundary maintenance is to be hidden. Thus these Gospel passages refer to the rejection of fasting within the Jesus group, with the later tradition noted by Matthew 6 altering the attitude to a rejection of only the horizontal, public dimensions of fasting for the Matthean community. In what social context did fasting have its primary locus?

Mourning Behavior: Vertical and Horizontal Dimensions

Matthew's retelling of Mark's discussion (Matt. 9:14–15) of fasting replaces the word "to fast" with the word "to mourn." It seems that the term "mourning" equally served to conjure up communicative non-consumption comparisons in Matthew 11:16–19 where the styles of John and Jesus are compared. The parallel statement in Luke 7:31–35 uses the word "weep" just as in the beatitudes prefacing the Sermon on the Plain Luke has

"Blessed are you that weep now" (Luke 6:21) to parallel Matthew's "Blessed are those who mourn" (Matt. 5:4). Both mourning/weeping statements refer to a line of behavior protesting the presence of evil and having fasting as integral parts. The collocations "hunger/weep" in Luke and "mourn/hunger/thirst" in Matthew point to this. The evil in question is whatever triggers the perception of a need for status reversal. Matthew discovers and assesses the evil requiring mourning behavior as the lack of righteousness, that is, proper interpersonal relations in the social body. Mourning/weeping behavior points to evil within the boundaries of the social body and fasting seems "natural" to communicate concern about the rupture of the social fabric, much as in the mourning that accompanies death in our society (cf. Hocart 1931 who sees fasting as symboling the condition of the dead person by the mourners; the problem with his explanation is that people fast in situations other than mourning for the dead, yet his insight is valuable too in that fasting in strong group/low grid makes immediate sense in situations that spell the "death" of the group, notably by having boundaries penetrated by evil).

From the foregoing it seems certain that Jesus rejected fasting from the time the Jesus movement was on its own. He probably fasted as a member of the John movement but ceased the practice when building his own group (cf. Hollenbach 1982 who underscores the change). What would account for the rejection of fasting? Minimally, non-fasting means non-non-consumption and hence a refusal to refuse to interact with God and neighbor as the other significant groups did. The positive injunctions to go out to others and to mix with others point to a rejection of defensiveness relative to boundaries. Openness is the rule, at least during the period of the Jesus movement; fasting would make no sense since status reversal has either begun or somehow been realized.

Word of Honor: Fasting to Bolster an Oath

Yet there is one instance in which Jesus does declare his intent to fast. This is the text-segment narrating the oath Jesus makes at the Last Supper (Mark 14:22–25). Oaths in honor and shame cultures function like a word of honor. The purpose of such oaths is to make known as clearly as possible the sincerity of intention of the person of honor. Oaths are necessary when persons with whom the person of honor interacts find the behavior or claims of that person ambiguous or incredible (cf. Malina 1981b: 37). By adding fasting to the word of honor the communicative redundancy simply gives greater salience to the behavior or utterance. Note here that fasting is directed horizontally (as also in the incident of Paul's opponents in Acts 23:12–22). This is, of course, what the Nazirite vow is all about, that is, adding some piece of non-consumption to the word of honor. According to Numbers 6:1–21, only grape non-consumption is involved, as in Mark

14:22–25 and Matthew 26:26–29; Luke 22:14–18, however, makes the vow an instance of full fasting.

FASTING IN NEW TESTAMENT TIMES: BROADER SOCIAL DIMENSIONS

The previous examples indicate that the specific receiver of the message communicated by fasting is determined by the social institution in which the communication is taking place. In the first-century Mediterranean world such fasting is normally political or familial since religion and economics are embedded in these institutions. Further, the receiver of the message likewise depends upon the structure of interaction within a given institution (e.g., corporate kinship, monolithic hierarchy, pluralistic and clientelistic structures).

In the first-century Mediterranean world the structure of fasting interaction is largely clientelistic (cf. Eisenstadt and Roniger 1980), to move the patron of the fictive kinship group to effect the required status reversal for the group (i.e., raise the grid in the grid and group model, cf. fig. 16 on pp. 194–195). In weak group/high grid U.S., fasting is largely political and horizontally directed to the wielders of power (voters, citizens) either to heighten their awareness or to have them take requisite political action (cf. Brooks et al. 1981).

DEFINING FASTING IN THE NEW TESTAMENT

In sum, it would seem that the following description adequately covers the meaning of fasting in the New Testament text-segments that mention and/or describe the practice. Fasting is a form of communicative non-consumption, a refusal to participate in the reciprocities that constitute social interaction. This refusal encodes a message of request for status reversal. Insofar as persons capable of effecting status reversal stand vertically above or horizontally on par with the one fasting, the message may have either a vertical or horizontal dimension. As indicated previously in chapter 4, in strong group, vertical direction seeks power to effect change, and horizontal direction seeks commitment or solidarity to effect change. The rejection of fasting in a social script that values such behavior points either to acquiescence in the status quo (hence recriminations of "sinner, glutton, drunkard" to shame the non-faster, as in Matthew 11:16–19; Luke 7:31–35) or to a perception that the requested status reversal has already been realized in some way (hence the rejection of fasting since it would be communicating the wrong information). Figure 16 on pp. 194–195 presents a summary of the discussion in this chapter within an overview deriving from the book as a whole.

Conclusion

This exercise in intellectual kitbashing has come to a close. The dimensions of similarity and difference between the modern Bible reader and the people described in various biblical texts should be all the more apparent, yet all the more understandable. People who have used the models presented here have found them thought-provoking and suggestive of other applications and insights. One person noted how SG/HG hierarchies are prone to grandiose and magnificent building projects, e.g., Roman emperors, Soviet planners, U.S. military chiefs, and corporate executives. Another suggested the book by Norman F. Dixon, *On the Psychology of Military Incompetence*, London: Futura, Macdonald & Co., 1979, as a perfect introduction to the SG/HG point of view, whether military, corporate, political, or ecclesiastical. The kitbashed models are intended to stand at a level of conceptualization that provides for easy cross-cultural comparison. It is hoped that the user of this book will make further connections and comparisons and thus fulfill the heuristic goals intended by the author of the book. And what better way to conclude the book than with another diagram that fixes the salient features of the grid and group matrix in retrospect (figure 17, pp. 206–207).

FIGURE 17. Summary

Weak Group/High Grid HIGH

The achievement-oriented, individualistic view.

Individuals have short term perspectives because of limited lifespan and temporal duration. In weak group/high grid, the individual has high moral status, makes demands for the present generation with a this-worldly morality [the individual is short-lived] and a this-worldly doctrine based on individual achievement/goals.

Heavy individual pressure on groups is possible, with the individual capable of accumulating great assets in his or her own name.

Emphasis on individual rights/obligations results in multiplicity of lawyers, unlike strong group in which groups and group representatives have rights/obligations.

WEAK GROUP

The contentment-oriented, individualistic view.

Individuals in weak group/low grid seek contentment in values/structures that oppose those of the quadrant from which individuals have emerged. E.g., individuals from weak group/high grid seek contentment by being anti-achievement, anti-competition; individuals from strong group/low grid seek contentment by being anti the maintenance of acquisitions (i.e., into "poverty" as a value/lifestyle or into heavy risk-taking speculation and opportunistic exploitation as a strategy).

Weak Group/Low Grid LOW

Group: Refers to the degree to which individuals perceive themselves embedded in primary social groups:
—strong group at the extreme refers to total embeddedness
—weak group at the extreme refers to total individualism

Ascription: The corporation view.

Corporations are endowed with eternal life, have a long-term time perspective, superior moral status that transcends individual representatives of the group, can make demands in the name of unborn generations focused on other-worldly morality since the group outlives its members.

Corporations develop other-worldly doctrine (generally, universally applicable systems) based on the strength of the group, purity rules that control admission and exclusion procedures, group strata, the privileges of each stratum, and uniformity of wealth characteristic of each.

There is a strong group pressure on individuals, with the group having greater capacity to accumulate assets in its own name, while individual members cannot.

STRONG GROUP

Acquisition maintenance: The competitive group view.

Points to multiple groups, each with an acquired corporation view that it seeks to maintain against others.

The aspirations of the individual group are perceived to be depredated from within or by more powerful rivals without. Attempts to ward off depredation are expressed in terms of focusing on honor and shame, luck, fate, and providence. There is heavy interest in the formation of alliances—marital, defensive, financial—on the group's behalf.

Purity rules test fitness for extremely limited upward mobility and serve as technique for selective exclusion from the group. Rules are about equality of competition between group representatives (e.g., challenge/riposte).

Grid: Refers to the degree to which socially held values and individual experience match:
    —high grid means high match
    —low grid means low match

References

Arbesmann, Rudolph
    1949–51   "Fasting and Prophecy in Pagan and Christian Antiquity" *Traditio* 7: 1–71.

Arendt, Hannah
    1958   "What Was Authority?" Pp. 81–112 in Carl J. Friedrich (ed.), *Nomos I: Authority*. Cambridge, MA: Harvard University Press.

Bailey, Kenneth D.
    1973   "Monothetic and Polythetic Typologies and Their Relation to Conceptualization, Measurement and Scaling" *American Sociological Review* 38: 18–33.

Barbour, Ian, Harvey Brooks, Sanford Lakoff, and John Opie
    1982   *Energy and American Values*. New York: Praeger.

Barthes, Roland
    1979   "Toward a Psychosociology of Contemporary Food Consumption." Pp. 166–173 in Robert Forster and Orest Ranum (eds.), *Food and Drink in History*. Selections from the Annales, 5. Baltimore: Johns Hopkins University Press.

Bellah, Robert, Kenelm Burridge, and Roland Robertson
    1982   "Responses to Louis Dumont's 'A Modified View of Our Origins: The Christian Beginnings of Modern Individualism' " *Religion* 12: 83–88.

Black, Donald
    1976   *The Behavior of Law*. New York: Academic Press.

Bogdan, Robert and Steven J. Taylor
    1975   *Introduction to Qualitative Research Methods: A Phenomenological Approach to the Social Sciences*. New York: John Wiley and Sons.

Bohannan, Paul
    1973   "The Differing Realms of the Law." Pp. 306–317 in Donald Black and Maureen Mileski (eds.), *The Social Organization of Law*. New York: Seminar Press.

Boissevain, Jeremy
    1974   *Friends of Friends: Networks, Manipulators and Coalitions*. New York: St. Martin's Press.

References   **209**

Boys, Mary C.
1980   *Biblical Interpretation in Religious Education: A Study of the Kerygmatic Era.* Birmingham: Religious Education Press.

Brander, Bruce
1983   "How Civilizations Got Sick and Died—And Now Ours Has the Symptoms" *National Catholic Reporter* 19 no. 16 (February 11, 1983): 11–13, 22–24.

Brongers, H. A.
1977   "Fasting in Israel in Biblical and Post-biblical Times" *Oudtestamentische Studiën* 20: 1–21.

Brooks, Svevo, John Burkhart, Dorothy Granada, and Charles Gray
1981   *A Guide to Political Fasting.* Eugene, OR: Nonviolent Tactics Development Project.

Brown, Raymond E. and John P. Meier
1983   *Antioch and Rome: New Testament Cradles of Catholic Christianity.* New York/Ramsey, NJ: Paulist Press.

Burke, Kenneth
1969   *A Grammar of Motives.* Berkeley/Los Angeles: University of California Press.

Burke, Peter
1970   *The Renaissance Sense of the Past.* Documents of Modern History. New York: St. Martin's Press.

Carney, T. F.
1973   *The Economies of Antiquity: Controls, Gifts and Trade.* Lawrence, KS: Coronado Press.

1975   *The Shape of the Past: Models and Antiquity.* Lawrence, KS: Coronado Press.

Charlesworth, James H.
1982   "The Historical Jesus in Light of Writings Contemporaneous with Him." Pp. 451–476 in Hildegard Temporini and Wolfgang Haase (eds.), *Aufstieg und Niedergang der römischen Welt,* II, 25, 1. Berlin/New York: Walter de Gruyter.

Chesnut, Glenn F.
1977   *The First Christian Histories: Eusebius, Socrates, Sozomen, Theodoret, and Evagrius.* Théologie Historique, 46. Paris: Editions Beauchesne.

Cohen, Yehudi A.
1968   "Food: II. Consumption Patterns." Pp. 508–513 in David L. Sills (ed.), *International Encyclopedia of the Social Sciences,* Volume 5. New York: The Macmillan Company/The Free Press.

Collins, Randall
1979   *The Credential Society: An Historical Sociology of Education and Stratification.* New York: Academic Press.

Countryman, L. William
1981   "Christian Equality and the Early Catholic Episcopate" *Anglican Theological Review* 63: 115–138.

Coyle, J. Kevin
1981   "Empire and Eschaton: The Early Church and the Question of Domestic Relationships" *Eglise et Théologie* 12: 35–94.

Dalton, George
1961   "Economic Theory and Primitive Society" *American Anthropologist* 63: 1–25.

De Beaugrande, Robert
1980   *Text, Discourse and Process: Toward a Multidisciplinary Science of Text*. Advances in Discourse Processes, 4. Norwood, NJ: Ablex.

De Garine, Igor
1972   "The Socio-cultural Aspects of Nutrition" *Ecology of Food and Nutrition* 1: 143–163.

De Ste. Croix, G. E. M.
1975   "Early Christian Attitudes to Property and Slavery." Pp. 1–38 in Derek Baker (ed.), *Church Society and Politics*. Studies in Church History, 12. Oxford: Basil Blackwell.

Deal, Terrence E. and Allan A. Kennedy
1982   *Corporate Cultures: The Rites and Rituals of Corporate Life*. Reading, MA: Addison-Wesley.

Desroche, Henri
1973   *Jacob and the Angel: An Essay in Sociologies of Religion*. Trans. John K. Savacool. Amherst: University of Massachusetts Press.

Diamond, Stanley
1973   "The Rule of Law Versus the Order of Custom." Pp. 318–341 in Donald Black and Maureen Mileski (eds.), *The Social Organization of Law*. New York: Seminar Press.

Diener, Paul and Eugene E. Robkin
1978   "Ecology, Evolution, and the Search for Cultural Origins: The Question of Islamic Pig Prohibition" *Current Anthropology* 19: 493–540.

Dodd, C. H.
1954   *The Bible and the Greeks*. London: Hodder and Stoughton.

Doty, William G.
1980   "Mythophiles' Dyscrasia: A Comprehensive Definition of Myth" *Journal of the American Academy of Religion* 48: 531–562.

Douglas, Mary T.
1966   *Purity and Danger: An Analysis of Concepts of Pollution and Taboo*. London: Routledge and Kegan Paul.

1969   "Social Preconditions of Enthusiasm and Heterodoxy." Pp. 69–80 in Robert F. Spencer (ed.), *Forms of Symbolic Action*. Proceedings of the

1969 Annual Spring Meeting of the American Ethnological Society. Seattle: University of Washington Press.

1971   "Do Dogs Laugh? A Cross-Cultural Approach to Body Symbolism" *Journal of Psychosomatic Research* 15: 387–390-pp. 83–89 in *Implicit Meanings*. London: Routledge and Kegan Paul, 1975.

1972   "Deciphering a Meal" *Daedalus* 101: 61–81.

1973   *Natural Symbols: Explorations in Cosmology*. New York: Vintage Books, reprint of 1970.

1978   *Cultural Bias*. Occasional Paper No. 35 of the Royal Anthropological Institute of Great Britain and Ireland. London: Royal Anthropological Institute.

Douglas, Mary and Baron Isherwood
1979   *The World of Goods*. New York: Basic Books.

Douglas, Mary and Aaron Wildavsky
1982   *Risk and Culture*. Berkeley/Los Angeles: University of California Press.

Dumont, Louis
1982a   "A Modified View of Our Origins: The Christian Beginnings of Modern Individualism" *Religion* 12: 1–27.

1982b   "Reply" (to Bellah et al.) *Religion* 12: 89–91.

Eisenstadt, S. N.
1963   *The Political System of Empires*. New York: The Free Press.

1978   *Revolution and the Transformation of Societies: A Comparative Study of Civilizations*. New York: The Free Press.

1983   "Transcendental Visions—Other Worldliness—and its Transformations: Some More Comments on L. Dumont" *Religion* 13: 1–17.

Eisenstadt, S. N. and L. Roniger
1980   "Patron–Client Relations as a Model of Structuring Social Exchange" *Comparative Studies in Society and History* 22: 42–77.

Elliott, John H.
1981   *A Home for the Homeless: A Sociological Exegesis of 1 Peter, Its Situation and Strategy*. Philadelphia: Fortress Press.

Farb, Peter and George Armelagos
1980   *Consuming Passions: The Anthropology of Eating*. Boston: Houghton Mifflin Company.

Farwell, Lyndon J.
1976   *Betwixt and Between: The Anthropological Contributions of Mary Douglas and Victor Turner Toward a Renewal of Roman Catholic Ritual*. Dissertation, Claremont (John A. Hutchison). Ann Arbor: University Microfilms.

Fennell, William O.
1977   *God's Intention for Man: Essays in Christian Anthropology*. Studies in

Religion Supplements, 4. Waterloo, Ont.: Wilfrid Laurier University Press.

Fiorenza, Elisabeth Schüssler
1983   *In Memory of Her: A Feminist Theological Reconstruction of Christian Origins.* New York: Crossroad.

Fishman, Joshua A.
1971   *Sociolinguistics: A Brief Introduction.* Rowley, MA: Newbury House Publishers.

Fortes, Meyer
1949   *The Web of Kinship Among the Tallensi.* London: Oxford University Press.

Foster, George M.
1965   "Peasant Society and the Image of Limited Good" *American Anthropologist* 67: 293–315.

Fowler, Roger
1977   *Linguistics and the Novel.* London: Methuen.

Freedman, Robert L.
1981   *Human Food Uses: A Cross-cultural, Comprehensive Annotated Bibliography.* Westport, CT: Greenwood Press.

Geertz, Clifford
1973   *The Interpretation of Cultures.* New York: Basic Books.

1976   " 'From the Native's Point of View': On the Nature of Anthropological Understanding." Pp. 221–237 in Keith H. Basso and Henry A. Selby (eds.), *Meaning in Anthropology.* Albuquerque: University of New Mexico Press.

Goldwert, Marvin
1981   *The Suicide and Rebirth of Western Civilization: A Collage of Psychohistorical Analogies.* Washington, DC: University Press of America.

Golob, Eugene O.
1980   "The Irony of Nihilism." Pp. 55–65 in Metahistory: Six Critiques. *History and Theory Beiheft,* 19. Middletown, CT: Wesleyan University Press.

Gottwald, Norman K.
1979   *The Tribes of Yahweh: A Sociology of the Religion of Liberated Israel, 1250–1050 B.C.E.* Maryknoll, NY: Orbis Books.

Grant, Robert M.
1980   "Dietary Laws Among Pythagoreans, Jews, and Christians" *Harvard Theological Review* 73: 299–310.

Greanias, George C. and Duane Windsor
1982   *The Foreign Corrupt Practices Act: Anatomy of a Statute.* Lexington, MA: Lexington Books.

Gregory, James R.
1975   "Image of Limited Good, or Expectation of Reciprocity?" *Current Anthropology* 16: 73–92.

Grivetti, Louis E.
1978   "Culture, Diet, and Nutrition: Selected Themes and Topics" *Bio-Science* 28: 171–177.

Grivetti, Louis E. and Rose Marie Pangborn
1973   "Food Habit Research: A Review of Approaches and Methods" *Journal of Nutrition Education* 5: 204–208.

1974   "Origin of Selected Old Testament Dietary Prohibitions" *Journal of the American Dietetic Association* 65: 634–638.

Halliday, Michael A. K.
1978   *Language as Social Semiotic: The Social Interpretation of Language and Meaning.* Baltimore: University Park Press.

Harvey, A. E.
1982   *Jesus and the Constraints of History.* Philadelphia: Westminster Press.

Herbst, P. G.
1976   *Alternatives to Hierarchies.* International Series on the Quality of Working Life, 1. Leiden: Martinus Nijhoff Social Sciences Division.

Hobsbawm, E. J.
1971   "From Social History to the History of Society" *Daedalus* 100: 20–45.

Hocart, A. M.
1931   "Fasting." Pp. 144–146 in Edwin R. A. Seligman and Alvin Johnson (eds.), *Encyclopaedia of the Social Sciences.* Volume 6. New York: The Macmillan Company.

Hochschild, Jennifer L.
1981   *What's Fair? American Beliefs About Distributive Justice.* Cambridge, MA: Harvard University Press.

Hollenbach, Paul W.
1979   "Social Aspects of John the Baptizer's Preaching Mission in the Context of Palestinian Judaism." Pp. 850–875 in Hildegard Temporini and Wolfgang Haase (eds.), *Aufstieg und Niedergang der römischen Welt,* II, 19, 1. Berlin/New York: Walter de Gruyter.

1981   "Jesus, Demoniacs, and Public Authorities: A Socio-Historical Study" *Journal of the American Academy of Religion* 49: 567–588.

1982   "The Conversion of Jesus: From Jesus the Baptizer to Jesus the Healer." Pp. 196–219 in Hildegard Temporini and Wolfgang Haase (eds.), *Aufstieg und Niedergang der römischen Welt,* II, 25, 1. Berlin/New York: Walter de Gruyter.

1984   "Recent Historical Jesus Studies and the Social Sciences." Pp. 61–78 in Kent H. Richards (ed.), *Society of Biblical Literature 1984 Seminar Papers.* Chico, CA: Scholars Press.

Hopkins, Keith
1978   *Conquerors and Slaves*. Sociological Studies in Roman History, 1. Cambridge: Cambridge University Press.

Hudson, R. A.
1980   *Sociolinguistics*. Cambridge: Cambridge University Press.

Isenberg, Sheldon R. and Dennis E. Owen
1977   "Bodies, Natural and Contrived: The Work of Mary Douglas" *Religious Studies Review* 3: 1–17.

Jacoby, Neil H., Peter Nehemkis, and Richard Eells
1977   *Bribery and Extortion in World Business: A Study of Corporate Political Payments Abroad*. New York: Macmillan Company.

Janowitz, Morris and Roger W. Little
1974   *Sociology and the Military Establishment*. Third edition. Beverly Hills/ London: Sage Publications.

Kellner, Hans
1980   "A Bedrock of Order: Hayden White's Linguistic Humanism." Pp. 1–29 in Metahistory: Six Critiques. *History and Theory Beiheft*, 19. Middletown, CT: Wesleyan University Press.

Kideckel, David A.
1983   "Introduction: Political Rituals and Symbolism in Socialist Eastern Europe" *Anthropological Quarterly* 56: 52–54.

Kraft, Charles H.
1979   *Christianity in Culture: A Study in Dynamic Biblical Theologizing in Cross-Cultural Perspective*. Maryknoll, NY: Orbis Books.

Küng, Hans
1967   *The Church*. Trans. Ray and Rosaleen Ockenden. New York: Sheed and Ward.

Langness, Lewis L.
1974   *The Study of Culture*. San Francisco: Chandler & Sharp.

Lassey, William R.
1976   "Dimensions of Leadership." Pp. 10–15 in William R. Lassey and Richard R. Fernandez (eds.), *Leadership and Social Change*. La Jolla, CA: University Associates Inc.

Leach, Edmund
1976   *Culture and Communication: The Logic by Which Symbols Are Connected*. Cambridge: Cambridge University Press.

Lieber, Elinor
1973   "The Pythagorean Community as a Sheltered Environment for the Handicapped." Pp. 33–41 in H. Karplus (ed.), *International Symposium on Society, Medicine and Law: Jerusalem, March 1972*. Amsterdam/London/New York: Elsevier Scientific Publishing Company.

Lowry, S. Todd
1979   "Recent Literature on Ancient Greek Economic Thought" *Journal of Economic Literature* 17: 65–86.

Maclean, Arthur John
1912   "Fasting (Christian)." Pp. 765–771 in James Hastings (ed.), *Encyclopaedia of Religion and Ethics*. Volume 5. New York: Charles Scribner's Sons.

MacCulloch, John Arnott
1912   "Fasting (Introductory and non-Christian)." Pp. 759–765 in James Hastings (ed.), *Encyclopaedia of Religion and Ethics*. Volume 5. New York: Charles Scribner's Sons.

Malina, Bruce J.
1979   "The Individual and the Community—Personality in the Social World of Early Christianity" *Biblical Theology Bulletin* 9: 126–138.

1980   "What Is Prayer?" *The Bible Today* 18: 214–220.

1981a   "The Apostle Paul and Law: Prolegomena for an Hermeneutic" *Creighton Law Review* 14: 1305–1339.

1981b   *The New Testament World: Insights from Cultural Anthropology*. Atlanta: John Knox Press.

1982   "The Social Sciences and Biblical Interpretation" *Interpretation* 36: 229–242, reprinted in slightly expanded form as pp. 11–25 in Norman K. Gottwald (ed.), *The Bible and Liberation: Political and Social Hermeneutics*. Maryknoll, NY: Orbis Books, 1983.

1983   "Why Interpret the Bible with the Social Sciences?" *American Baptist Quarterly* 2: 119–133.

1984   "Jesus as Charismatic Leader?" *Biblical Theology Bulletin* 14: 55–62.

1985   *The Gospel of John in Sociolinguistic Perspective*. Forty-eighth Colloquy of the Center for Hermeneutical Studies, ed. Herman Waetjen. Berkeley: Center for Hermeneutical Studies.

Mandelbaum, Maurice
1980   "The Presuppositions of *Metahistory*." Pp. 39–59 in Metahistory: Six Critiques. *History and Theory Beiheft*, 19. Middletown, CT: Wesleyan University Press.

McGregor, Douglas
1976   "An Analysis of Leadership." Pp. 16–21 in William R. Lassey and Richard R. Fernandez (eds.), *Leadership and Social Change*. La Jolla, CA: University Associates Inc.

Meeks, Wayne A.
1972   "Epilogue: The Christian Proteus." Pp. 435–444 in Wayne A. Meeks (ed.), *The Writings of St. Paul*. New York: W. W. Norton.

1983   *The First Urban Christians: The Social World of the Apostle Paul*. New Haven: Yale University Press.

Merton, Robert K.
1968   *Social Theory and Social Structure*. New York: The Free Press.

Meyer, Ben F.
1979   *The Aims of Jesus*. London: SCM Press.

Milgrom, Jacob and Moshe Herr
1971   "Fasting and Fast Days" *Encyclopaedia Judaica* 6: 1189–1195. New York: Macmillan.

Millar, Fergus
1977   *The Emperor in the Roman World (31 BC–AD 337)*. Ithaca, NY: Cornell University Press.

Miller, Dean A.
1969   *Imperial Constantinople*. New York: John Wiley and Sons.

Miller, George A.
1956   "The Magical Number Seven, Plus or Minus Two: Some Limits on Our Capacity for Processing Information" *Psychological Review* 63: 81–97.

Miller, John
1980   "Jesus' Personality as Reflected in His Parables." Pp. 55–72 in William Klassen (ed.), *The New Way of Jesus*. Newton, KS: Faith and Life Press.

Miyahara, Kojiro
1983   "Charisma: From Weber to Contemporary Sociology" *Sociological Inquiry* 53: 368–388.

Mol, Hans J.
1977   *Identity and the Sacred: A Sketch for a New Social-Scientific Theory of Religion*. New York: The Free Press.

Needham, Rodney (ed.)
1973   *Right and Left: Essays on Dual Symbolic Classification*. Chicago: University of Chicago Press.

Nelson, John S.
1980   "Tropal History and the Social Sciences: Reflections on Struever's Remarks." Pp. 80–101 in Metahistory: Six Critiques. *History and Theory Beiheft,* 19. Middletown, CT: Wesleyan University Press.

Nineham, Dennis
1976   *The Use and Abuse of the Bible: A Study of the Bible in an Age of Rapid Cultural Change*. London: The Macmillan Press Ltd.

Parsons, Talcott
1958   "Authority, Legitimation, and Political Action." Pp. 197–221 in Carl J. Friedrich (ed.), *Nomos I: Authority*. Cambridge, MA: Harvard University Press.

1969   *Politics and Social Structure*. New York: The Free Press.

Patte, Daniel
1976   *What Is Structural Exegesis?* Philadelphia: Fortress Press.

Pepper, Stephen C.
1942   *World Hypotheses: A Study in Evidence*. Berkeley/Los Angeles: University of California Press.

1945   *The Basis of Criticism in the Arts*. Cambridge, MA: Harvard University Press.

1967   *Concept and Quality: A World Hypothesis*. The Paul Carus Lectures, Series 13, 1961. La Salle, IL: Open Court.

Perinbam, B. Marie
1977   "Homo Africanus: Antiquus or Oeconomicus? Some Interpretations of African Economic History" *Comparative Studies in Society and History* 19: 156–178.

Pilch, John J.
1983   *Galatians and Romans*. Collegeville Bible Commentary, 6. Collegeville, MN: Liturgical Press.

Pixley, George V.
1977   *God's Kingdom: A Guide for Biblical Study*. Trans. Donald D. Walsh. Maryknoll, NY: Orbis Books.

Pomper, Philip
1980   "Typologies and Cycles in Intellectual History." Pp. 30–38 in Metahistory: Six Critiques. *History and Theory Beiheft,* 19. Middletown, CT: Wesleyan University Press.

Reason, Peter and John Rowan (eds.)
1981   *Human Inquiry: A Sourcebook of New Paradigm Research*. New York: John Wiley and Sons.

Riches, John K.
1980/1982   *Jesus and the Transformation of Judaism*. London/New York: Darton, Longman & Todd/Seabury.

Rogers, Everett M., with F. Floyd Shoemaker
1971   *Communication of Innovations: A Cross-Cultural Approach*. Second Edition. New York: The Free Press.

Ruch, Michel
1972   "Le thème de la croissance organique dans la pensée historique des Romains, de Caton à Florus." Pp. 827–841 in Hildegarde Temporini (ed.), *Aufstieg und Niedergang der römischen Welt*, I, 2. Berlin/New York: Walter de Gruyter.

Sagan, Carl
1980   *Cosmos*. New York: Random House.

Sahlins, Marshall
1972   *Stone Age Economics*. Chicago: Aldine-Atherton Inc.

Sanders, Ed Parish
1982   "Jesus, Paul and Judaism." Pp. 390–450 in Hildegard Temporini and Wolfgang Haase (eds.), *Aufstieg und Niedergang der römischen Welt*, II, 25, 1. Berlin/New York: Walter de Gruyter.

Sanford, A. J. and S. C. Garrod
    1981   *Understanding Written Language: Explorations of Comprehension Beyond the Sentence*. New York: John Wiley and Sons.

Satran, David
    1980   "Daniel: Seer, Philosopher, Holy Man." Pp. 33–49 in John J. Collins and George W. E. Nickelsburg (eds.), *Ideal Figures in Ancient Judaism: Profiles and Paradigms*. Chico, CA: Scholars Press.

Scarborough, John
    1981/82   "Beans, Pythagoras, Taboos, and Ancient Dietetics" *Classical World* 75: 355–358.

Schilling, Robert
    1980   "La Déification à Rome: tradition latine et interférence grecque" *Revue des études latines* 58: 137–152.

Schmidt, Steffen W., James C. Scott, Carl Lande, and Laura Guasti (eds.)
    1977   *Friends, Followers, and Factions: A Reader in Political Clientelism*. Berkeley: University of California Press.

Schmitt, John J.
    1983   "The Gender of Ancient Israel" *Journal for the Study of the Old Testament* 26: 115–125.

Schottroff, Luise
    1979   "Die Schreckensherrschaft der Sünde und die Befreiung durch Christus nach dem Römerbrief des Paulus" *Evangelische Theologie* 39: 497–510.

Schwartz, Barry
    1981   *Vertical Classification: A Study in Structuralism and the Sociology of Knowledge*. Chicago: University of Chicago Press.

    1983   "George Washington and the Whig Conception of Heroic Leadership" *American Sociological Review* 48: 18–33.

Schwartz, Howard and Jerry Jacobs
    1979   *Qualitative Sociology: A Method to the Madness*. New York: The Free Press.

Selznick, Philip, Leon Mayhew, Phillippe Nonet, Jerome E. Carlin, and Paul Bohannan
    1968   "Law." Pp. 49–78 in David L. Sills (ed.), *International Encyclopedia of the Social Sciences*. Volume 9. New York: The Macmillan Company/The Free Press.

Semple, Ellen Churchill
    1921   "Geographic Factors in the Ancient Mediterranean Grain Trade" *Annals of the Association of American Geographers* 11: 47–74.

    1922   "The Influence of Geographic Conditions upon Ancient Mediterranean Stock-Raising" *Annals of the Association of American Geographers* 12: 3–38.

Simoons, Frederick J.
1978   "Traditional Use and Avoidance of Foods of Animal Origin: A Culture Historical View" *BioScience* 28: 178–184.

Smart, Ninian
1983   *Worldviews: Crosscultural Explorations of Human Beliefs.* New York: Charles Scribner's Sons.

Smith, Morton
1978   *Jesus the Magician.* San Francisco: Harper and Row.

Smith, Wilfred C.
1963   *The Meaning and End of Religion: A New Approach to the Religious Traditions of Mankind.* New York: Macmillan Company.

Spence, Janet T. (ed.)
1983   *Achievement and Achievement Motives: Psychological and Sociological Approaches.* San Francisco: W. H. Freeman.

Stavely, E. Stuart
1982   "The Nature and Aims of the Patriciate" *Historia* 32: 24–57.

Steinmetz, David C.
1980/81   "The Superiority of Pre-Critical Exegesis" *Theology Today* 37: 27–38.

Struever, Nancy S.
1980   "Topics in History." Pp. 66–79 in Metahistory: Six Critiques. *History and Theory Beiheft,* 19. Middletown, CT: Wesleyan University Press.

Thom, Rene
1969   "Topological Models in Biology" *Topology* 8: 313–335 - pp. 89–116 (with minor changes) in C. H. Waddington (ed.), *Towards a Theoretical Biology.* Volume 3. Edinburgh/Chicago: University of Edinburgh Press/Aldine Publishing Company, 1970.

Thompson, Michael
1979   *Rubbish Theory: The Creation and Destruction of Value.* Oxford: Oxford University Press.

Thornton, M. K. and R. L. Thornton
1983   "Manpower Needs for the Public Works Programs of the Julio-Claudian Emperors" *Journal of Economic History* 43: 373–378.

Turner, Victor W.
1969   *The Ritual Process: Structure and Anti-Structure.* Chicago: Aldine Publishing Company.

Van Dijk, Teun A.
1972   *Some Aspects of Text Grammars: A Study in Theoretical Linguistics and Poetics.* Janua Linguarum Series Maior, 63. The Hague: Mouton.

Van Parijs, Philippe
1981   *Evolutionary Explanation in the Social Sciences: An Emerging Paradigm.* Totowa, NJ: Rowman and Littlefield.

Via, Dan O.
1975   *Kerygma and Comedy in the New Testament: A Structuralist Approach to Hermeneutic.* Philadelphia: Fortress Press.

Wallace, Walter L.
1981   "Hierarchic Structure in Social Phenomena." Pp. 191–234 in Peter M. Blau and Robert K. Merton (eds.), *Continuities in Structural Inquiry.* Beverly Hills/London: Sage Publishing.

Weaver, P. R. C.
1972   *Familia Caesaris: A Social Study of the Emperor's Freedmen and Slaves.* Cambridge: Cambridge University Press.

White, Hayden
1973   *Metahistory: The Historical Imagination in Nineteenth Century Europe.* Baltimore: Johns Hopkins University Press.

Wilcox, Max
1982   "Jesus in the Light of his Jewish Environment." Pp. 131–195 in Hildegard Temporini and Wolfgang Haase (eds.), *Aufstieg und Niedergang der römischen Welt*, II, 25, 1. Berlin/New York: Walter de Gruyter.

Williams, Robin M.
1970   *American Society: A Sociological Interpretation.* New York: Alfred A. Knopf.

Wilson, Christine S.
1979   "Food–Custom and Nurture: An Annotated Bibliography on Sociocultural and Biocultural Aspects of Nutrition" *Journal of Nutrition Education* 11, no. 4, (Supplement) 1: 211–264.

Wimmer, Joseph F.
1980   *The Meaning and Motivation of Fasting According to the Synoptic Gospels.* Rome: Pontifical Gregorian University.

Wrong, Dennis H.
1976   "Competent Authority: Reality and Legitimating Model." Pp. 262–272 in Lewis A. Coser and Otto N. Larsen (eds.), *The Use of Controversy in Sociology.* New York: The Free Press.

Ziesler, J. A.
1972/73   "The Removal of the Bridegroom: A Note on Mark ii.18–22 and Parallels" *New Testament Studies* 19: 190–194.

Topical Index

Scripture Index